Western Democracies and Extreme Right Challenge

Should democratic societies shun extreme right parties or treat them as 'normal' political parties? Is the solution to the extreme right challenge to be found in new laws banning 'hate speech' or individual parties? To what extent must we search beyond political and legal answers and focus on educational programmes and civil society responses?

For long periods, western democracy, especially its European form, seemed in danger of eclipse by a series of radical forces, most notably communism and fascism. Yet by the beginning of the 1990s, western democracy appeared destined to become the universal governmental norm. However, as we move into the new millennium there are growing signs that extremism is far from dead. In recent years, the extreme right has gathered notable support in many western countries, such as Austria, France and Italy. Racist violence, initially aimed at 'immigrants' is on the rise, and in the US – and increasingly in Europe – the state itself has become a major target. This book considers the varying trajectories of the 'extreme right' and 'populist' parties and focuses on the problems of responses to these trends, an issue which has hitherto been neglected in academic literature.

Based on extensive and original research, this work combines both nationally specific and comparative chapters to give a detailed picture of the new extreme right challenge in the western world. Its considered approach to the responses available to democratic governments will prove essential reading to students of European and American Politics and Law, and those more generally concerned with the future of democracy.

Roger Eatwell is Professor of European Politics at the University of Bath, and specializes in fascism and the contemporary extreme right.

Cas Mudde is Lecturer in Political Science at the University of Antwerp, and specializes in issues of extremism and democracy.

Routledge Studies in Extremism and Democracy
Series Editors: Roger Eatwell
University of Bath
and
Cas Mudde
University of Antwerp

This new series encompasses academic studies within the broad fields of 'extremism' and 'democracy'. These topics have traditionally been considered largely in isolation by academics. A key focus of the series, therefore, is the (inter-)*relation* between extremism and democracy. Works will seek to answer questions such as to what extent 'extremist' groups pose a major threat to democratic parties, or how can democracy respond to extremism without undermining its own democratic credentials?

The books encompass two strands:

Routledge Studies in Extremism and Democracy includes books with an introductory and broad focus which are aimed at students and teachers. These books will be available in hardback and paperback. Titles include:

Understanding Terrorism in America
From the Klan to al Qaeda
Christopher Hewitt

Fascism and the Extreme Right
Roger Eatwell

Routledge Research in Extremism and Democracy offers a forum for innovative new research intended for a more specialist readership. These books will be in hardback only. Titles include:

1. Uncivil Society?
Contentious politics in post-Communist Europe
Edited by Petr Kopecký and Cas Mudde

2. Political Parties and Terrorist Groups
Leonard Weinberg and Ami Pedahzur

3. Western Democracies and the New Extreme Right Challenge
Edited by Roger Eatwell and Cas Mudde

4. Confronting Right-Wing Extremism and Terrorism in the USA
George Michael

5. Anti-Political Establishment Parties
A comparative analysis
Amir Abedi

6. American Extremism, History Politics and the Militia Movement
Darren J. Mulloy

Western Democracies and the New Extreme Right Challenge

Edited by
Roger Eatwell and Cas Mudde

LONDON AND NEW YORK

First published 2004
by Routledge
2 Park Square, Milton Park, Abingdon, Oxon, OX14 4RN

Simultaneously published in the USA and Canada
by Routledge
270 Madison Ave, New York NY 10016

Routledge is an imprint of the Taylor & Francis Group

Transferred to Digital Printing 2009

© 2004 editorial matter and selection, Roger Eatwell and Cas Mudde; individual chapters, the contributors

Typeset in Sabon by Wearset Ltd, Boldon, Tyne and Wear

All rights reserved. No part of this book may be reprinted or reproduced or utilized in any form or by any electronic, mechanical, or other means, now known or hereafter invented, including photocopying and recording, or in any information storage or retrieval system, without permission in writing from the publishers.

British Library Cataloguing in Publication Data
A catalogue record for this book is available from the British Library

Library of Congress Cataloging in Publication Data
Western democracies and the new extreme right challenge / edited by Roger Eatwell and Cas Mudde. — 1st ed.
    p. cm. — (Routledge studies in extremism and democracy)
"Simultaneously published in the USA and Canada."
  1. Conservatism—Europe. 2. Right-wing extremists—Europe.
3. Political parties—Europe. 4. Europe—Politics and government—20th century. 5. Conservatism—United States. 6. Right-wing extremists—United States. 7. Political parties—United States.
8. United States—Politics and government—20th century. I. Eatwell, Roger. II. Mudde, Cas. III. Series.
    JC573.2.E85W47 2004
    324.2'13—dc21
                                                        2003010829

ISBN10: 0–415–36971–1 (hbk)
ISBN10: 0–415–55387–3 (pbk)

ISBN13: 978–0–415–36971–8 (hbk)
ISBN13: 978–0–415–55387–2 (pbk)

Contents

List of illustrations vii
List of contributors viii
Preface x
Acknowledgements xvi
List of abbreviations xvii

Introduction: the new extreme right challenge 1
ROGER EATWELL

PART I
Right-wing extremism in contemporary democracies 17

1 Between adaptation, differentiation and distinction: extreme right-wing parties within democratic political systems 19
ALEXANDRE DÉZÉ

2 The American radical right: the 1990s and beyond 41
MARK POTOK

3 The extreme right in Britain: the long road to 'modernization' 62
ROGER EATWELL

PART II
Democratic responses to right-wing extremism 81

4 Defence of democracy against the extreme right in inter-war Europe: a past still present? 83
GIOVANNI CAPOCCIA

5	The defending democracy and the extreme right: a comparative analysis AMI PEDAHZUR	108
6	Institutional inclusion and exclusion of extreme right parties LAURENT KESTEL AND LAURENT GODMER	133
7	The diversified approach: Swedish responses to the extreme right ANDERS WIDFELDT	150
8	Right-wing extremism in the land of the free: repression and toleration in the USA GEORGE MICHAEL	172
	Conclusion: defending democracy and the extreme right CAS MUDDE	193
	Index	213

Illustrations

Figures

4.1	Political processes and political outcomes in inter-war Europe	86
4.2	Peak results of extremist parties 1919–39	88
4.3	Party system propensities in the electoral and parliamentary arena	89
7.1	A typology of responses to political extremism	153

Tables

4.1	Defensive actions of the Head of State and the Government	92
4.2	Mechanisms of democratic defence (Finland, Belgium, First Czechoslovak Republic)	100
5.1	Defending democracy: the militant and the immunized route	115
8.1	Financial assets and annual income of leading watchdog groups	187

Contributors

Giovanni Capoccia is Tutorial Fellow in Politics at Magdalen College and Lecturer in the Department of Politics and International Relations at the University of Oxford. He is the author of *La Germania unita fra continuità e rinnovamento* (1995) and *Defending Democracy: The Extremist Threat in Inter-war Europe* (2004), and various articles. His current research project analyzes politico-institutional responses to extremism in 16 European countries.

Alexandre Dézé is currently a Visiting Fellow at Princeton University. He holds an MA in politics from Sciences Po, Paris, where he is also submitting his PhD. His main research and publications concern the relationship between extreme right parties and democratic political systems, and the political iconography of the extreme right.

Roger Eatwell is Professor of European Politics at the University of Bath. His main field of research is fascism and the contemporary extreme right. Recent publications include a new edition of his book *Fascism. A History* (2003) and articles on charisma and political religions. A collection of some of his most important articles and chapters, together with new material, will be published as *Fascism and the Extreme Right* in 2004.

Laurent Godmer is Lecturer in Political Science at the University of Marmara, a graduate of the Institute of Political Studies (Sciences Po) and Paris-1 Sorbonne. His research and publications mainly focus on the selection of political elites in West European countries, especially France.

Laurent Kestel currently teaches political science at Paris-1 (Sorbonne) University. He has a BA in history and an MA in politics, specializing on the Front National, and is finishing a PhD on the French Popular Party for Paris-1.

George Michael is a military veteran and has worked as an operations research analyst for the US Army. He holds a PhD from George Mason

University, and is currently an Assistant Professor of Political Science and Administration of justice at the University of Virginia's College at Wise. His publications include *Confronting Right-Wing Terrorism and Extremism in the USA* (2003).

Cas Mudde is Lecturer in Political Science at the University of Antwerp. He is Chair of the European Consortium for Political Research's (ECPR) Standing Group on Extremism & Democracy and editor of its newsletter, *e-Extreme*. He is the author of various publications on political extremism, including *The Ideology of the Extreme Right* (2000). Currently, he is working on a new book entitled *Xenophobic Nationalist Parties in Wider Europe: Concepts, Issues, Explanations*.

Ami Pedahzur is a Senior Lecturer at the Department of Political Science at the University of Haifa. He has published extensively on issues relating to extremism and the defence of democracy. Recent publications include *The Israeli Response to Jewish Extremism and Violence: Defending Democracy* (2002) and (with Leonard Weinberg) *Political Parties and Terrorist Groups* (2003).

Mark Potok is a prize-winning journalist, who is currently the Editor of the Alabama-based Southern Poverty Law Center's quarterly *Intelligence Report* – an important source on extremism, especially in the USA. He has written extensively on the American radical right. Related activities include testimony to the US Senate on hatred on the Internet, and presentations at various international fora.

Anders Widfeldt is Lecturer in Politics at the University of Aberdeen. His main area of research is political parties, especially in Scandinavia. He has published various articles on this subject, including the extreme right, and his book *Consensus under Threat? Racism and Right-Wing Extremism in Scandinavia* should appear in 2004.

Preface

i

For much of the 'short twentieth century', history was characterized by the clash of great ideologies, internal violence and major wars. Although the most catastrophic events took place outside the Western world, Europe and the USA were not immune from the turmoil. Two world wars and a series of lesser conflicts led to countless horrors and losses. Moreover, for long periods Western democracy – especially in its European homeland – seemed in danger of eclipse by a series of radical forces, most notably communist and fascist.

Yet by the beginning of the 1990s, liberal democracy appeared destined to become the universal governmental norm. Dictatorial Soviet communism had collapsed, to be replaced in most successor states by multi-party electoral politics. Chinese communism remained autocratic, but in the economic sphere it was moving rapidly towards greater freedoms and marketization. The main manifestations of fascism had gone down to catastrophic defeat in war. Overtly neo-fascist parties were damned by omnipresent images of brutality and genocide, and exerted little appeal outside a fringe of ageing nostalgics and alienated youths.

In the Western World, political violence had disappeared, or was of minimal importance in terms of system stability. Where it lingered on as a regularly-murderous phenomenon, for instance in Northern Ireland or Spain, it seemed a hangover from the past – a final flicker of the embers of old nationalist passions. It was easy to conclude that such tribal atavism was doomed in an increasingly-interconnected 'capitalist' world, characterized by growing forms of multi-level governance that were transcending the antagonism and parochialism of old borders.

However, as we move into the new millennium there are growing signs that extremism, even in the West, is far from dead – that we celebrated prematurely the universal victory of democracy. Perhaps the turn of the twenty-first century was an interregnum, rather than a turning point? In Western Europe there has been the rise of 'extreme right' and 'populist' parties such as Jean-Marie Le Pen's Front National, which pose a radical challenge to existing elites – even to the liberal political system. In the USA, the 1995 Oklahoma mass-bombing has not been followed by another major extreme right attack, but there is simmering resentment towards the allegedly over-powerful state among well-armed militias and successor groups. More generally across the West, new forms of green politics, often linked by a growing hostility to globalization–Americanization, are taking on more violent forms. The issue of animal rights is also of growing importance in this context.

In the former Soviet space, there are clear signs of the revival of 'communist' parties, which often masquerade as 'socialists' or 'social democrats', and whose allegiance to democracy is (in varying degrees) debatable. In Latin America, there remain notable extremist movements on the left, although these tend not to be communist. This trend may well grow both in response to globalization–Americanization and to the (partly-linked) crises which many of these countries, such as Argentina, are experiencing. This in turn increases the threat to democracy from the extreme right, ranging in form from paramilitary groups to agro-military conspiracies.

The rise of Islamic fundamentalism has been an even more notable feature of recent years. This is not simply a facet of Middle Eastern politics. It has had an impact within some former Soviet republics, where the old nomenklatura have used the Islamic threat to maintain autocratic rule. In countries such as Indonesia and India, Muslims and other ethnic groups have literally cut each other to pieces. More Al-Qaeda-style bombings of the 2002 Bali-type threaten economic ruin to Islamic countries that attract many Western tourists.

Moreover, growing Islamic fundamentalism has had an impact within some Western countries. The terrorist attacks in the USA on September 11, 2001 are perhaps the most graphic illustration of this impact. But in democracies generally, the rise of religious and other forms of extremism poses vital questions about the limits of freedom, multiculturalism, and tolerance. This is especially the case in democracies that have experienced notable Islamic immigration and/or which face the greatest threat of further terrorist attack – especially Britain and the US in the wake of the 2003 Iraq war.

Democracy may have become a near-universal shibboleth, but its exact connotations are being increasingly challenged and debated. As long as the 'evil empire' of communism existed, Western democracy could, in an important sense, define itself by the 'Other' – by what it was not. It did not have overt dictatorial rule, censorship, the gulags, and so on. But with the collapse of its great external foe, the spotlight has turned inward (although Islam is in some ways replacing communism as the 'Other'). Is liberal-Western democracy truly democratic? Can it defend itself against terrorism and new threats without undermining the very nature of democracy, in particular by the growing surveillance of a Big Brother state?

xii *Preface*

These broad opening comments provide the rationale for the *Routledge Series on Extremism and Democracy* – the series in which this book appears. In particular, there are three issues we seek to probe in this series.

- Conceptions of democracy and extremism.
- Forms of the new extremism in both the West and the wider world.
- How democracies are responding to the new extremism.

ii

This book relates to all three of these themes – especially the third. The recent revival of the extreme right has led to a burgeoning literature. However, much of the analytical literature adopts an essentially socio-economic, structuralist approach. Stressing factors such as the dramatic impact of globalization on both cultural identities and the economy is important in the sense that it underlines that the rise of the extreme right is unlikely to be a merely passing phenomenon. However, it is a notably blunt tool when it comes to explaining the different patterns of extreme right support not just between countries, but also within them. A full understanding of these issues requires a careful analysis of agency and political institutions.

We believe that there is, in particular, a need for a book that considers the delicate relationship between the extreme right and other players in the democratic system. We especially want to stress *political* issues, as they have become crucial given the advance of the extreme right on many fronts. Even more specifically, the focus is on what might be termed short-run rather than long run responses. Long-run *social policies*, such as developing forms of anti-racist education through the creation of new school curricula, or programmes aimed at integrating recidivist youths from both white and non-white communities, offer important perspectives. However, they require detailed and systematic treatment in their own right. Thus, the focus here is on issues such as the following. How do extreme right parties deal with the inherent tensions of functioning in a liberal democracy? What role do the various democratic actors (especially political parties and NGOs) play in response? And what are the effects of various anti-extremist measures currently in use?

We decided that in order fully to comprehend the problems involved in judging how to respond to the extreme right, it is necessary to understand more about the chameleon nature of the 'beast'. Thus, whereas Part II of this book contains five chapters that focus mainly on responses, Part I uses three case studies to probe the recent nature and trajectory of the extreme right.

In the Introduction, Roger Eatwell sets the scene, particularly for Part I. In the first section of this chapter, he highlights the key reasons why the extreme right has become a major topic of concern in recent years. The second section stresses the chameleon and variegated nature of the 'extreme right'. However, in different ways, all versions pose dangers to (liberal) democracy.

Part I begins with a comparative study by Alexandre Dézé of how the Austrian Freedom Party, the Flemish Block, the Italian National Alliance and especially the French National Front have adapted their discourses over the years as they pursue attempts at accommodation, differentiation and distinction. His subtle analysis points to the complex interactions between these groups and the political system more generally.

The next two chapters turn the spotlight on the USA and Britain, which are typically seen as countries with a weak extreme right tradition. These chapters, therefore, are important to understanding how contemporary groups operate in what is, in many ways, unfertile soil. At the same time, they point to very different patterns of recent extreme right mutation.

Mark Potok's survey of the US scene particularly focuses on what many people see as the archetypal form of the extreme right – namely, actually or potentially violent groups. Various organizations of this type have arisen in the USA to replace the Patriot militias which were a characteristic of the 1990s. In some cases, these groups increasingly espouse anti-Americanism and fascist-inspired views, especially anti-semitic sentiments.

Roger Eatwell's analysis of the British National Party shows how it has moved in the opposite direction by seeking to 'modernize' its more extreme policies, such as the compulsory expulsion of non-whites. At the same time, it has sought to develop a form of community politics, portraying itself as the party of ordinary people whose views are largely ignored by Establishment elites. The result has been growing electoral support in some areas.

Giovanni Capoccia opens Part II by examining lessons to be drawn from the inter-war era in Europe, in which many democracies collapsed. Focusing especially on Belgium, Czechoslovakia and Finland, all of which survived strong extremist challenges, he draws lessons for the present by stressing the importance of the role of the mainstream right, and of flexible elite responses that can encompass both inclusion and repression.

Ami Pedahzur contrasts America's historic constitutional protection of free speech with the very different concept of *wehrhafte Demokratie* (defensive democracy) in Germany and a similarly protective approach in Israel. From this comparison, he develops two ideal types of democratic response – the militant (which seeks to destroy the enemy through restrictions and bans) and immunized (which conceives protection in much wider terms, including education).

Laurent Godmer and Laurent Kestel also adopt a comparative approach, demonstrating how the extreme right's ability to gain access to local coalition 'markets' has had a crucial effect on its success or failure. They contrast two important ideal types – the German exclusionary oligopoly, which has always excluded the extreme right, with the Austrian maximum integration model, seeing France as exhibiting a mixture of the two.

Anders Widfeldt focuses on Sweden, which has seen off an extremist electoral challenge, but where violence has proved more enduring. He develops a fourfold typology: general accommodation (such as adopting part of the extreme right's platform); specific accommodation (for instance, accepting the extremists as coalition partners); general marginalization (e.g. laws against racist discourse); and specific marginalization (such as bans), arguing the need for a flexible response.

In the final chapter of Part II, George Michael analyses the American scene, where until recently the First Amendment encouraged government caution in curtailing right-wing extremists. Here NGOs, such as the Anti-Defamation League and Southern Poverty Law Center, have played a particularly important role in countering the extreme right by such means as providing intelligence to law enforcing agencies and the media, and by filing lawsuits against extremists.

In the Conclusion, Cas Mudde offers a general commentary on responses to the extreme right, and looks forward by setting an agenda for further research. His final words contend that: 'scholars of extremism and democracy should become more involved in studying, and perhaps even solving, the dilemma that has been summarized in a succinct and simple way by Hans-Gerd Jaschke (2000, p. 22): "Too much state is dangerous, too little as well."'

On the one hand, there are unquestionable dangers in adopting a pure First Amendment approach, or complacently holding that the main extremist parties have been tamed and have accommodated to the democratic system. Even the more moderate 'populist' groups pose significant problems. For example, they tend to set out Manichaen dichotomies and offer simplistic solutions, whereas at the heart of successful liberal democracy lies widespread trust between groups and the ability to broker compromise between different interests and programmes. Moreover, some of the more moderate extremist parties appear to have a (partly) hidden side, which inevitably raises questions about whether their commitment to democracy can be taken at face value.

On the other hand, there are problems with banning even the more extreme groups. They may simply reform with new names and/or previous restraints may be removed, leading them to turn to even greater violence! There are also dangers in adopting a politically correct position, which demonizes as 'extremist', even makes illegal, discourse that fails to correspond to liberal academic or judicial standards. The language of the streets may in some ways be racist and unsophisticated, but it can also raise legitimate questions about the limits of multi-culturalism, or about the capacity of some countries to take significant numbers of immigrants without adverse economic and social effects. There can be a very narrow line between politicians pandering to prejudice, and asking reasonable questions about outsiders – as the late Pim Fortuyn showed when, as the 2002 elections approached, he attacked Islamic immigration in the cause of the defence of Dutch liberalism. Moreover, extremists can raise legitimate questions about whether *liberal* democracy corresponds even to its own norms, let alone to *direct* democratic ones. For example, major political decisions often seem to be reached in smoke-filled rooms with little sense of accountability or transparency. Mainstream political parties are arguably more divorced from civil society than at any time in the post-1945 era – with apparently little chance of them becoming re-embedded in the declining traditional milieus of social class and religion. Clearly, there is much to ponder . . .

Roger Eatwell and Cas Mudde
Bath and Antwerp
May 2003

Acknowledgements

This book is written by members of the European Consortium for Political Research's (ECPR) Standing Group on Extremism & Democracy, which the Editors set up in 1999. This now has more than 600 members around the world. Its web-based members' interests list and quarterly newsletter, *e-Extreme*, are key sources not just for fellow researchers, but also for conference organizers, government officials, journalists and others (http://www.bath.ac.uk/esml/ecpr/ecpr.htm).

The key date in the birth of this book was April 2001, when over 20 members of the Extremism & Democracy Standing Group met at the ECPR's Joint Sessions in Grenoble, spending several days listening to papers and discussing related general issues. We are grateful to all the participants at this workshop – including those who gave papers on themes that proved too diverse to be included in a single volume. This book is largely made up of revised papers which began their lives at this conference. We are especially grateful to all the contributors for (on the whole) taking note of editorial comments, and (not always so efficiently) producing work on time. We are particularly pleased that the chapters have been updated where appropriate to the spring of 2003, so that this book does not suffer from the musty-chapter syndrome which is a frequent characteristic of books that emanate from long-forgotten conferences. Furthermore, we must thank Professor Jan van Deth for agreeing that we could publish this book in our own series rather than in the ECPR-Routledge Studies in European Political Science, which he edits. Last, but by no means least, we want to thank Craig Fowlie, Senior Politics Editor at Routledge, for his encouragement and expert advice.

Abbreviations

Abbreviation	Full name	Country
ADL	Anti-Defamation League	US
AEL	Arab European League	Belgium
AFA	Anti-Fascist Action	Sweden
AFS	Anne Frank Foundation	Netherlands
AN	National Alliance	Italy
ARA	Anti-Racist Action	US
BATF	Bureau of Alcohol, Tobacco and Firearms	US
BdL	German Agrarian Party	Czechoslovakia
BfVS	Federal Bureau for the Protection of the Constitution	Germany
BNP	British National Party	Britain
C18	Combat 18	Britain
CAR	Committees of Republican Action	France
CD	Center Democrats	Netherlands
CDR	Center for Democratic Renewal	US
CDU	Christian Democratic Union	Germany
CERD	Committee on the Elimination of Racial Discrimination	
CNIP	National Centre of Independents and Peasants	France
CP'86	Center Party'86	Netherlands
CSA	Covenant, Sword and the Arm of the Lord	US
CSU	Christian Social Union	Germany
DN	National Right	Italy
DVU	German People's Union	Germany
EUMC	European Monitoring Centre on Racism and Xenophobia	
FBI	Federal Bureau of Investigation	US
FDP	Free Democratic Party	Germany

FN	National Front	France
FPÖ	Austrian Freedom Party	Austria
FrP	Progress Party	Norway
GSS	General Security Service	Israel
HRT	Hostage Rescue Team	US
IKL	People's Patriotic Movement	Finland
KVV	Flemish Catholic People's Party	Belgium
LI	Liberal International	
MDR	Movement of Reformers	France
MNR	Republican National Movement	France
MOM	Militia of Montana	US
MSI	Italian Social Movement	Italy
NAFTA	North American Free Trade Agreement	
NF	National Front	Britain
NGO	Non-Governmental Organization	
NPD	National Democratic Party of Germany	Germany
NRA	National Rifle Association	US
NSDAP	German National Socialist Workers' Party	Germany
NSF	National Socialist Front	Sweden
NSPA	National Socialist Party	US
NWC	Northwest Coalition Against Malicious Harassment	US
ÖVP	Austrian People's Party	Austria
ON	New Order	France
PACA	Provence-Alpes-Côte d'Azur	France
PCF	Communist Party of France	France
PRA	Political Research Associates	US
PS	Socialist Party	France
REP	Republicans	Germany
RN	National Rally	France
RPR	Rally for the Republic	France
SdP	Sudeten German Party	Czechoslovakia
SGP	Political Reformed Party	Netherlands
SHF	Sudeten German Home Front	Czechoslovakia
SPD	Social Democratic Party of Germany	Germany
SPLC	Southern Poverty Law Center	US
SPÖ	Austrian Socialist Party	Austria
SRP	Socialist Reich Party	Germany
SWC	Simon Wiesenthal Center	US
UDF	Union for French Democracy	France
UKIP	UK Independence Party	Britain
VAM	White Aryan Resistance	Sweden
VB	Flemish Block	Belgium
VNV	Flemish National League	Belgium

Introduction
The new extreme right challenge

Roger Eatwell

Prelude

For many years after 1945, the contemporary Western 'extreme right' and related phenomena were not a central concern for academics, politicians and the policy community. However, during the last 20 or so years, a series of developments has significantly raised the extreme right's profile (for recent surveys of the extreme right see Merkl and Weinberg 2003 and Schain *et al.* 2002). Five trends highlight why the extreme right has become a growing cause for concern.

First, in Europe, there has been a pattern of mounting electoral success for many extreme right parties. For example, Jean-Marie Le Pen, the leader of French National Front (FN), made it into the run-off ballot of the 2002 Presidential elections, while 'King' Carl Hagen's Norwegian Progress Party (FrP) topped the opinion poll ratings in 2002 with over 30 per cent of popular support. Even Britain, which historically has been characterized by a weak extreme right electorally, has, since 2001, witnessed the election of several British National Party (BNP) councillors. It is important to stress that support for such groups has often been volatile: the populist List Pim Fortuyn's support slumped from 17 per cent of the vote in 2002 to a third of this in the 2003 Dutch elections, while support for Jörg Haider's Austrian Freedom Party (FPÖ) fell in 2002 to just over half its record 27 per cent achieved in the 1999 elections. Nevertheless, there is growing academic acceptance that the general rise of parties such as the FN and FrP cannot be dismissed simply as a form of passing protest. Voters in general are losing their traditional partisan allegiances, as the hold of factors such as class and religion decline. Some are strongly attracted by extreme right and populist policies on issues such as immigration and law and order, and by 'charismatic' personalities such as Le Pen[1] (on general theories of support see Eatwell 2003; for a good recent study of France see Mayer 2002).

Second, there has been an apparently mounting wave of harassment and outbursts of violence aimed at asylum seekers and ethnic minorities in Europe (other extreme right targets include the gay community and abortionists in the USA). Since the attacks on the Twin Towers and Washington on 11 September 2001, Muslims in particular have become a particularly notable target.[2] Especially in the USA, there has also been a growth of radical groups willing to use violence against the state – a state often seen by extremists as under the control of ZOG (the Zionist Occupation Government). War against Iraq in 2003 is likely to increase this sentiment by appearing to make the US an agent of Israeli interests – especially if the search for Weapons of Mass Destruction (the publicly-stressed cause of invasion) proves largely fruitless and/or Israel continues to block the creation of a Palestinian state. This may further encourage links between Islamic and hard-core extreme right militants, such as those within the American National Alliance and the German National Democratic Party (NPD), who praised the 11 September attack (although it is important to note that some anti-semitic groups, such as those influenced by the American Christian Identity doctrine, remain hostile to Islam).

Third, there are signs that ethnic minorities in Europe are increasingly asserting a sense of their own identity and/or feeling significant alienation from the political system. For example, this is very much the case among second and third generation Arab immigrants in France, who reject the traditional French policy of assimilation. In America, the Nation of Islam and the New Black Panther Party reflect similar disaffection. Such alienation can lead to violent behavior, both between and within ethnic communities, which in turn can help the extreme right. Indeed, its hard core sometimes seeks to promote racial violence as a way of radicalizing whites. Certainly the surprise electoral breakthrough of the BNP in 2001–03 came after ethnic disturbances in northern England, which were partly fomented by white extremists (although not directly by the BNP). At the same time, even among elites, there is a growing debate about the limits of multi-culturalism, and the need to unite society around shared values and symbols in order to avoid ethnic strife and other dysfunctional activities. Pushing the emphasis back towards a shared culture can provide succour to populist politicians like Pim Fortuyn, who do not argue along classic racist lines that immigrants are inferior, but rather that they – especially Muslims – cannot be integrated into indigenous cultures.

Fourth, there has been a dramatic increase in extremist propaganda. In some cases this stems from intellectual developments, such as the post-1970s' French Nouvelle Droite of Alain de Benoist. More generally, the Internet has opened up a plethora of new opportunities. It allows small radical American groups to preach views such as 'leaderless resistance' and race war – views that have been picked up by Europeans, such as the man who planted three bombs in London in 1999 aimed at ethnic minorities and gays. All European parties, like the FN, now operate extensive and usually well-presented websites. Indeed, the FN's site even has an English section – a reflection of the way in which this party sees itself as part of a family of European nationalist parties, and also an indication of its importance as a model to others. Some of the smaller extreme right coteries, such as Blood and Honour, part of the burgeoning neo-Nazi music scene, also have extensive sites.[3] However, the European groups face notable problems in claiming their 'right' to free speech, as no country has the equivalent of the American First Amendment. Indeed, the constitutions of some European countries are based on the idea of defensive or protective democracy, and permit the banning of non-democratic political parties, and the curtailing of free speech on issues such as Holocaust Denial.

Finally, there are growing concerns about the future of democracy. Whereas the beginning of the 1990s was characterized by an 'end of history' triumphalism, recent discussion has focused more on democracy's failings. One crucial problem is that democracy can no longer legitimize itself by demonizing the communist 'Other'. Anti-Islamism is, in some ways, a substitute, but this helps legitimate anti-immigrant and nationalist sentiment, which in turn poses problems for mainstream parties. Political scientists debate whether democracy is anything more than the organization of elite competition, mediated via television? Even more ominously, they ponder whether increasing economic globalization and political internationalization has undermined democracy at the national level? In future, will it be necessary to focus on *output* rather than *input* democracy – namely, factors such as constitutional rights and securing an underlying healthy economy rather than on democracy as active citizens and party competition? Post-modernist academics attack democratic universalism, holding that there are no universal values. Religious fundamentalists (including Christian as well as Islamic ones) attack democracy for the opposite reason – because of its moral pluralism, its failure to delineate a more worthy life than the pursuit of individual self-interest. Although most voters have not responded by rejecting the democratic system, there is widespread antipathy to politicians, which is reflected in declining turnouts at elections. Predictably, many extreme right and populist parties respond by stressing 'Rights for Whites' rather than for ethnic minorities, and legitimize themselves by claiming that they are the true representatives of the 'people' who are ignored by a distant Establishment (Canovan 1999; Mény and Surel 2002).

These opening comments raise a variety of major issues. One concerns the issue of how have others responded to these developments? This is an issue that is largely ignored in the extensive existing literature on the extreme right, which tends to concentrate on explaining support for the insurgent parties. This is an important omission because it raises vital perspectives. For example, to what extent have mainstream parties imposed a *cordon sanitaire* around extremist groups, sending out a moral signal that these groups support morally unacceptable policies? – a fate which has befallen the Flemish Block (VB) in Antwerp, where it is the largest party. And does this risk further alienating voters from an already distant 'Establishment'? Do the cases where the more moderate 'extremist' groups have been admitted into coalitions indicate that this tames and/or tends to split the parties between more purist and pragmatic wings? The problem of responses also involves non-party perspectives: for instance, what role do the law, civil society or education play in coming to terms with a more multicultural society?

The issue of response poses the especially important question of, to what extent is it possible for a democracy to inoculate itself against extremism without itself adopting measures which are undemocratic – such as curbing free speech, limiting the right to association, and even banning groups. For instance, Radical Unity was banned in France after one of its members attempted to assassinate President Chirac in the summer of 2002 – although it seems unlikely that the group was aware of this plan. Similarly, in 2001, the German government sought the banning of the National Democratic Party (NPD), in spite of the fact that there was no clear evidence that it specifically directed racial attacks and other criminal activities (the attempt was thrown out by the Constitutional Court in 2003 after it was revealed that the case relied heavily on paid informers, some of whom acted as *agents provocateurs*). These actions were taken in spite of the fact that the Council of Europe's Venice Commission for Democracy through the Law specifically stated in 1999 that: 'A political party as a whole can not be held responsible for the individual behaviour of members not authorized by the party' (though it accepts the possibility of bans on openly violent groups).[4]

A second issue raised by the five opening perspectives listed above concerns the fact that there appear to be major differences between the 'extreme right', 'populists' and others who are sometimes grouped into the party family. For example, Fortuyn recruited members of some ethnic minorities to his party and stated shortly before his assassination in 2002 that he had nothing in common with the 'racist' Jean-Marie Le Pen. Fortuyn claimed that his position was not based on any belief in racial hierarchies or hatred, but on his belief that the Netherlands could not take more immigrants, and the need to assimilate those who were already there. He added that if he were French, he would have voted for Jacques Chirac in the second ballot, and compared himself on economic policies more with Margaret Thatcher and Silvio Berlusconi than with the extreme right (although these 'mainstream' right leaders would have disagreed with Fortuyn's liberalism on many social issues). A similar point was made about Le Pen in 2002 by Gianfranco Fini, the leader of the Italian Alleanza Nazionale (AN), which had emerged in 1994 out of the clearly neo-fascist Italian Social Movement (MSI).

Fini, a former leader of the MSI, has in turn been accused of opportunistic moderation by hard liners such as Pino Rauti, who broke away from the AN to form the Fiamme Tricolore, which has remained far more clearly part of the fascist heritage. Filip Dewinter, a leading figure in the Flemish

Block, has accused Haider of being moderate, because the FPÖ's leader only sought to slow the rate of immigration into Austria whereas the VB sought to reverse it and make Flanders ethnically pure! Among fringe groups like the French Radical Unity, abuse for politicians like Le Pen, Fini and Haider is even greater. Indeed, hard-core groups, such as the British Combat 18 (its name taken from the first and eighth letters in the alphabet – (A(dolf) and H(itler)) have even carried out physical attacks on more moderate members of the putative extreme right 'family'.

The main thrust of this chapter concerns the second of these issues – namely, the problem of categorization. Is it reasonable to term all or most of the various individuals and groups referred to above as 'extreme right'? The simple answer given here, and reinforced by Part I of this book, is 'no' in the sense that few advocate violence or the creation of any form of dictatorship. Indeed, much of the 'extreme right' today does not appear to seek the overthrow of some form of democracy (although it is important to stress that there are good reasons, given the widespread support for democracy, to hide contrary views). In some ways 'populist' is a better term for many of the groups analysed in this book. However, these groups still pose a major challenge to liberal democracy, as well as a threat to specific groups within society. By highlighting these threats, the following discussion also sets the scene for Part II of this book, which focuses on the issue of how others have responded to such groups.

A plethora of terms – and threats?

A remarkable variety of terms have been used by academics and others to refer to groups like the FPÖ and Combat 18. In some cases the labels are used as synonyms, often in thesaurus-like ways. So a reference to the 'extreme right' can be followed by the substitution of a 'radical right', and so on. On other occasions, an attempt is made to distinguish between different types of groups. Thus, the 'populist' Norwegian Progress Party can be distinguished from the more Nazi-nostalgic NPD, and so on (see, for instance, Betz and Immerfall 1998). Sometimes such distinctions are diachronic rather than synchronic. A common approach distinguishes between the 'new extreme right' or 'radical right' and the 'old' one (for instance, Ignazi 1992, Kitschelt 1995) – though on closer examination the differences often turn out to be remarkably close to what some people term 'fascism' and 'populism', which is somewhat curious as populist movements pre-dated fascist ones.[5]

In recent years, two terms have become pre-eminent in the academic discussion of these contemporary phenomena – the 'extreme right' and 'populism'. Seeking to deconstruct both terms helps us to understand the threats they pose. However, before analysing these central terms, I will briefly consider 'fascism' and the 'radical right', which also often feature in discussions of current developments.

Fascism

The first self-styled 'fascist' movement was set up by Benito Mussolini in 1919, the term deriving from the Italian word '*fasci*', meaning leagues or unions in a political context (etymologically the word is linked to the ancient Roman *fasces*, an axe bound in rods, which became a key symbol of both authority and tradition for the Italian fascist movement). However, few subsequent groups have termed themselves 'fascist'. Indeed, a major debate rages among academics about whether a form of 'generic' fascism existed even in the inter-war era (many historians stress the differences between the putative 'fascisms' rather than similarities, especially the uniqueness of Nazi genocide). In spite of this, 'fascist' and 'Nazi' are common epithets among journalists for parties such as the FN, as well as for overtly Nazi groups like racist skinheads. Some academics on the left are also willing to identify widespread forms of contemporary fascism, continuing a tradition of seeing fascism as a form of 'capitalist' politics that deludes ordinary people about their true interests, and/or which appeals particularly to a 'petit bourgeoisie' which lacks a broad class and party home (for instance, Renton 1999).

Outside the left, only a handful of academics are willing to identify significant fascist strands in groups like the FN or FPÖ, or within intellectual groups such as the Nouvelle Droite. Usually the argument here focuses on ideology rather than structure. For example, fascism has been identified with the quest for the rebirth (palingenesis') of 'ultra nationalism' after a period of decadence (Griffin 1995), or the quest to forge a 'holistic nation' and pursue a 'Third Way' (neither capitalist nor socialist) political economy (Eatwell 1995). Such approaches raise important questions about the extent to which contemporary fascism must be a clone of the past, and about whether successful new forms would completely destroy democracy, as happened in Germany and Italy in the inter-war period. For example, whilst FN does not reject democracy, it supports a strong Presidency and the regular use of referendums to test the will of a re-forged holistic French people. The resulting government would hardly be a Nazi style dictatorship, but would it really be a form of liberal democracy either?

However, most political scientists use the term 'fascism' in the contemporary context within a rigid inter-war template. Sometimes the point of contact is essentially stylistic – for example, the wearing of fascist style uniform or insignia. Common ideological parallels include current groups that more or less openly support violence, which are critical of liberal democracy, and which advocate statist (typically corporatist) economics – groups such as the Italian Armed Revolutionary Nuclei (NAR), several of whose leading members have been prosecuted for various plots against the state. The term 'Nazism' is used for groups that overtly link themselves with the German model and/or which are highly anti-semitic[6] – groups such as the American National Alliance, whose overt extremism has been protected by the First Amendment (the writings of the party's leader at the time, Dr William Pierce, were a major source of inspiration for the 1995 bombing of a government building in Oklahoma, which killed well over 100 people).

Radical right

After 1945, the term 'radical right' became a commonplace in the academic political lexicon. The concept of the 'right' is another elusive one. In the past it has often been associated with a situational hostility to the left's commitment to change. In more essentialist terms, it is most typically associated with varying forms of inegalitarian and anti-universal views (Bobbio 1996; Eatwell and O'Sullivan 1989). Use of the term 'radical right' after 1945 was sometimes part of a wider tripartite typology, encompassing the reactionary right (opposed to all change, or desiring a return to the status quo ante), and the resistant right (a more flexible and pragmatic conservatism) (Weber 1965, pp. 15–16). On this approach, the radical right did not necessarily involve violence or advocate dictatorship. For instance, the 'radical right' American Senator Joe McCarthy and the John Birch Society in the USA sought to restrict the freedoms of the left on the grounds that these constituted 'un-American' activities (Bell 1963).

Today, the radical right remains a common generic term, especially among American academics. For instance, an influential recent work has distinguished between a 'New Radical Right' epitomized by the FN, and which is based on a 'winning formula' of liberal economics and conservative social values (including anti-immigrant politics), and an electorally unsuccessful old right linked more to the fascist tradition (Kitschelt 1995).

However, there are major typological problems involved in using the term 'radical right' to include disparate groups such as those who claim to support the democratic order, such as the John Birch Society or FN, latter-day extremists such as the Ku Klux Klan, which since 11 September 2001 has increasingly dropped its white garb and embraced combat fatigues and black shirts emblazoned with Nazi symbols, and those who even more overtly support violence. Moreover, the term 'radical right' has also been applied to clearly democratic developments, such as the post-1960s Anglo-American 'New Right', which advocated free market economics and smaller government, and to linked politicians such as Margaret Thatcher. Arguably, the only issue that really links this broad array of groups is that they in some way reject consensus or the status quo.

In Germany since the 1970s, there has been a legal distinction between 'radical' groups, which oppose aspects of (West) Germany's constitution, the Basic Law, and 'extremist' ones, which are overtly or implicitly hostile to it. However, it is often difficult to operationalize, as the radical category is mainly seen as a half-way house towards extremism. Thus, the Republikaner Party, formed in the early 1980s after a break-away from the

Bavarian Christian Social Union, was re-classified in the early 1990s from radical to extreme – although changes in the party programme were relatively minor. Indeed, some critics claimed that reclassification was an attempt to defuse the party's apparent growing threat to the mainstream and/or to appear to be doing something to halt growing attacks on immigrants, which many blamed on the extreme right. Whatever the merits of this particular case, it illustrates the difficulty in deciphering some parties' basic ideology in a world in which democracy seems the only game in town.

Extreme right

The most common academic term today grouping together parties such as the FN and organizations such as the NAR is 'extreme right'. In political contexts, the term 'extreme' is commonly associated with violence. The term is also commonly associated with intensity of belief, especially rigidly held beliefs. There is even a long tradition in Western thought, stemming back to Aristotle, which has associated direct democracy with forms of extremism. The liberal philosopher, John Stuart Mill, famously warned in the nineteenth century of the 'tyranny of the majority', which threatened minority rights and effective government.

Recent academic attempts to define the 'extreme right' have tended to drop violence as a necessary characteristic (although it is a notable feature of many groups on the fringes). Today four other traits feature most prominently in definitions: (1) anti-democracy; (2) nationalism; (3) racism; and (4) the strong state (Backes 2001; Hainsworth 2000; von Beyme 1988; and especially Mudde 1996 and 2000).

Arguably the most common feature stressed in definitions is anti-democracy. However, there are problems with this formulation. There are different forms of democracy, including 'direct' and 'liberal'. Extremism has sometimes presented itself as representing the former – the true will of the people (thus extremists can ask: who really wanted immigrants in Europe or Ivy League East Coast elites in the US?). Moreover, direct democracy in its original Greek form stressed the holistic community and Greek identity was based on a demonization of the 'Other' – a very different conception to the pluralism and internationalism that lie at the heart of modern liberal democracy. As a result, some argue that 'anti-parliamentarianism' is a better term (for instance, Fennema 1997). Extremists in the post-1945 era are usually more willing to attack parliamentary government openly. This form of government is associated with weakness, division, and, especially in America, with smoke filled rooms distant from the real people. Nevertheless, many extremists are willing to work through the parliamentary system to gain power, and their exact desires about democracy can be difficult to discern given the obvious reasons in the contemporary West to hide anti-democratic sentiments.

A more fertile variation on the anti-democracy theme holds that at the heart of democratic thinking is a willingness not just to tolerate diversity, but to accept different points of view as legitimate (Lipset and Raab 1971). Extremists are 'monists' rather than 'pluralists', believing that there is only one true way. This is accompanied by a commitment to authoritarianism, in particular a desire to impose the correct line on others. If there is only one truth, then those who disagree with this truth must be fools – or worse, evil people, involved in some kind of conspiracy (a characteristic assertion on the fringes of the American right and Nazism). Most contemporary extreme right-wingers do not say that they seek to repress all different points of view. However, the way in which the FN used its control of several French municipalities after the late 1990s to weed out mainly left-wing books from libraries, withdraw subsidies from undesired groups, and pursue other restrictive policies illustrates their limited view of 'pluralism'.

The extreme right is typically seen as highly nationalistic. To be more precise, it defends a particular type of nationalism – one that in Europe stresses the holistic community over the individual, and tends towards intolerance of diversity (American versions historically have been more individualistic). Nationalism can encompass both biological and cultural forms – although, in general, in the post-war era there has been a decline in the Nazi-like belief that nations are primordial or genetically determined. Although this discussion of the extreme right began with anti-democracy, a strong case could be made that it is nationalism that is the key. Indeed, other extreme right values – such as the critique of party politics – tend to derive from a view of the nation (in this case, they are related to the belief that the nation has fallen into decadence, that it is divided, and so on). But even nationalism is fading among some of the theorists of the extreme right. For example, de Benoist has argued that the ethnic region is the more natural unit of immediate association – and Europe, although not the bureaucratic European Union, is sometimes seen as the key wider unit of cultural identity.

It is especially important to note that nationalism can be polycentric and is perfectly consistent with a form of Europeanism based around 'Europe of the nation states' – a view now espoused by the leadership of the BNP (whereas the earlier line had been close to 'Wogs begin at Calais'). European extremists sometimes portray the First and Second World wars as 'civil wars', and seek to form a 'Fortress Europe' against immigration and economic threats. Nationalism should also not necessarily be equated with the defence of existing state forms. Some extremist movements, for instance the Flemish Block in Belgium, have sought the break up of the existing state on the grounds that it was polyglot. The Northern League in Italy has at times similarly sought the breakaway of a mythical Padania, and the purging of unwanted outsiders (who can include southern Italians as well as those from the Balkans and North Africa). In the USA, white supremacists have even advocated setting up a new heartland state, most typically in the more white, rural-based north west area of the country.

An increasing concern of the post-1945 European extreme right has been protecting the nation against outsiders – delineating people who should be expelled, or forced to conform. Although this prejudice can be aimed at homosexuals, female liberationists and 'anti-fascists', most typically it has involved targeting Jews and even more commonly 'immigrants' (the last term is frequently used very loosely, sometimes referring to people whose families have lived in a country for one or more generations). There are some differences between the main European extreme right parties about how to deal with 'immigrants'. For instance, the BNP in the past sought the compulsory expulsion of non-whites, whereas the FPÖ sought more to halt new inflows and assimilate those already in Austria. However, with the exception of the Alleanza Nazionale, until recently all the most successful European parties since the 1980s have featured some form of anti-immigrant politics. In the US, anti-immigrant politics has never fired a new electoral movement, but hostility to new arrivals, such as Hispanics and South East Asians, has increasingly reinforced more traditional racist sentiments.

When examining racism on the extreme right, it is important to note that, historically, racism mainly dealt in hierarchies, or pointed to conspiracies (especially Jewish ones). In recent decades, there has been a growth of a 'new racism'. This holds that nations and races are not so much superior or inferior, as different: each should live 'naturally' in its own home, respecting others (Taguieff 1994). This form of Nouvelle Droite-influenced 'differencialism' has been common in the FN and has helped it deflect charges of racism (as has the fact that the wife of one of its leading members is Japanese, and the FN has included a small number of non-white members). However, such differencialism is clearly designed to make prejudice and exclusionism more respectable. Moreover, at times Le Pen has let the mask slip and talked openly about differences between races (other such slips include his reference to the Holocaust as a 'detail' of history). More generally at the extremist rank and file level, 'old' racism is far from dead.

Traditionally, extreme right support for the strong state encompasses features such as the elevation of strong leadership, authoritarian control and militarism. The first trait remains common among extremists, although some parties, such as the German People's Union and the BNP until recently, have hardly been characterized by 'charismatic' leadership. But commitment to authoritarian politics and militarism is now much less common. European extremist groups now rarely display any military style – though this is in part explained by the fact that, in many countries, the wearing of political uniforms is banned, a very different situation to the US where groups like the 1990s' Militias donned battle fatigues. Gun control

Introduction 11

is also very strict in Western Europe. Most recent European extreme right groups have also not been notably warlike. Indeed, many opposed the 2003 Iraq war – though this also reflected anti-Israeli and anti-US sentiments (since the turn of the 1990s, the latter has become much stronger in an extreme right that no longer fears Soviet communism).

Statism can also be considered in the economic sphere. Historically, the extreme right has tended to be suspicious of capitalism as a social solvent and potential threat to the nation. However, the growing popularity of free market views after the 1970s had an effect on some European parties like the FPÖ and Alleanza. Nevertheless, support for lower taxes and a rolling back of the state tend to be accompanied by support for 'national preference' or 'welfare chauvinism' – namely, the belief that the fruits of the national economy should first and foremost go to their own people. Moreover, some parties, which exhibited relatively free market views in the 1980s, such as the FN, are now increasingly stressing anti-globalization views, including national or European protectionism. Once again, anti-Americanism is often an important factor in this equation. But it is interesting to note that some right-wing Americans, such as Pat Buchanan, have also been critical of free markets and globalization, fearing for the fate of 'ordinary' Americans as more and more goods are manufactured in low cost countries.

Populism

In the US, the term 'populism' has for many years been employed to describe groups which, in some ways, hark back to the US Populist Party of the late nineteenth century, which eulogized the ordinary working man and was hostile to urban elites (Berlet and Lyons 2000). More generally in recent years, there has been a tendency to use the term loosely to refer to non-ideological politicians and parties that seem to be driven by opinion polls and spin doctors, and the quest to tell voters what they want to hear.

Among academics, there has been a growing number who have adopted the term 'populist' rather than extreme right. In some cases, this reflects the argument that the term 'extreme right' has never been a form of self-reference for any party, and that it is essentially an academic and anti-fascist construct designed to delegitimize groups. More common is the argument that many of the major manifestations of so-called right-wing extremism are not really extreme (for instance, Betz 1994; Betz and Immerfall 1998; Taggart 1995, 2000). Some parties, for instance the Scandinavian Progress ones, have no historical connection with the fascist tradition. They also, unlike the FN at times, do not appear to have a hidden agenda or the desire to use office to restrict the rights of others whose views they do not share.

Four features are central to populism. First, populists claim to represent the true will of the people, which is failing to be heard. Widespread use of the referendum is advocated to enable the voice of the true majority to be ascertained. Second, populists are anti-Establishment, portraying parties and especially elite politicians as distant and often corrupt. Le Pen, for example, frequently contrasts penthouse (*d'en haut*) with basement (*en bas*) France. The Italian Northern League is a good example of a linked third trait, the tendency to use 'low' rather than 'high' concepts, language and style.[7] The League's garrulous leader, Umberto Bossi, is a frequent exponent of the language of the streets, and party propaganda has played on machismo with slogans like 'The League's got a hard one'. Fourth, populist movements tend to produce charismatic leaders, who portray themselves as the embodiment of what people really think. Le Pen, for instance, has claimed that he only says out loud what most French people think in private.

Undoubtedly there are very good arguments for not using the term 'extremist' in the case of, say, the Norwegian Progress Party or the List Pim Fortuyn. Some would even extend these cases to include parties like Haider's or Le Pen's, arguing that whilst some of their views, especially in relation to immigration, are reprehensible, they have basically come to accept the liberal democratic system. To put it a different way, within the context of the German legal definition, they are 'radical' rather than 'extremist' parties. Certainly most of these parties would accept the label 'populist'.

However, populism in both the US and Europe is best seen as a style, rather than as a specific body of thought (Canovan 1981). In particular, it has no clear ideology, and tends to be negative. Especially in America it has supported 'producers' against spongers, but this has not produced any clear economic body of thought. For example, early American populism sought an expansion of the state, whereas contemporary groups, including European ones, typically advocate the rolling back of what is seen as an inflated state. Moreover, there is populism of the left as well as the right – it is a language and style that can be used by groups which genuinely support a radical redistribution of income and power within society. As a result, some academics prefer compound terms, especially 'national populism' (for instance, Taguieff 1994). But given that nationalism is a 'thin' ideology, perfectly consistent with left-wing thought (Freeden 1998), such terminology is still consistent with left-wing groups.

Moreover, the term 'populism' poses the opposite danger to classifying parties as 'extreme right' – namely, it tends to legitimize them as in some ways genuinely democratic. However, 'populist' (in most cases also read 'extreme right') groups pose a variety of threats to liberal democracy, of which I will focus on six.

First, populism tends to dichotomize issues, into black and white, good and evil. This makes a politics of bargaining and compromise, which are at the very heart of liberal democracy, more difficult. The desire by some extremists to use referendums as a major form of policy making is a particularly clear indication of hostility to compromise. Referendums encourage 'yes' or 'no' answers, rather than nuanced discussion. Populism essentially seeks to mobilize people rather than make them think about complex issues.

Second, populism's celebration of the charismatic leader, often characterized by a sense of mission more than by a particularly clear programme, is part of a more general attack on parties as the basis of democracy. Populist parties are paradoxical in the sense that they are political parties that reject the legitimacy of parties. As such, they encourage growing anti-party sentiment among the electorate, which risks broadening into a more general attack on democracy. Thus, even if they do not overtly reject liberal democracy, they effectively become 'anti-system parties'.

Third, populism is hostile to many individual rights, as these are associated with liberal elites, who use them to the disadvantage of the majority. True rights belong to the majority – for instance, to preserve their traditional way of life or to enjoy the economic benefits provided by previous efforts. Thus, old age pensioners have a right to a decent standard of living, but immigrants, even asylum seekers, have limited or no rights to claim on the state.

Fourth, populism tends to make international cooperation more difficult. As well as the fact that it stresses the will of the (national) 'people', it also tends to portray bodies like the European Union as the epitome of backroom deals. The United Nations is portrayed at best as corrupt, and at worst as central to various conspiracies. In the US especially, this is often linked to claims that there are plans for a 'New World Order', with the UN occupying the land of the free!

Fifth, the relatively coarse language of populist leaders poses a challenge to the impartial judicial discourse that is central to the concept of reason for modern liberal thinkers like John Rawls. This does not simply mean that populists pander to the lowest prejudices. Populists can also invoke a moral language that is opposed to liberalism's value neutrality and pluralism. In the US especially, populists have often adopted a fundamentalist Christian line to challenge dominant liberal norms on abortion or the teaching of the Creation.

Finally, it is vital to consider the impact of populist parties on other parties. Regardless of whether 'populist' parties are admitted into local or national coalitions, they tend to have an effect on mainstream parties, especially in the realm of immigration and related issues. In France in the 1980s and 1990s, there was much talk of the 'Le Penization' of politics, with even parties of the left borrowing from the FN's programme and rhetoric. Similarly, in Italy recently, Silvio Berlusconi's conservative government has been influenced on immigration policy by his Northern League and Alleanza allies.

Conclusions

This Introduction has not set out to delineate a full typology of groups such as the FN, FrP, National Alliance and Combat 18: to do so, would require far more space than is available here. Rather, this chapter has sought to do two main things. First, it points to the problems involved in using terms such as 'extreme right' and 'populism'. Even as Weberian 'ideal types', both raise major issues concerning the extent to which they can be applied to contemporary movements. Second, this chapter has sought to show that even the more moderate groups pose notable challenges to contemporary democracy.

The question of how others have responded to these threats is picked up particularly in Part 2 of this book, and the Conclusion. So here I will limit my final comments to expanding briefly on the use of the term 'extreme right' in the title and elsewhere in this book.

Some of the groups referred to above, such as the NAR and Combat 18, are unquestionably extreme. However, most do not espouse violence and many do not clearly seek the overthrow of some form of liberal democracy. Moreover, it is important to note that some of the questions raised by these groups relate to growing problems within liberal democracy. Whilst extremism is often defined in terms of opposition to, or at least fundamental criticism of, liberal democracy it is important to remember that existing democracies are in many ways flawed. This is not simply a question of modern democracy's failure to provide what some see as adequate provision for more direct participation. Even in its own terms, contemporary democracy has many problems – including growing power for multinational corporations, of the mass media, and of national and international bureaucracies.

The use of the term 'extreme right' in this book's title constitutes, therefore, more a convenient but flawed shorthand, with an inbuilt warning for complacent democrats, than an attempt to damn all who are discussed in this book. Indeed, it is especially important to underline that this book seeks to be a work of political science, not normative pleading. Our main concerns involve analysing questions concerning how 'extremists' have adapted to the pre-eminence of democracy, and how others have responded to 'extremists', rather than to answering questions about how we ought to respond to related threats.

Notes

1 The term 'charismatic' is used here in the sense of a leader becoming the personification of politics, especially for more alienated voters, rather than in the Weberian mass-affective sense. On this, and the concept of 'coterie charisma', where the leader exerts a special appeal over core supporters, see Eatwell 2002.
2 Countries collect statistics in very different ways, which makes it difficult to compare across borders. Even within countries, it is difficult to compare figures

across areas and over time because of varying collection techniques, etc. For instance, the British Crime Survey includes racial 'incidents', which can include verbal harassment, whereas German statistics have mainly logged violent activities, and the French government has adopted a policy which seems designed to create the impression of minimal racist activity.
3 http://www.skrewdriver.net.
4 http://venice.coe.int/docs/2000/CDL-INF(2000)001-e.html, pp. 3–4. Downloaded 15 March 2003.
5 In some cases, the distinction is a structural rather than an ideological one. Thus the 'new' extreme right is often seen as based on a form of reverse post-materialism, in which less skilled males in particular react to new politics agendas concerning issues such as feminism, and to new threats such as globalization.
6 Italian fascism in its early years was not anti-semitic: indeed, many Jews were active in the party and Mussolini for many years had a Jewish mistress.
7 The distinction borrows from the distinction between high and low styles of Islam, which can be found in Gellner (1992).

Bibliography

Backes, U. (2001) 'L'extrême droite. Les multiples facettes d'une catégorie d'analyse', in Perrineau, P. (ed.) *Les Croisées de la société fermée. L'europe des extrêmes droites*, Paris: Editions de l'Aube.

Bell, D. (1963) *The Radical Right*, New York: Doubleday.

Berlet, C. and Lyons, M.N. (2000) *Right-Wing Populism in America*, New York: the Guilford Press.

Betz, H.-G. (1994) *Radical Right-Wing Populism in Western Europe*, Basingstoke: Macmillan.

Betz, H.-G. and Immerfall, S. (eds) (1998) *The New Politics of the Right*, New York: St. Martins.

Bobbio, N. (1996) *Left and Right*, Cambridge: Polity Press.

Canovan, M. (1981) *Populism*, London: Junction Books.

Canovan, M. (1999) 'Trust the people! Populism and the two faces of democracy', *Political Studies* XLVII, 1: 2–16.

Eatwell, R. (1995) *Fascism. A History*, London: Chatto and Windus (new edn. 2003, London: Pimlico).

Eatwell, R. (2002) 'The rebirth of right-wing charisma?: the cases of Vladimir Zhirinovsky and Jean-Marie Le Pen', *Totalitarian Movements and Political Religions* 3, 3: 1–23.

Eatwell, R. (2003) 'Ten theories of the extreme right', in Merkl, P.H. and Weinberg, L. (eds) *The Extreme Right in the Twenty-First Century*, London: Frank Cass.

Eatwell, R. and O'Sullivan, N. (eds) (1989) *The Nature of the Right*, London: Pinter.

Fennema, M. (1997) 'Some conceptual issues and problems in the comparison of anti-immigrant parties in Western Europe', *Party Politics* 3, 4: 473–492.

Freeden, M. (1998) 'Is nationalism a distinct ideology?', *Political Studies* XLVI, 4: 746–765.

Gellner, R. (1992) *Postmodernism, Reason and Religion*, London: Routledge.

Griffin, R. (1995) *Fascism. A Reader*, Oxford: Oxford University Press.

Hainsworth, P. (ed.) (2000) *The Politics of the Extreme Right*, London: Pinter.

Ignazi, P. (1992) 'The silent counter-revolution: hypotheses on the emergence of extreme right-wing parties in Europe', *European Journal of Political Research* 22, 1: 3–34.

Kitschelt, H. (with M. McGann) (1995) *The Radical Right in Western Europe*, Chicago: University of Michigan Press.

Lipset, S.M. and Raab, E. (1971) *The Politics of Unreason. Right-Wing Extremism in America, 1790–1970*, London: Heinemann.

Mayer, N. (2002) *Ces français qui votent Le Pen*, Paris: Flammarion.

Mény, Y. and Surel, Y. (eds) (2002) *Democracies and the Populist Challenge*, Basingstoke: Palgrave.

Merkl, P. and Weinberg, L. (eds) (2003) *The Extreme Right in the Twenty-First Century*, London: Frank Cass.

Mudde, C. (1996) 'The war of the words. Defining the extreme right party family', *West European Politics* 19, 2: 225–248.

Mudde, C. (2000) *The Ideology of the Extreme Right*, Manchester: Manchester University Press.

Renton, D. (1999) *Fascism. Theory and Practice*, London: Pluto.

Schain, M. Zolberg, A. and Hossay, P. (eds) (2002) *Shadows Over Europe: the Development and Impact of the Extreme Right in Western Europe*, New York: Palgrave.

Taggart, P. (1995) 'New populist parties in Western Europe', *West European Politics* 18.1: 34–51.

Taggart, P. (2000) *Populism*, Milton Keynes: Open University Press.

Taguieff, P.-A. (1994) *Sur la Nouvelle Droite*, Paris: La Découverte.

Von Beyme, K. (ed.) (1998) *Right-wing Extremism in Europe*, London: Frank Cass.

Weber, E. (1965) 'The right. An introduction', in Rogger, H. and Weber, E. (eds) *The European Right*, London: Weidenfeld and Nicholson.

Part I

Right-wing extremism in contemporary democracies

1 Between adaptation, differentiation and distinction
Extreme right-wing parties within democratic political systems

Alexandre Dézé

Introduction

On the whole, classical approaches to extreme right parties have analyzed the question of their relationship to European democratic political systems in four different ways: first, by considering extreme right movements as a danger for democracy (e.g. Taguieff and Tribalat 1998); second, by examining the responses of democratic regimes to extremist challenges (e.g. Capoccia and Pedahzur 2003); third, by evaluating the impact of extremist formations on political systems (e.g. Schain 2001); finally, by interpreting the phenomenon's emergence in Europe as the consequence of factors such as the transformation (Kitschelt and McGann 1995) or the crisis of West European party systems (e.g. Ivaldi 1999a). In this chapter, I would like to suggest another way of exploring the relationship between extremism and democracy, and more specifically its consequences for extreme right parties.

Some of these parties can now be considered as full members of the political arena. This is particularly true in Belgium, Austria, Italy, and France. However, it does not entail that the relationship between these parties and European democratic systems is less problematic. Although based on an ideology whose roots are in contradiction to essential liberal democratic principles, such parties have nonetheless tried to win power through proper constitutional means. How have these parties managed, and how do they still manage, to deal with this contradiction – institutional logic versus doctrinal orthodoxy? My hypothesis is that the manner in which these parties have managed this contradiction partly explains their present evolution. I will try to test this hypothesis through the comparative analysis of four organizations – the French National Front (FN), the Flemish Block (VB), the National Alliance-Italian Social Movement (AN-MSI) and the Austrian Freedom Party (FPÖ). The comparative approach to the extreme right in Europe raises several taxonomic problems (Backes 2001; Mudde 1996). However, using Piero Ignazi's (1992, 1994a) definition, I will consider these as extreme right parties.[1]

Adaptation, differentiation and distinction

According to the main teachings of the systemic and environmentalist approaches to political parties, parties are both dependent and independent from their global environment.[2] The dependency factor forces them to 'adapt themselves' to it. As emphasized by Jean and Monica Charlot, it is a 'matter of life and death' (Charlot and Charlot 1985, p. 431). Thus, parties are 'dependent variables' of the systems in which they operate. Nevertheless, they also 'always manage to maintain [...] sufficient autonomy so as to be independent variables as well' (Charlot and Charlot, p. 471). Parties are free to decide not to adapt to the environment; however, this choice partly excludes them from it. Whether parties abide by liberal democratic values depends on the ideological distance separating these values from those on which the identity of a given party is built.

In the particular instance of extreme right formations, this distance is important enough for the relationship with democratic political systems to be problematic. We can formulate, theoretically, that this interaction leaves extreme right parties with one alternative: either adapt themselves to the system, hence running the risk of losing a part of their original identities and of the support of their most orthodox members, or distinguish themselves from the system, thereby running the risk of being excluded from it, or of being marginalized.

It is necessary, at this point, to clarify notions and to specify how this theoretical schema works. First, I think that the strategic alternative between *adaptation* and *distinction* is an alternative between terms that are contradictory for extreme right parties. However, I do not think that for any party, there is any contradiction or 'paradox' (Villalba 1997) between *adaptation* and *differentiation*. Political systems in representative democracies create a competitive game: parties are therefore forced to use strategic differentiation (Parodi 1991; Ysmal 1985). Hence, adapting themselves to the system and differentiating themselves within the system are 'two essential rules of the political game' (Birenbaum 1992, p. 18).

However, a party wishing to participate in the electoral game must reconcile these two imperatives (adaptation and differentiation), which creates an intra-party tension centering around the relationship to ideology. The changing pattern of positions occupied within the system implies that, in some circumstances, parties are led to stress their differentiation strategy and propose some of the most controversial elements in their ideologies and platforms. In other circumstances, particularly while allying themselves with other parties or while trying to broaden their electoral base, these singular aspects in their ideologies are marginalized (Bourdieu 1981; Michels 1962).

However, the tension at work in the relationship of these parties to their ideologies does not simply vary according to the position occupied within the system. It also, and more importantly, depends on the nature of the relationship with this system. For contemporary extreme right parties, who show 'opposition of principle' (Kirchheimer 1966, p. 237) to democratic systems, differentiating themselves can imply putting forward, in some circumstances and on some topics, an ideology and a platform that contradict the principles on which the system is based. In this case, extreme right parties not only stress their difference *within* the system but also *with* the system: they distinguish themselves *from* it.

An 'alternative *within* the system' and an 'alternative *to* the system': an irreducible dilemma?

It is now time to test the validity of this schema from an empirical point of view. Now that they have become full-time actors in the political game, how have extreme right parties managed to deal with this paradoxical relationship with the system? To answer this question, it is important to grant full attention to the contextual evolution of the global environment which, from the mid-1980s onward, has been rather favorable to the emergence and implantation of extreme right organizations in representative democracies (Kitschelt and McGann 1995; Ignazi 1994a).

Incidentally, political organizations are far from able to control the full process granting them access to, and survival within, a given political system. Their recognition, which is the key to access the decision-making process (Charlot and Charlot 1985), comes from a host of complex institutional, cultural, economic, social and political mechanisms that they can only partially control (Lagroye 1985). Still, these organizations use strategies and discourses, in the competitive game over power, which are clear testimonies of the type of political behaviors that they have adopted towards both the system and the other political actors. I will use the – inevitably summary and fragmentary – analysis of these strategies and discourses as a basis for empirical verification, while taking the environmental global context into consideration as a constraint on the elaboration and the implementation of these strategies and discourses.

The MSI: from the 'excluded' to the 'integrated' pole

Founded in 1946 by ex-dignitaries of the Italian Social Republic, the Italian Social Movement (MSI) positioned itself from the start at the fringe of the Italian democratic political system. As the movement 'owed its *raison d'être* to its bond with fascism, accepting [...] the "anti-fascist" system was a painful operation as it was difficult to reconcile with its manifest ideology' (Ignazi 1994b, pp. 1016–17). In a first phase, the party clearly refused to compromise with the system. It overtly used strategic distinction and violently criticized the institutional regime. Its platform was unambiguous – 'to keep on calling on the spirit of fascism and the spirit of the Italian Social Republic' (in Simon 1992, p. 73) – and its activities focused on activism and anti-communism.

In spite of this rejection, the political system still functioned as the MSI's inescapable center of attraction. As early as 1947, the MSI endeavored to implement both a strategy of adaptation and of electoral participation. As underlined by Roberto Chiarini, 'the very fact of entering Parliament [in 1948] and local councils [in 1947] forced the MSI to moderate its ideology' (Chiarini 1995, p. 98), i.e. to reduce the distance between their own values and those of representative democracy. This strategic participation raised the sensitive question of the relationship with the political system. As such, it became the issue of a heated conflict between the two wings of the party – the intransigents hostile to any type of compromise, and the moderates in favor of an anti-communist alliance with the Christian Democrats and the monarchists.[3]

In 1950, Augusto de Marsanich, the leader of the moderate wing, acceded to the leadership of the party. From this year onward, the MSI planned to become a 'credible' political force, the 'hub of a future government of national union' (Milza 1991, p. 481). They concluded a 'pact of alliance' with the Monarchist Party, and supported successive moderate governments. This change had immediate positive electoral consequences. However, it gave rise to strong tensions with the intransigent, revolutionary and social wing. Remaining faithful to the tradition of the Social Republic, Giorgio Almirante, Principal Private Secretary at the Ministry of Popular Culture (Minculpop) under the Social Republic and an irreconcilable opponent to the regime, resigned from the national leadership of the party in April 1956. Pino Rauti, likewise, parted with the Almirantian group of the party to form the Evolian movement Ordine Nuovo (New Order).

In 1960, the strategic insertion of the MSI seemed complete (Ignazi 1996) when Tambroni's Christian Democrat government obtained a vote of confidence thanks to the support of the neo-fascist party. But this event triggered a strong reaction from the Italian population, and violent confrontations between leftist militants and the police took place during the congress of the MSI, which was held in Genoa (the former capital of the Resistance). Twelve people died in the street battles and hundreds were injured, leading the government to resign.

From this date, the MSI entered a phase of political decline, during which the moderate leadership was increasingly contested. However, when Arturo Michelini (de Marsanich's successor) died in 1969, the MSI was once again faced with the 'contradiction between theoretico-verbal maximalism and the daily practice of a somewhat receptive attitude towards the moderation of the Christian Democrats' (Ignazi 1989, p. 133). Paradoxically, the election of Giorgio Almirante as Secretary General did not lead to radicalization of the movement's strategy. Strengthened by increasing electoral support, Almirante asserted his intention to pursue and update the strategy of insertion by reconciling the extremes within a vast 'autonomous' union. The party was then redefined as the party of 'the alternative to the system *and* of the alternative within the system' (Almirante 1969).

The outcome of this strategy of conciliation was the creation of the Destra Nazionale (National Right, DN) with a view to contesting the legislative elections. The aim of the DN was clearly to broaden their electoral base as well as their political staff (Monarchists, Liberals, Christian Democrats, whose presence helped grant legitimacy to the party). This process contributed to changing the party label to MSI-DN, and to effacing a part of the original ideological grounding. Henceforward, in their speeches 'any subversive or revolutionary attempts were rejected' (Almirante 1970) while 'democracy' and 'liberty' were redefined as 'priority values that cannot be renounced' (Almirante 1972).

The party could not totally renounce its ideological grounding without estranging part of its electorate and its most orthodox militants. Nevertheless, MSI leaders were conscious that it was no longer possible to 'present fascism in a grotesque [...], old-fashioned, anachronistic and stupidly nostalgic manner' (Almirante cited in Cheles 1986, p. 29). The party therefore developed a latent ideology, expressed through the use of a 'double' discourse perfectly illustrated by the slogan found on a poster of the 1970 regional elections campaign – '*Nostalgia dell'avvenire*' (Nostalgia for the future), a conceptual expression of this search for compromise between the past (fascism) and the future (the integration of the MSI). The results of the 1972 election initially seemed to confirm Almirante's strategy. However, unable to complete this ideological revision because of strong criticism among the more militant, intransigent fringes of the party, he was faced with the failure of the DN project during the 1976 elections.

Jeopardized by a context of gruesome terrorism, abandoned by the advocates of ideological renovation (the faction led by Ernesto De Marzio having decided to leave the party in order to extend 'the limits of the DN strategy into a right-wing conservative party' (Ignazi 1996, p. 698) by founding National Democracy), the MSI relaunched its policy of an alternative *to* the system (one of their slogans was 'Struggle against the regime') and became increasingly isolated. More than 30 years after its creation, the issue of its relationship with the political system centered around contradictory ideas, as it failed to overcome the alternative between loyalty to fascism and adaptation to the system. As Almirante had underlined in 1956, 'the ambiguity [...] is to be fascists within democracy' (cited in Campi 1995, p. 121).

At the end of the 1980s, the death of the historical leaders (Almirante, Romualdi) did not change anything. As the 'Dauphin' of Almirante, Gianfranco Fini, the young and new Secretary of the party whose nomination had been strongly debated, maintained the traditional line of opposition to the system and kept stressing the continuity of the party's ideals with fascism. His strategy left things unchanged, and Fini was criticized and defeated by Pino Rauti at the 1990 Congress. Both leaders disagreed about strategic options: while Fini, inspired by the French FN, tried to put forward immigration issues as a means of electoral mobilization (Simon 1992), Rauti elaborated a program combining elements of both neo-rightist thought and early Fascist radicalism with the intention of attracting leftist voters. At the 1990 municipal and regional elections, the MSI obtained the worst results of its history (3.9 per cent of the vote). As the 1991 Sicily elections were no better, Rauti resigned and Fini was re-elected. The following year the MSI commemorated the 70th anniversary of the 'March on Rome'.

At the dawn of the 1990s, everything seemed to indicate that the neo-fascist movement was doomed to remaining a marginal force in the Italian political system. However, its recent evolution, based on full integration into the system and, consequently, on the acceptance of the founding principles of representative democracy, proves different. How did the MSI succeed in overcoming the historic dilemma with which it had been faced during 50 years?

First, a series of exogenous factors contributed to the progressive rehabilitation of the MSI, as well as encouraging the constitution of the 'List of Agreement of the Good Government' linking it to the new Forza Italia, and the Northern League.[4] Thus, a political pariah became one of the main actors of the 'Pole of Liberty'. It is at this moment that the neo-fascist movement adopted the label National Alliance-Italian Social Movement (AN-MSI), thereby stressing its will to change and renew the party.

The ensuing 1994 legislative elections were a triumphant success. The AN-MSI got 13.5 per cent of the vote, 107 deputies and five ministers. Now a member of the Berlusconi government, the MSI went much further than simply changing labels: it also stopped referring to corporatism, and accepted the market economy as well as the fundamental principles of democracy. Finally, the party clearly distanced itself from fascism; for example, Fini (re)defined anti-fascism as 'a moment which was historically essential to the return of democratic values in Italy'. The 1995 Fiuggi Congress made the party transformation official. In protest, Rauti left the party together with a militant radical group and subsequently created the Movimento Sociale Fiamma-Tricolore.

Returning to opposition after the fall of Berlusconi's government, the AN-MSI did not return to the fringes. The party recognized the fundamental principles of democracy, and officially rejected the 1938 racial laws, together with anti-Semitism and racism (reasserted again at the 1998 Verona Congress). It developed a program in line with those of moderate European right-wing parties (which rejected the state-controlled, nationalist and centralist tradition of the neo-fascist project). In spite of disappointing results in the 1999 European elections and the 2001 national election, the AN is now a strong institutionalized political force: it has four ministers in the post-2001 Berlusconi government in which Fini became Vice President of the Council of Ministries.

Hence, the recent evolution of the former neo-fascist movement confirms the validity of the theoretical hypotheses previously expressed. It was only by giving up its original identity, and helped by a particularly favorable context, that the AN succeeded in overcoming the constituent dilemma in the history of the MSI. However, even though the AN can now be considered as a 'postfascist' party (Ignazi 1994c), there still is a clearly 'nostalgic' culture within the movement. It is true that the profiles of the party's intermediate leaders appear less and less radical, but ties with fascist culture are still strong (Bertolino and Chiapponi 1999; Baldini and Vignati 1996). This was again confirmed recently by the vigorous debates within the movement about the eventual erasing of MSI historical symbols from the AN logo (the three letters MSI and the tricolor flame). 'It's our patrimony', Alessandra Mussolini, granddaughter of the Duce and an AN Deputy – 'Leaving it behind is out of the question' (*Le Monde*, 8 April 2002).

The FN: a 'Necessarily partial and unfinished institutional strategy'?[5]

At the beginning of the 1970s, the MSI represented a model for the French extreme right (Duprat 1972). Inspired by recent Italian experience, the leaders of the activist and nationalist-revolutionary group New Order (ON) decided to 'widen the penetration of the movement' and to increase their participation in the competition for power, by creating, in October 1972, a more 'respectable' political organization: the party of the 'Droite nationale, sociale et populaire' (The national, social and people's right), i.e. the Front National.

Hence, the creation of the FN proceeded from strategic adaptation to the political system, which implied giving up all forms of activism on the one hand (which, in turn, led to the disappearance of ON within the Front), and adjusting to the access conditions of the electoral competition on the other hand (implying the adoption of moderate speech and images). The appointment of Jean-Marie Le Pen (who embodied, at that time, the more legalist face of the French extreme right) to head the new party was supposed to meet this second requirement, as well as the elaboration of a programme that was based on a compromise between revolutionary-nationalism and conservatism (Camus 1996).

However, poor early electoral results seemed to prove the failure of this strategy and led to a split between those who called for intensified activism and a return to a radical conception of doctrine, and the national Lepenist tendency. The latter began a long 'crossing of the desert' (in their own words); a period during which the party, under the influence of the revolutionary-nationalist wing of François Duprat, first expressed full ideological opposition to the democratic system and parliamentary government, before changing strategy under the influence of the 'solidarist' wing of Jean-Pierre Stirbois.

Therefore, at the beginning of the 1980s, the Front National was only a very small organization on the French political scene. In 1981, Le Pen could not even gather the 500 signatures required to stand in the Presidential election, and in the parliamentary election that year the FN obtained just 0.18 per cent of the vote. An isolated and weakly implanted organization, the FN seemed doomed to remain a marginal party, incapable of presenting itself as either an alternative to the system or an alternative within the system.

However, three years later, the FN obtained 11.2 per cent in the European elections. Its sudden emergence corresponded with a very clearcut change in the image, the style and the speech of the party (Dézé 1995) and with the appearance of a double discourse: a traditional radical one for loyal militants, and a softer and respectable one for the electorate in general. This showed the constraints that emerged from the party's more active participation in political competition (Birenbaum 1985) as well as the necessity for the FN to adapt to the system without giving up its political identity.

The problematic management of this double discourse was partly resolved by the use of strategic euphemisms, such as the notion of 'national preference' (the equivalent of the 'French First!' slogan). It is necessary to underline that the use of this notion in Frontist speech from 1985 onward not only showed the need to adapt racist ideology to the standards of political expression of the time, but also, by playing on the implicit, this notion contained the radical aspirations of the militants and turned an exclusive conception of racism into an 'acceptable' preferential one (Taguieff 1988, 1986).

The political history of the FN from that moment onwards can be read in the light of the alternation between and/or the concomitance of:

- strategic phases of *adaptation*: the creation of the label 'Rassemblement National' for the 1986 parliamentary election to attract some members of the moderate right; particularly active parliamentary participation between 1986 and 1988 (Maisonneuve 1991); the 'Presidentialization' of Le Pen's image; the creation by Bruno Mégret of a set of 'new [party] instruments' in order to implement the strategy of 'conquête du pouvoir' (conquest of power); where possible, local coalitions with the moderate right; the emergence of new themes in FN platforms, such as ecology, agriculture or social questions;
- strategic phases of *differentiation*: recurring attacks on the political class and the 'Gang of the Four'; a competitive quest for legitimacy by

- strategically attacking in turn the right and the left (Taguieff 1990); and
- strategic phases of *distinction*: statements about gas chambers as 'a detail' of the Second World War; the play on word 'Durafour-crématoire'; comments on the 'inequality of races'; radicalization of the immigration theme, as well as the issues of insecurity and unemployment; the celebration of the twentieth anniversary of François Duprat's death (see Birenbaum 1992, 1985; Ysmal 1989).

As in the case of the MSI, these different strategies caused tensions between the two main wings of the party; on the one hand, the General Delegation of the movement ran by Mégret, a supporter of an electoral strategy based on alliance with fringe members of the moderate right (a project supported by Jean-Yves Le Gallou, Yvan Blot and Pierre Vial *inter alia*); on the other hand the Lepenist wing, gathered around the Secretary General Bruno Gollnish and grouping, among others, Jean-Claude Martinez, Dominique Chaboche, Samuel Maréchal, Marie-France Stirbois, Roger Holeindre). This aggravated conflict between these two wings explains the major split in the FN during 1998–99 (Ivaldi 1999b), an event that needs to be briefly discussed here.

After the 1989 municipal elections, in which the FN managed to form some 30 alliances with the moderate right, the leaders of latter agreed on a policy of ostracism towards the FN, condemning the Lepenist movement 'to marginality by considerably reducing their possibilities of tactical choices' (Ivaldi 1998, p. 11). The FN was left with no other option but to 'amplify their difference and their capacity to embody an alternative by means of great change' (*Le Monde*, 13 February 1996). It was by applying a strategy of differentiated adaptation (*'ni droite, ni gauche'*) that the party aspired to establish itself within the political system. However, the penetration of its theses into both public opinion and mainstream politics (Pasqua laws on immigration, Sauvaigo report on clandestine immigration, Debré bill) forced the FN to reassert its monopoly on the political representation and treatment of the immigration, law and order, and unemployment themes.

Forced to accentuate their differentiation, the party abandoned the discursive register of differential neo-racism to make a vivid comeback in 'the field of ideological racism' (Ivaldi 1998, p. 13) – a phenomenon expressed through the elaboration of the 50 propositions of the FN on immigration or through Le Pen's comments on 'the inequality between races'. This strategy proved successful in the 1995 Presidential election.

This phase also corresponded with the growing power within the movement of the advocates of ideological orthodoxy: fights between the two different wings intensified. Le Pen sought to fire a warning shot by sarcastically commenting on 'those that dream about a union of the rights' (*Le Monde*, 22 February 1997), implicitly referring to the Mégret wing.

1997 was a real turning point. The Megretist conquest of the municipality of Vitrolles enabled the Delegate General to strengthen his position within the leadership of the party. In addition, the defeat of the moderate right at the 1997 parliamentary elections, together with the isolation of the FN in Parliament (14.9 per cent of the votes but only one Deputy, Jean-Marie Le Chevallier) lent credibility to the electoral project of the Delegate General. The explicit policy of seeking an opening to disillusioned mainstream right-wing electors was a sign of this new strategic reversal. This reversal was finally confirmed during the national convention of the party in January 1998.

The results of the March 1998 elections, as well as local alliances with the right on the basis of a 'minimum common program' (*Le Monde*, 18 March 1998), confirmed the Megretist strategy. In spite of profound contextual differences between the two countries, the hypothesis of an 'Italian-style' evolution emerged, helped by the apparition, at the right of the political scene, of a political space favoring the bringing together of a fringe of the classic right and the FN. The creation of La Droite (The Right), the party of Charles Millon that was meant to be a rallying point of 'all temperaments and of all wings of the right, from nationals to Europeans, from Girondins to Jacobins, from traditionalists to reformists' (*Libération*, 20 April 1998), first seemed to satisfy Mégret's expectations. In an interview with *Le Monde* (20 April 1998), he asserted that 'there is space for a right-wing party, different from the FN, but ready to make alliances with him. This coalition can quite quickly come to power'.

However, aggravated internal tensions between the two wings of the movement, mirrored by the confrontation between Le Pen and Mégret, made this perspective unlikely and led the FN to a split which undoubtedly came from the clash of ambitions, as well as the 'merciless confrontation of two strategies [...]. On the one side: Le Pen and his own people, obsessed by the conservation of the ideological "purity" of the movement and rejecting the slightest compromise with the parties of "*the establishment*"; on the other side: Mégret and his clan, concerned with "*the conquest of responsibilities*", and convinced that they will need to make alliances in order to succeed' (*Libération*, 7 December 1998).

Thus, as far as the French case is concerned, the split of the FN into two different organizations – Mégret created the National Movement in January 1999, which was renamed the National Republican Movement (MNR) in October – confirms the validity of the theoretical schema previously described, i.e. the incapacity of an extreme right party to overcome the political struggle between 'tradition vs. modernity, historic legitimacy vs. program *aggiornamento*' (Osmond 1999, p. 118).

Following the split of the FN, the French extreme right found itself considerably weakened, from an organizational point of view. Its cadres and elected members were divided,[6] it faced declining membership, and suffered electoral setbacks in the European and 2001 local elections (despite high scores for the FN and the MNR in some cities). Most importantly, the relationship of the two parties with the political system has reversed. Hesitating over their strategic and programmatic choices, and eventually unable to seduce the right-wing electorate as well as the working-class electorate of the FN, the MNR quickly renounced their alliance politics, and reverted to an orthodox National Frontist doctrine, thus becoming a 'gathering place' for the most radical members of the 'national camp' (Camus 2001: 210).

Compared to Mégret, Le Pen came to appear a moderate candidate. The FN president tried to appear responsible and worthy, without exploiting an already favorable societal context (Chombeau 2002). Coupled with classic populist discourse, this strategy largely explains his success in the presidential election, which for the first time saw an extreme right candidate winning through to the second ballot.

The MNR has subsequently appeared close to collapse, unsure as to its political strategy. In stark contrast, strengthened by its Presidential results, the FN seems determined to maintain the orientation of moderate integration. During the 2002 parliamentary campaign, Secretary General Carl Lang clearly came down in favor of a strategy of '*main-tendue*' (i.e. helping hand) towards right-wing representatives, as well a strategy of electoral agreements (Ivaldi 2002). In spite of disappointing results, Le Pen seems committed to continue the strategy of presenting the FN as a party of government. Nevertheless, before the 2004 elections, the FN President will have to deal with rising internal tensions concerning both various programmatic points and the central issue of the leader's succession (which has led to a 'youth' camp gathered around daughter Marine Le Pen and her association 'Generations Le Pen', and old party leaders such as Bernard Anthony and Bruno Gollnisch, the current Delegate General).

The FPÖ: the long conquest of the power

The FPÖ was founded in 1956 with the intention of restructuring the German liberal-national 'Lager' and of creating a political alternative to the two dominant parties, the Austrian Socialist Party (SPÖ) and the Austrian People's Party (ÖVP). From its creation to the early 1960s, the FPÖ experienced a 'ghetto period' (Luther 2001, p. 2), i.e. it was treated as a Nazi party and utterly isolated within the Parliament. Yet, from 1958, the new leader Friedrich Peter set about establishing a new profile for the party. Although a former *Waffen-SS* officer, Peter turned out to be a pragmatic, moderate conservative who sought to transform the FPÖ into a respectable party of opposition or cooperation. But this strategy, which implied breaking with the German-national tradition – a tradition 'invalidated by its association with Nazism according to the FPÖ's president' (Riedlsperger 1992) – was rejected by the radical *Grossdeutsche* wing.

Despite a rapprochement with the SPÖ in the mid-1960s (notably during the debate over the return of Otto von Habsburg to Austria), the FPÖ was still perceived as an extremist party and failed in its attempt to enter the Austrian government. Notwithstanding this failure, Peter maintained his strategy of integration and 'planned to move the FPÖ toward the liberal center' (Riedlsperger 1998, p. 29). This aroused tensions within the party; in 1966, several radicals left the FPÖ to form the National Democratic Party, a neo-Nazi formation banned in 1988.

Early in the 1970s, the right extremists, made up of the rank and file, and the liberal leaning partisan elite, who considered German nationalism to be out of date, began their 'struggle for power' (Neugebauer 2000, p. 66). Under Friedhelm Frischenschlager's leadership, this partisan elite met within the 'Atterseer Circle' and elaborated the *Freiheitliches Manifest*, which was eventually adopted in 1973 and became the program for liberalizing the FPÖ until the middle of the 1980s (Riedlsperger 1987).

On the eve of the 1975 national elections, Federal Chancellor and SPÖ-president Bruno Kreisky considered forming a coalition with the liberalizing party. At the same time, Simon Wiesenthal, the famous Nazi hunter, revealed the FPÖ president's past as an ex-SS officer. An internal crisis within the SPÖ ensued, and the coalition project was abandoned while the FPÖ experienced a new electoral failure. Nonetheless, the liberalization of the party continued. In 1978, the liberals, who included the rapidly-rising Jörg Haider, forced Peter, whose past was considered too embarrassing, to leave the party. The next year the FPÖ joined the Liberal International (LI) and obtained its best electoral score since 1962 (6.1 per cent of the vote).

Norbert Steger's election as chairman against the rightist candidate Harald Ofner in 1980 marked a new stage in the liberals' rise to power. The same year Steger also became Vice President of the LI. Finally, in 1983, the integration of the FPÖ and its transformation into a modern liberal party seemed complete when, for the first time in the FPO's history, it came to power in a 'small coalition' together with the SPÖ. Steger was made Vice Chancellor and the FPÖ obtained the Justice and Defense Ministries.

Far from being the beginning of some sort of political normalization, the FPÖ's participation in government created a new series of internal tensions. The lack of electoral backing for the liberalization of the party, the loss of the FPO's protest vote, together with the fact that Steger's attitude within the coalition was viewed as arrogant by the party's elite, were all factors that contributed to creating a favorable breeding ground for the internal revolt led by Haider. Since his contribution to the party's liberal renovation in the 1970s, Haider had become a convinced pan-German through his contact with the (German-nationalist leaning) Carinthian federation. From the early 1980s, Haider gradually began to climb the party ladder, making sure of gaining the national-German wing's support in the successful 'putsch' at the 1986 Innsbruck Congress (Camus 2000; Moreau 1999; Riedlsperger 1987) – a victory which was greeted by bursts of 'Sieg

Heil'. Reacting to this sudden radicalization, Chancellor Vranitzky broke up the governmental coalition and called for new elections, putting a temporary end to the FPÖ's integration efforts.

If we rely on theoretical logics, the November 1986 national elections should have condemned the FPÖ, which was now in the hands of nationalists, back to the political fringes. However, contrary to this reasoning, Haider's party achieved the first in a long series of electoral successes. So how did the FPÖ manage to escape this fate?

First, despite the takeover of the party by the radical wing, the FPÖ was not transformed into a neo-Nazi organization. From 1986 to 1990, Haider's FPÖ looked a lot like the initial FPÖ: a populist protest party that denounced the practice of the '*Proporz*' system, with German nationalist demands as secondary to their agenda. Second, because it was excluded from the SPÖ-ÖVP national government, the FPÖ maintained its anti-system credentials during the 1990s. However, the aim of the party remained the conquest of power. Faced with the impossibility of forming an alliance with one of the two major formations, Haider implemented a strategy of vote maximization (Luther 2001), showing amazing political opportunism.

Beginning in the early 1990s, the FPÖ entered a phase of political radicalization, adopting a program and a rhetoric similar to the other European extreme right parties (making law and order and immigration its principal issues), and through the voice of their leader made repeated provocative statements that borrowed explicitly from Nazism (see Riedlsperger 1998). This change in the political line aroused deep tensions among the liberals in the party. In 1992, the parliamentary fraction chairman Norbert Gugerbauer resigned, one of the last true liberals within the party's leadership. In 1993, five liberal representatives, including Heide Schmidt and Friedhelm Frischenschlager, left the FPÖ in order to protest against the anti-immigrant 'Austria First' petition, and subsequently founded the *Liberales Forum*. Meanwhile, the FPÖ withdrew from the LI before being excluded from it.

The FPÖ's strategy of radicalization worked. In a context of economic crisis, social fragmentation and increasing flow of Eastern immigration, Haider's authoritarian and xenophobic discourses seduced a large portion of the Austrian electorate. Nevertheless, in the middle of the 1990s, the FPÖ changed its strategy again. The '"national potential" of the extreme right [was] exhausted' (Neugebauer 2000, p. 71). Haider, who aimed at conquering the Chancellery in 1999, modified the party's position towards the political system in order to present the FPÖ as a respectable formation.

Beginning in 1995, Haider showed his intention of putting an end to German-nationalist chauvinism, calling for Austrian patriotism instead. Formerly referred to as an 'ideological miscarriage', the Austrian nation was now celebrated for its values and traditions (Riedlsperger 1998). In the 1997 program, the term '*Volksgemeinschaft*', which had been historically defined as a key Nazi concept, was abandoned. Now, the German people, together with the 'Croatian, Roma, Slovakian, Slovenian, Czech and Hungarian peoples', were considered as 'historically domiciled' groups in Austria. The same program marked another major change for the party: the abandonment of their anticlerical positions, the recognition of Christianity as a foundation for Europe, and the will to become a 'partner of the Christian Churches'. Seeking to gain a wider electorate (most notably the Catholic electorate of the ÖVP), these new pragmatic measures impacted the pan-German, anti-clerical and radical wing of the party. At the beginning of 1998, internal criticism increased to such an extent that Haider threatened to take disciplinary measures against party members and to resign.

There is no denying that, until the 1999 elections, the FPÖ's Chairman showed great talent in dealing with internal tensions – including expulsions of opponents of his politics (Moreau 1998) – as well as in changing strategic orientation. On the other hand, Haider seems to have been less successful after 2000. In this respect, the FPÖ's participation in the government has seriously challenged the party, emphasizing the contradictions that underlie the institutional integration of a protest and anti-system formation faced with ministerial functions and unable to overcome its own internal conflicts.

It is obvious that Haider himself is largely responsible for the turbulent FPÖ governmental experience, and even more so for the fall of the ÖVP-FPÖ in September 2002. His position can, nevertheless, be explained by his will to maintain, from a distance, the protest and anti-system vocation of the party. On this point, it seems that Haider was right to want to draw lessons from the first FPÖ governmental experience during the 1980s: in 1998, the FPÖ's leader confided to Richard K. Luther that they 'must resist the temptation of entering government' until the party 'has achieved such a share of the vote that the inevitable electoral losses' entailed by such a move would not plunge it into 'the kind of existential crisis it had experienced under Steger's leadership' (Luther 2001, p. 10).

The loss of electoral support after entering coalition in 2000 undoubtedly played a role in the final crisis that led Susanne Riess-Passer to resign from her post as the government's Vice Chancellor and as President of the FPÖ. This crisis was also a clear testimony to the increasing struggle which began in 2000 between the pragmatic and moderate wing of the party, led by Susanne Riess-Passer, which was seeking to transform the FPÖ into a party of government, and the radical wing, which called for the implementation of the original program. The fall of the government produced an important wave of criticism of Haider (including from his close colleagues) who finally gave up the leadership of the party. The particularly weak results obtained in the November 2002 elections (a loss of 16 points), inevitably relaunched the ongoing debate within the FPÖ since its inception: to protest or to govern.

The VB: an impossible final integration?

The VB was officially created as a common list of the moderate nationalist Flemish People's Party of Lode Claes and the Flemish National Party of Karel Dillen. Regrouping extreme right nationalists, the VNP was a direct successor of the Flemish National Union, a collaborationist party created in 1933 and a Flemish version of German National Socialism. In the December 1978 elections, only Dillen was elected, in the district of Antwerp – one of the bastions of Flemish nationalism and of the Flemish extreme right. Claes failed and soon after left the VB, which then entirely adopted the ultranationalist Flemish program of the VNP.

The nature of the VB's creation is particularly helpful to understand the initially ambivalent position of the party towards the political system. On the one hand, the VB was clearly opposed to this system. Claiming the independence of Flanders, they refused to compromise with the Belgian state, whose suppression they called for, and they turned down in advance any offer of a ministerial job (Delwit and De Waele 1996; Govaert 1992). On the other hand, from the very beginning the VB has participated in that system and was originally conceived as an electoral cartel created with 'the hope of achieving a breakthrough at the 1978 general elections' (Delwit and De Waele 1996, p. 18).

In this respect, it must be noted that the creation of this new party and its participation in elections aroused some distrust among the radical nationalist circles (and notably within youth movements not bound to political parties), which were profoundly marked by the VU's 'betrayal' and by its participation in the Belgian government (Spruyt 1996). Thus, although supported by radical organizations such as *Were Di*, *Vlaamse Militanten Orde* or *Voorspost*, the VB was faced with important difficulties in recruitment until the mid-1980s. Until then, the party remained tiny (3700 members in 1985), with no real political representation (in 1985, the VB only had one representative and two provincial councilors), and with a program centered around the independence of Flanders, anti-communism, anti-immigration and amnesty for collaborationists. Sticking to their strong anti-system line, the 'One against all' party experienced a 'crossing of the desert' (in their own words) until the end of the 1980s.

At first glance, the VB's evolution confirms the validity of the 'schema' of the alternative. It is only at the end of a 'Rejuvenation Operation' (Mudde 2000, p. 88) initiated by Filip Dewinter that the VB succeeded in breaking free from the political marginality to which it seemed more or less condemned at the beginning of the 1980s. As Marc Spruyt (1996, p. 206) underlines, 'the program of the party is refreshed: political marketing is introduced; the vocabulary of the old right is replaced by modern right-wing language; young intellectuals are bringing a new style, and above all things respectability is sought'. Filip Dewinter, in his own way, confirmed this new trend, when he argued: 'Without changing anything to our program, we have tried hard to modify the image of the party [...] It was necessary to prove wrong the people who wrongly accuse us of being racists, fascists and neo-Nazis' (*Le Monde*, 8 October 2000).

This new political 'modernity', together with an effort to build party organization and distance itself from the various militant movements supporting the party, led the VB to experience electoral takeoff. As Marc Swyngedouw (2000, p. 135) observed, 'the 1987 and 1988 elections marked the beginning of a "second phase" characterized by the geographical and political extension of the VB's field of action'. Undoubtedy, this extension can be attributed (at least partially) to the modernized image of the party.

But it is necessary to keep in mind that the 1987–88 period corresponds to the moment when Filip Dewinter, among others, put the immigration theme forward. As in the case of the FN, the political 'modernity' of the VB is coupled with authoritarian positions but also with 'culturally racist' ones (*Eigen volk eerst!*), centering around the defense of 'the principle of fundamental and natural inequality between communities' which implies 'ethnic hierarchy' (Swyngedouw, 1998, p. 191).

However, this emphasis caused tensions between the 'Lepenist' wing (Dewinter), accused of giving up the Flemish issue and 'defending unacceptable theses on immigration' (*De Standaard*, 16–17 November 1991), and the Flemish nationalist wing. A few members of the latter (including General Secretary Jack Peeters and party council Chairman Geert Wouters) decided to leave the VB, after having tried to 'squeeze the VBJ-group around Dewinter out of the ranks of the party leadership' (Mudde 2000, p. 89), and they created a nationalist pressure group, the *Nationalistisch Verbond* (Nationalist Union).

These tensions did not slow down the progress of the VB in Antwerp or in Flanders. The real 'breakthrough' was achieved in the 1991 parliamentary election, while the results of the 1994 municipal election finally sealed the political implantation of the party (28 per cent in Antwerp, 10.3 per cent in Flanders) and raised the issue of its participation in the city's administration. However, the implementation of the second *cordon satinaire*, made official by the 'Democratic Charter' and signed by all major parties in 1993, prevented it from participating in power.

Since then, the issue of the VB's relationship towards the system has become increasingly problematic. Experiencing uninterrupted electoral growth, the party has remained isolated in the Belgian political scene. This situation led the leaders to modify their strategy and positions, and to show that the VB was 'able to take its responsibility' (in Mudde 2000, p. 111). From 1996 onward, and despite the unbroken *cordon sanitaire*, the VB tried to become more respectable and to be considered as 'a normal political partner'.

Evidence of this are Gerolf Annemans's contributions to the activities of the Dutroux Inquiry Parliamentary Commission, the rallying of the VB to the parliamentary consensus on the first final report of the Commission, and its participation in the Flemish Parliament debates over a new political culture (Maddens and Fiers 1998), the evolution of party literature that appears more populist (Mudde 2000) and less focused on immigration issues (Breuning and Ishiyama 1998), or the recent dismissal of Roland Raes from its functions after he minimized the reality of the Holocaust during an interview on Dutch TV. Nevertheless, the fact remains that while transforming into a more acceptable party, the VB has dreaded being perceived as too respectable, which could have weakened its – electorally very advantageous – image of an anti-system party (Maddens and Fiers, 1998).

Torn between the possibility of coming to power and of maintaining its identity, the VB seems to have reached a sort of balance, thanks to the existence of the triumvirate currently leading the party. Franck Vanhecke, the successor of Karel Dillen, became president of the party in 1996. He represents a sort of neutral point between Filip Dewinter, the representative of the hard anti-immigrant and anti-system members of the VB, and Gerolf Annemans, the representative of the nationalist wing in favor of making the party more respectable. This has allowed the Vlaams Blok to conduct differentiated strategies and to target different electoral clienteles – on the one hand, traditionalist Catholics, by laying the emphasis on the fight against abortion and against 'the permissive society and sexual dissoluteness' (a strategic pole run by Alexandra Colen); on the other hand, the labour movement, by putting forward a social program associating classic socialist claims (increasing pensions and fighting against unemployment) with Flemish ultranationalist and ethnocentric positions (De Witte and Scheepers 1998). At the moment, this balance appears to be stable, although the emphasis laid on some topics is not unanimously approved within the party and tension is emerging.

Conclusion

The ambition of this study was not to elaborate a predictive, normative model of the evolution of extreme right formations, but to try to understand better the specificity of the relationship that these formations have with the political system. In this perspective, I tried to demonstrate that this relationship is based on a triple strategic dimension – adaptation to the system, distinction from the system, differentiation within the system – and that, from a theoretical as well as an empirical point of view, the issue of this relationship implied making conflicting choices for the parties studied. Thus, the manner in which these parties have dealt with the tension induced by their relationship towards the system partly explains their present evolution.

All these parties have chosen to adapt to the system, and it is precisely this choice which forced them to play constantly with various strategic styles. Except for the MSI, whose evolution created a precedent in the contemporary history of extreme right parties, all the parties still face the necessity of integrating while dealing with both ideological and strategic internal conflicts between the different wings. The FN's split and the current emergence of a new line of opposition between the young and the old leaders, as well as the recent collapse of the Austrian government, show how difficult dealing with this issue is, while the VB seems to have succeeded in establishing a sort of political balance.

It would be particularly interesting, in order to clarify even more the modalities of this specificity, to make a comparative analysis of the relationship of other formations with the system. In this respect, we could learn a great deal from a comparison with communist parties. The fact nonetheless remains that, in the case of extreme right formations, the conflict on which the question of the relationship with the system rests is not only ideological, it is also moral. Undoubtedly, this constitutes a unique specificity of extreme right parties.

Notes

1 Though the AN in recent years is no longer 'extreme', adopting a more mainstream–conservative outlook on most issues.
2 The systemic approach (Easton 1953) and the environmentalist approach to political organizations (Charlot and Charlot 1985; Panebianco 1982) emphasize the necessity of including the political system into a larger environment, an institutional, cultural, social, and economic one, with which the political system (defined as the 'sum of the political interactions'), together with all the elements that compose it, interact.
3 These two wings embody the two historical fascist trends distinguished by Renzo de Felice (1975): the 'fascist-movement' (revolutionary, anti-bourgeois, socialist leaning, futuristic) and the 'fascist-regime' (conservative, clerical, capitalist, corporatist). See Ignazi (1994b, pp. 1015–16).
4 These exogenous factors included the de-radicalization of political conflict (namely the end of the terrorism and of political violence), the renewal of the historiography on fascism, the 'Mani Pulite' Operation and the 'Tangentopoli' trials, the legitimizing support of Silvio Berlusconi to Gianfranco Fini during the Rome 1993 municipal elections, and the adoption of a new mixed majority electoral system for the 1994 legislative elections.
5 This is a quote from Donegani and Sadoun (1992, p. 767).
6 59 per cent of the district secretaries and 51 per cent of the regional councilors left the FN to join the MNR.

Bibliography

Almirante, G. (1969) 'L'unità del MSI, garanzia per la nazione', *Il Secolo d'Italia*, 23 September.
Almirante, G. (1970) 'I nostri anni settanta', *Il Secolo d'Italia*, 3 January.
Almirante, G. (1972) 'Conferenza Stampa', *Il Secolo d'Italia*, 20 April.
Backes, U. (2001) 'L'extrême droite: les multiples d'une catégorie d'analyse', in

Perrineau, P. (ed.) *Les croisés de la société fermée. L'Europe des extrêmes droites*, Paris: editions de l'Aube.
Baldini, G. and Vignati R. (1996) 'Dal MSI ad AN: una nuova cultura politica?', *Polis* 10, 1: 81–101.
Bertolino, S. and Chiapponi, F. (1999) 'I militanti di Alleanza nazionale: ancora "esuli in patria?"', *Quaderni di scienza politica* 2: 211–249.
Birenbaum, G. (1985) *Les stratégies du Front national: participation au champ politique et démarcation*, DEA Thesis of Political Sociology, University Paris I.
Birenbaum, G. (1992) *Le Front national en politique*, Paris: Balland.
Bourdieu, P. (1981) 'La représentation politique. Eléments pour une théorie du champ politique', *Actes de la recherche en sciences sociales* 36–37: 3–24.
Breuning, M. and Ishiyama, J. (1998) 'The rhetoric of nationalism: rhetorical strategies of the Volksunie and Vlaams Blok in Belgium (1991–95)', *Political Communication* 15, 1: 5–26.
Campi, A. (1995) 'What is National Alliance?', *Telos* 105: 112–132.
Camus, J.Y. (1996) 'Origine et formation du Front national', in Mayer, N. and Perrineau, P. (eds) *Le Front national à découvert*, Paris: Presses de Sciences Po, pp. 17–36.
Camus, J.Y. (2000) 'Le phénomène Haider en Autriche: une droite extrême ultra-libérale et xénophobe', *Pensée* 321: 103–112.
Camus, J.Y. (2001) 'La structure du "camp national" en France: la périphérie militante et organisationnelle du FN et du MNR', in Perrineau, P. (ed.) *Les croisés de la société fermée. L'Europe des extrêmes droites*, Paris: Editions de l'Aube, pp. 199–223.
Capoccia, G. and Pedahzur, A. (2003) 'Defending democracy: how can democratic regimes respond to extremist challenges', proposal for workshop at the ECPR 30th Joint Sessions of Workshops, Edinburgh. Available at: http://www.essex.ac.uk/ecpr/jointsessions/edinburgh/list.htm#4
Charlot, J. and Charlot, M. (1985) 'Les groupes politiques dans leur environnement', in Grawitz, M. and Leca, J. (eds) *Traité de science politique*, vol. 3, Paris: PUF, pp. 429–495.
Cheles, L. (1986) 'Le new-look du néo-fascisme italien. Thèmes, styles et sources de la récente propagande de l'extrême droite parlementaire', *Mots* 12: 29–42.
Chiarini, R. (1995) 'The Italian far right', in Cheles, L., Ferguson, R. and Vaughan, M. (eds) *The Far Right in Western and Eastern Europe*, Harlow: Longman, pp. 91–111.
Chombeau, C. (2002) 'Comment le président du Front national a poli son image et profité du thème de l'insécurité', *Le Monde*, 22 April.
Delwit, P. and De Waele, J.M. (1996) 'Origines, évolutions et devenir des partis politiques en Belgique', in Delwit, P. and De Waele, J.M. (eds) *Les partis politiques en Belgique*, Brussels: Editions de l'Université de Bruxelles, pp. 17–21.
Dézé, A. (1995) *La propagande par l'affiche du Front national*, Master's Thesis of Contemporary History, University of Reims.
de Felice, R. (1975) *Intervista sul fascismo*, Bari: Laterza.
De Witte, H. and Scheepers, P. (1998) 'En Flandre: origines, évolution et avenir du Vlaams Blok et de ses électeurs', *Pouvoirs* 87: 95–113.
Donegani, J.M. and Sadoun, M. (1992) 'Le jeu des institutions', in Sirinelli, J.F. (ed.) *Les Droites en France. De la révolution à nos jours*, Paris: Folio-Gallimard, pp. 663–830.

Duprat, F. (1972) *Les mouvements d'extrême droite en France*, Paris: Edition Albatros.
Easton, D. (1953) *The Political System. An Inquiry into the State of Political Science*, New York: Knopf.
Govaert, S. (1992) 'Le Vlaams Blok et ses dissidences', *Courrier hebdomadaire du CRISP* 1365: 1–42.
Ignazi, P. (1989) *Il Polo escluso. Profilo del Movimento sociale italiano*, Bologna: Il Mulino.
Ignazi, P. (1992) 'The silent-counter revolution. Hypotheses on the emergence of extreme-right-wing parties in Europe', *European Journal of Political Research* 22, 1: 3–34.
Ignazi, P. (1994a) *L'Estrema Destra in Europa*, Bologna: Il Mulino.
Ignazi, P. (1994b) 'La force des racines. La culture politique du MSI au seuil du gouvernement', *Revue française de science politique* 44, 6: 1014–33.
Ignazi, P. (1994c) *Postfascisti? Dal Movimento sociale italiano ad Alleanza nazionale*, Bologna: Il Mulino.
Ignazi, P. (1996) 'From neo-fascists to post-fascists? The transformation of MSI into the AN', *West European Politics* 19, 4: 693–714.
Ivaldi, G. (1998) 'Le Front national à l'assaut du système', *Revue politique et parlementaire* 995: 5–22.
Ivaldi, G. (1999a) 'L'extrême droite ou la crise des systèmes de partis', *Revue internationale de politique comparée* 6, 1: 201–246.
Ivaldi, G. (1999b) 'La scission du Front national', *Regards sur l'actualité* 251: 17–32.
Ivaldi, G. (2002) 'Retour à une stratégie de la main-tendue', *Le Figaro*, 18–19 May.
Kirchheimer, O. (1966) 'The vanishing opposition', in Dahl, R. (ed.) *Political Opposition in Western Democracies*, New Haven and London: Yale University Press, pp. 237–259.
Kitschelt, H. and McGann, A. (1995) *The Radical Right in Western Europe. A comparative Analysis*, Ann Arbor: University of Michigan Press.
Lagroye, J. (1985) 'La légitimation', in Grawitz, M. and Leca, J. (eds) *Traité de science politique*, vol. 1, Paris: PUF, pp. 395–467.
Luther, K.R. (2001) 'From populist protest to incumbency: the strategic challenges facing Jörg Haider's Freedom Party of Austria', Keele European Parties Research Unit, Working Paper 5.
Maddens, B. and Fiers, S. (1998) 'Les partis flamands face au poids du Vlaams Blok', in Delwit, P., De Waele, J.M. and Rea, A. (eds) *L'extrême droite en France et en Belgique*, Brussels: Complexe, pp. 247–265.
Maisonneuve, C. (1991) *Le Front national à l'Assemblée Nationale: histoire d'un groupe parlementaire (1986–88)*, DEA Thesis of Contemporary History, Institute of Political Studies of Paris.
Michels, R. (1962), *Political Parties*, New York: the Free Press.
Milza, P. (1991) *Les Fascismes*. Paris: Editions du Seuil.
Moreau, P. (1998) 'Le Freiheitliche Partei Österreichs, parti national-libéral ou pulsion austro-fasciste?', *Pouvoirs* 87: 61–82.
Moreau, P. (1999) 'Le FPÖ: l'année décisve', Paper presented at the 6th Congress of the Association française de science politique, IEP de Rennes, 28 September–1 October 1999.

Mudde, C. (1996) 'The war of words: defining the extreme right party family', *West European Politics* 19, 2: 225–248.
Mudde, C. (2000) *The Ideology of the Extreme Right*, Manchester and New York: Manchester University Press.
Neugebauer, W. (2000) 'Extrémisme de droite et pangermanisme: continuité traditions, changements', *Austriaca*, 51: 63–72.
Osmond, E. (1999) 'FN: la déchirure', *Mouvements* 3: 118–122.
Panebianco, A. (1982) *Modelli di partito. Organizzazione e potere nei partiti politici*, Bologna: Il Mulino.
Parodi, J.L. (1991) 'Le nouvel espace politique français', in Mény, Y. (ed.) *Idéologies, partis politiques et groupes sociaux*, Paris: Presses de la FNSP, pp. 49–59.
Riedlsperger, M. (1987) 'Der Haider Jörg (HJ) and the FPÖ Election Victory of 1986', paper presented at the German Studies Association meeting, St. Louis. Available at: http://www.ulb.ac.be/soco/cevipol/documentation/Contributions_en_ligne.htm.
Riedlsperger, M. (1992) 'Heil Haïder! The revitalization of the Austrian Freedom Party since 1986', *Politics and Society in Germany, Austrian and Swiss* 4, 3: 18–47. Available at: http://www.ulb.ac.be/soco/cevipol/documentation/Contributions_en_ligne.htm
Riedlsperger, M. (1998) 'The Freedom Party of Austria: from protest to radical right populism', in Betz, H.G. and Immerfall, S. (eds) *The New Politics of the Right. Neo-Populist Parties and Movements in Established Democracies*, New York: St. Martin's Press.
Schain, M. (2001) 'L'impact du Front national sur le système politique français', in Perrineau, P. (ed.) *Les croisés de la société fermée. L'Europe des extrêmes droites*, Paris: Editions de l'Aube, pp. 287–302.
Simon, E. (1992) 'Italie: les héritiers du Duce', in *L'Europe en chemise brune. Néo-fascistes, néo-nazis et nationaux-populistes en Europe de l'Ouest depuis 1945*, Paris: Reflex, 72–86.
Spruyt, M. (1996) 'Le Vlaams Blok', in Delwit, P. and De Waele, J.M. (eds) *Les partis politiques en Belgique*, Brussels: Editions de l'Université de Bruxelles, pp. 205–214.
Swyngedouw (1998) 'L'idéologie du Vlaams Blok: l'offre identitaire', *Revue Internationale de Politique Comparée* 5, 1: 189–202.
Swyngedouw (2000) 'Belgium: explaining the relationship between Vlaams Blok and the city of Antwerp', in Hainsworth, P. (ed.) *The Politics of the Extreme Right. From Margins to the Mainstream*, London and New York: Pinter, pp. 121–143.
Taguieff, P.A. (1986) 'L'identité nationale saisie par les logiques de racisation. Aspects, figures et problèmes du racisme différencialiste', *Mots* 12: 91–116.
Taguieff, P.A. (1988) 'De l'anti-socialisme au national-racisme. Deux aspects de la recomposition idéologique des droites en France', *Raison présente* 8: 15–54.
Taguieff, P.A. (1990) 'Mobilisation nationale-populiste en France: vote xénophobe et nouvel antisémitisme politique', *Lignes* 9: 91–136.
Taguieff, P.A. and Tribalat, M. (1998) *Face au Front national. Arguments pour une contre-offensive*, Paris: La Découverte.
Villalba, B. (1997) 'Les petits partis et l'idéologie: le paradoxe de la différencia-

tion', in Laurent, A. and Villalba, B. (eds) *Les petits partis. De la petitesse en politique*. Paris: L'Harmattan, pp. 67–89.

Ysmal, C. (1985) 'Elites et leaders politiques', in Grawitz, M. and Leca, J. (eds) *Traité de science politique*, vol. 3, Paris: PUF, pp. 603–42.

Ysmal, C. (1989) *Les partis politiques sous la Ve République*, Paris: Montchrestien.

2 The American radical right
The 1990s and beyond

Mark Potok

The 1990s were a heady time for the American radical right. From the scattered pockets of tiny groups and individuals that had characterized the extreme right of the 1980s, something approaching a genuine mass movement developed. The militia movement, more than many of its predecessors, was directly fueled by the actions of the federal government – from deadly confrontations between police and heterodox groups, to gun control and other federal regulations that angered many millions of Americans. At the same time, the government's failure to significantly restrict non-white immigration helped spark radical groups with an explicitly racist agenda. The clear endorsement of multiculturalism by both government and many political elites also helped to provoke a backlash that is being felt to this day.

It was, by any account, a remarkable decade. The militia movement – a uniquely American expression of extreme anti-government ideology mixed with overt paramilitarism – rose and fell. Right-wing terrorists bombed the Oklahoma City federal building, killing 168 people in what many radicals saw as the opening shot in an apocalyptic race war. White Southern nationalism – the so-called neo-Confederate movement – burst energetically onto the scene. Holocaust Denial and neo-Nazism spread, along with racist neo-Pagan creeds. The tentacles of extremist ideology – and its hatred of government – reached into mainstream politics.

In part, the radical right fared so well because the American two-party system made it particularly difficult to deal with the concerns of extreme groups within mainstream politics. Rather than being co-opted into the political process, with a concomitant softening of their ideology, extremists were isolated both politically and by the increasing attentions of law enforcement in the wake of Oklahoma City. As a result, much of the radical right grew more radical still during the 1990s. Indeed, as militias and other self-described "Patriot" groups started to disappear toward the end of the decade, they were replaced by a rising number of harder-line, race-based, and often Nazified groups. These new groups were not mere updated versions of the Ku Klux Klan or other nativist groups. Where the Klansman of the 1960s saw himself as a restorationist, wrapping himself in the flag and seeking to bring back an imagined golden era of American life, the contemporary radical rightist is a true revolutionary – anti-capitalist, anti-Semitic and, most remarkably of all, anti-American.

This was highlighted most dramatically in the immediate aftermath of the September 11, 2001, terrorist attacks on the World Trade Center and the Pentagon. In case after case, extremists applauded the murder of some 3000 of their countrymen. Billy Roper, an official of the neo-Nazi group National Alliance (NA), said it best in an e-mail to members: 'The enemy of our enemy is, for now at least, our friend. We may not want them marrying our daughters, just as they would not want us marrying theirs. We may not want them in our societies, just as they would not want us in theirs. But anyone who is willing to drive a plane into a building to kill Jews is all right by me.'[1]

It remains unclear precisely how the spread of these kinds of ideas will play out on the larger political scene in America. But as the twenty-first century begins to unfold, it is obvious how definitively the far right had broken with the government that it had once patriotically defended. Since the 1989 fall of the Berlin Wall and the disappearance of the Communist bogeyman, the radical right has turned into the foremost critic of the federal government, attacking a potential war with Iraq and what it sees as other 'imperial' enterprises. In fact, the far right now sounds increasingly like the far left, and it may find new allies as a result. In any event, what is clear is that the decade of the 1990s – and in particular the rise and fall of the militia movement – gave the radical right an importance it had not had for many years.

Roots of the militia movement

In many ways, the symbolic inauguration of the modern militia movement came on September 11, 1990, when then-President George Bush made a speech to a joint session of Congress as the Cold War came to an end and in the middle of the crisis in the Persian Gulf. 'Out of these troubled times ... a new world order can emerge', the president said, oblivious to the fact that he was about to set off a firestorm.

Although it would be over three years before the first militias appeared, the speech galvanized many on the radical right who saw the president's words as a slip of the tongue – a stunning admission that revealed federal officials' secret plans to establish a 'New World Order', a kind of dictatorial, one-world government (e.g. Snow 1999).[2] That idea was reinforced in 1991 when right-wing televangelist Pat Robertson came out with a book, *The New World Order*, alleging a conspiracy to take over America.

Since the 1989 fall of the Berlin wall, the American radical right had been groping about as it sought to reorient its world view to accommodate the sudden loss of its primary enemy, the Communist bogeyman. That it finally settled on the federal government as the chief culprit did not come as much of a surprise. Going back to the 1950s, extreme-right groups, such as the John Birch Society, had accused various administrations of being in the pay of the Communists. A tax protest movement with even deeper roots had been growing steadily for decades. Most importantly, perhaps, the 1970s and 1980s saw the rise of the violent and anti-Semitic Posse Comitatus, a group that viewed the county sheriff as the highest legitimate level of government (e.g. Levitas 2002).

In the largest sense, these attitudes built on a history of anti-government sentiment that goes all the way back to the colonial rebellion against the British. However, these attitudes had been exacerbated in modern America by angry disputes over environmental and other kinds of federal regulation – disputes that often seemed to pit the jobs of workers in the central and western states against the welfare of endangered species such as the rare spotted owl. The inveighing of mostly Republican politicians against new taxes and large government added fuel to the raging anti-government fire, as did the large number of ultra-conservative talk show hosts on AM radio stations.

Just how far this sentiment had penetrated American thinking was revealed in a remarkable poll by *USA Today* (26 April 1995), a national newspaper, a few days after the Oklahoma City bombing. The poll found that fully 39 per cent of Americans agreed with the proposition that the federal government was 'so large and powerful that it poses an immediate threat to the rights and freedoms of ordinary citizens.'

Ruby Ridge and the radical backlash

The militia movement drew on other strains of American culture as well. In particular, its fascination with guns – and with a whole culture of paramilitarism, as exemplified in the magazine for mercenaries, *Soldier of Fortune* – derives from a tradition that goes back to the frontier period. This paramilitary culture exploded in the 1970s (see Gibson 1994).

But the militia movement also had more proximate causes – virtually all of them actions of the federal government that enraged many Americans. A stand-off in Idaho, a bloody confrontation in Texas, and a series of gun control laws and free trade agreements passed in the early to mid-1990s ignited a movement that was also fueled by a visceral hatred of the neoliberal administration of Bill Clinton.

In August 1992, federal agents surrounded the cabin of Randy Weaver, a white supremacist living on an Idaho mountaintop known as Ruby Ridge, as they prepared to serve a warrant for weapons violations. As agents surveilled the cabin, they were discovered by Weaver's 14-year-old son and a shoot-out began. The boy and a federal marshal were killed. In the 11-day stand-off that ensued, an FBI sniper shot and killed Weaver's wife as she opened the cabin door, cradling an infant.

The incident infuriated the radical right. Crowds gathered at the base of the road leading to Ruby Ridge, bitterly denouncing the government and its agents. Years later, Weaver would be acquitted of murder charges, and the FBI would be severely criticized for loosening its rules of engagement to allow the shooting of the unarmed Vicki Weaver. The federal government would settle a civil suit Weaver brought on behalf of his surviving children, paying the family $3.1 million.

The confrontation did not receive national publicity and did not have much effect on the general public outside the area. But for the radical right, which viewed the incident as proof that the federal government would murder anyone who dared to deviate from political orthodoxy, it was critical. Two months after the stand-off ended, 160 far-right activists came together in Estes Park, Colorado, for the 'Gathering of Christian Men' that was intended to formulate a response to Ruby Ridge.

The importance of this meeting is disputed. Some believe that the militia movement was essentially shaped by the Klansmen, neo-Nazis and more 'moderate' rightists who attended.[3] What is certain is that a key theorist, former Klan leader Louis Beam (Kaplan 2000, pp. 17–23), made a famous and impassioned speech that de-emphasized doctrinal and even racial differences. And indeed, the militia movement that would arise in the next few years was marked far less by racism than by anti-federalism. Whether or not this was a conscious ploy to build a mass movement remains unclear.

The militia movement would also draw on the often stark resentment in rural America of federal regulation, and in particular of federal regulation of public lands. (In some western states, local, state and federal governments combined own as much as 80 per cent of all land.) An earlier right-wing phenomenon, the anti-environmentalist 'Wise Use' movement of the 1980s, helped supply activists who would later join the militia movement. In New Mexico's Catron County, for example, anti-government hard-liners, sounding a great deal like militia ideologues, won control of the local government for a period in the 1990s. They passed a total of 21 ordinances, claiming to supersede federal authority on public lands, urging every head of household to own a gun – and declaring federal officials 'a clear and present danger.'

Conflagration in Waco

However, the immediate catalyst for the movement was Waco. On February 28, 1993, the day after a local newspaper published a hard-hitting investigative report on a heavily armed religious cult in Waco, Texas, agents from the Bureau of Alcohol, Tobacco and Firearms (BATF) raided the cult's compound, known as 'Mount Carmel' or 'Ranch Apocalypse' (*Waco Tribune-Herald*, February 27, 1993). The raid was a disaster. The compound's inhabitants, tipped off by a member that the raiders were approaching, got into a massive firefight with the agents. At day's end, four federal agents and six cultists were dead.

The cultists – adherents of the obscure theology of Branch Davidianism and followers of authoritarian leader David Koresh – were not members of the radical right. In fact, close to half were black. But that did not prevent radicals, including white supremacists, from taking up the Davidian cause. As what would become a 51-day stand-off dragged on, the extreme right increasingly saw the cultists as people who were deeply interested in guns (the raid's justification was that illegal weapons were being manufactured on the compound) and held heterodox religious beliefs like their own. The Davidians, too, hated the federal government and its powers. In other words, right-wing extremists came to see the Davidians as ideological cousins.

Unlike Ruby Ridge, Waco was an international story, with televised reports every day of the confrontation. When, on April 19, federal agents used armored vehicles to inject gas into the compound and it burst into flames, virtually the entire nation watched the televised conflagration that followed. Seventy-four Davidians, including 21 children, died as the compound's main structure burned.

Millions of Americans were horrified. Despite strong evidence that suicidal Davidians had started the fire themselves – including audiotapes from listening devices smuggled into the compound – hundreds of thousands also came to believe that the fire was the intentional work of federal agents. This belief was abetted by wildly conspiratorial movement propaganda, but even more so, in ensuing years, by two 'documentaries' by filmmaker Michael McNulty. Despite very good reviews by naïve critics,[4] the films were highly selective and inflammatory propaganda pieces – tall tales that falsely suggested that federal agents engaged in mass murder.

Within months, citizen militias began to appear around America. For the first time since the Civil War, large numbers of armed Americans were mobilizing to resist their government. 'The movement was conceived at Ruby Ridge in 1992', the militia publication *U.S. Militiaman* (undated) concluded years later, and 'given birth on April 19, 1993, at Waco.'

Guns, free trade and the militias

Two other federal government actions with great resonance among Americans provided major fuel to the takeoff of the militias. In November 1993, in the culmination of seven years of congressional battles, the Brady Bill – imposing a five-day waiting period and background checks on handgun purchasers – was signed into law by President Clinton. Along with a September 1994 law that banned 19 types of assault weapons, the gun control measure ignited grass-roots fury and helped to turn many toward the militias. Militiamen emerged as champions of the controversial view that the Constitution's Second Amendment guarantees unfettered gun rights.

The second federal action was the January 1994 implementation of the North American Free Trade Agreement (NAFTA), a measure meant to spur international trade and economic growth. Within three years, according to a study by the advocacy group Public Citizen (2001), some 500,000 US jobs would be lost to other countries as a result, and downward wage pressure would affect millions more. The radical right won much sympathy as it railed against NAFTA and similar pacts, which it saw as evidence of the growing power of a global elite, or 'New World Order'.

The Militia of Montana (MOM), the first major modern militia, was officially inaugurated on January 1, 1994, although it may have existed for some months before that. (While militias would not be mainly characterized by racism or anti-Semitism, the case of MOM – whose leader John Trochmann had close ties to a leading neo-Nazi group – illustrated how white supremacists helped to build the movement.) In April of that year, a radical gun shop owner and another man formed the country's second major militia, the Michigan Militia. By the end of 1994, the movement was white hot, with militias forming weekly and ever more radical calls for violence.

The number of those who ultimately joined citizen militias is not certain. Estimates ranged from thousands to several million. What seems likely is that tens of thousands of people – perhaps 40,000 – formed the movement's activist core, while a far larger group was influenced by its rhetoric and conspiracy theories.[5] Anecdotal evidence strongly suggests that the militias, which were almost exclusively white, drew their members from the working, middle and even professional classes (see Aho 1990).[6]

Two of those affected by the increasingly charged political atmosphere were Gulf War veteran Timothy McVeigh and his Army buddy Terry Nichols. By the fall of 1994, these two men – and possibly others – were acquiring explosives, secretly renting storage sheds and in other ways preparing to bomb Oklahoma City's federal building. Much has been made of the fact that neither man apparently belonged to a militia. McVeigh, in particular, was enamored of *The Turner Diaries*, a novel of race war by America's leading neo-Nazi, a man from another sector of the radical right. But the clear reality is that both McVeigh and Nichols were very much products of militia culture. They flirted with a number of militias, imbibed conspiracy theories espoused by them, and adopted many of their beliefs.[7] Above all, both men fully agreed with the militia view of the federal government as a corrupt behemoth that was totally out of control – an evil entity in need of the severest reprimand.

Terror comes to the heartland

At 9:02 a.m. on April 19, 1995 – the second anniversary of the burning of the Branch Davidian compound – a 7,000-pound truck bomb exploded directly in front of the Alfred P. Murrah Federal Building in Oklahoma City. Concocted from a farm fertilizer (ammonium nitrate) and nitromethane racing fuel, the bomb tore away the front of the building, killing 168 people – including 19 children in a day-care center, infants and toddlers who McVeigh would later refer to as 'collateral damage'.

It was, until the 2001 attacks on the Pentagon and New York's World Trade Center, the worst-ever terrorist outrage on American soil. Although suspicions focused initially on foreign Muslim extremists, the chance arrest of McVeigh after the blast quickly made it clear that the mass murder had been the work of Americans – and, specifically, Americans from the still little-known extreme right. Within days, America and the rest of the world would learn much about this movement.

Before his 2001 execution, McVeigh would explicitly take credit for the attack. His rage stemmed from Ruby Ridge and, especially, Waco (Michel and Herbeck 2001). As it turned out, McVeigh had personally visited Waco during the 51-day stand-off. He saw himself as reining in an out-of-control and murderous federal government, a regime that he intended to teach a bloody lesson. 'To these people in Oklahoma who lost a loved one', McVeigh added, 'I'm sorry, but it happens every day'.

In the aftermath of the bombing, many analysts assumed the militia movement would shrink or fade away. Who, after all, would want to be tied to a movement that had produced mass murderers on the scale of McVeigh and Nichols? And who cared to brave the attentions of the newly aroused and angry federal government? But that is not what actually happened to the militia movement – at least not right away.

In 1995, the Southern Poverty Law Center (SPLC), a non-profit civil rights group that monitors the American radical right, counted 224 'Patriot' groups – militias and other groups characterized mainly by their extreme anti-government animus and their fondness for conspiracy theories about the New World Order.[8] In 1996, that number rocketed to 858. Only in the following year did a long decline begin.

Conspiracy theories and Oklahoma

The most likely explanation relates to the conspiratorial mindset of the movement – and of Americans in general. Throughout US history, especially since the 1963 assassination of President John Kennedy, Americans have had a proclivity for conspiracy theories. Explored in the 1967 classic by Richard Hofstadter, *The Paranoid Style in American Politics and Other Essays*, this proclivity may have reached its peak in the militia movement, many of whose members believed, for example, that a secret weather machine in Brussels was being used to ruin American farmers. To minds like these, the bombing did not pose much of a conundrum.

Indeed, within weeks of the attack, the militia movement had come up with an array of unsupported theories to explain it. Federal agents, the ideologues insisted, had been warned of the bomb in advance. A bomb squad truck was waiting a block away for the blast they knew was coming. Seismographic records proved there was more than one explosion – and the second came from deep inside the building. The list of theories went on, but they all boiled down to the same basic scenario: using McVeigh as a patsy, the federal government bombed its own building in order to so frighten Americans that they would accept draconian anti-terrorism legislation. In other words, to the movement, Oklahoma was just one more Ruby Ridge or Waco – yet another proof of the vicious barbarity of the federal government. Seen in that light, the bombing actually appears to have helped the movement grow.

If it seems hard to believe that sane people would accept this scenario, it is worth remembering some of the other fantastic ideas promoted by militias. Literally thousands of people, and probably tens of thousands, were convinced that 'black helicopters' were spying on them and other American patriots, preparing for an invasion of United Nations blue helmets and other forces of the New World Order. Tales of concentration camps, hidden inside mountains and under cities, were rife. Stickers on road signs, actually meant to tell highway crews when the signs needed replacement, were taken as cleverly coded directions for invading foreign troops. Blurry photographs of railroad cattle cars found in the desert, the insides of which were supposedly being fitted with shackles, were presented as evidence of imminent martial law. A militia publication in Montana asserted that global elites planned to divide the human race into seven classes, one of which would be used to provide organs for the ailing wealthy (*The Big Sky Patriot*, undated). Freemasons, Bilderbergers, Illuminati, 'international' Jewish bankers and others were each described as secretly running the world.

A virtual industry of conspiratologists sprang up to promote these ideas. And they were supported by some unlikely allies, including many right-wing Christians who saw Clinton as morally decadent. Jerry Falwell, a fundamentalist Baptist with a huge audience, produced 'The Clinton Chronicles', a paranoid video alleging the president was a mass-murdering drug smuggler (Harding 2000). Phyllis Schlafly's Eagle Forum, a group of right-wing Republican women, produced another video that described an array of liberal causes as part and parcel of a one-world government plot. In some rural states, sheriffs and other local officials with similar ideas were elected.

It also did not hurt that the National Rifle Association (NRA), a powerful right-wing gun rights lobby, claimed in a fundraising letter just days after the Oklahoma City bomb, that 'jack-booted government thugs' in 'Nazi bucket helmets' had 'the government's go-ahead to harass, intimidate, even murder law abiding citizens'. Former President Bush was so outraged that he quit the NRA in protest.

The reactions of the political apparatus did not help. The decision to hire 500 more FBI agents specifically to battle domestic terrorism helped fuel the paranoia of many 'Patriots', who felt they were being set up by the government. Congressional hearings in the fall of 1995 brought a series of militiamen and others to Washington to testify – but, thanks to the generally uncritical nature of the legislators' questions, the hearings actually seemed to give some support to the militias' views.

And so the movement continued to expand. It was becoming increasingly acceptable, it seemed, to see the federal government as the embodiment of evil.

The violence spreads

At the same time, violence spread. Even before the Oklahoma attack, the militias and other Patriot groups had produced a high level of criminality. In January of 1994, for instance, adherents of 'common-law' doctrine – men who believed that 'sovereign citizens' (typically, whites) were exempt from state and federal laws and who were setting up their own vigilante 'courts' – viciously attacked a court official in California. Ambushed in her garage, Stanislaus County Recorder Karen Mathews was severely beaten, stabbed and sodomized with a gun by radicals enraged that she had refused to remove a $416,343 federal tax lien entered against one of them. Similarly, in September of that year, Linda Thompson, an Indianapolis attorney and self-declared 'acting Adjutant General of the Unorganized Militia of the United States', urged an armed march on Washington to force the repeal of gun control laws, trade pacts and three constitutional amendments. It was called off after other radicals warned that Thompson's plan was an invitation for a bloodbath.

In the aftermath of Oklahoma City, the pace picked up. There were hundreds of minor confrontations between Patriots and government officials, often agents of environmental agencies such as the US Forest Service and the federal Bureau of Land Management. But the most remarkable development, galvanized by McVeigh's attack, was the large number of domestic terrorist plots uncovered after Oklahoma. One measure of this was the fact that the FBI was carrying an average of about 100 open domestic terrorism cases before the Oklahoma bombing; in the following years, agency officials say they averaged between 900 and 1,000 cases at a time (*Intelligence Report*, 92, 1998, p. 8).

The Oklahoma bombing turned out to be an opening shot in a deadly new phase of right-wing terror in America. McVeigh had opened the door to attacking not just 'enemy' targets, but large and essentially random groups of citizens – something that had not occurred in either right-wing or left-wing terrorist attacks of the 1960s, 1970s or 1980s. Before the 1990s were out, almost 30 major plots were discovered, most of them foiled before conspirators could take action (*Intelligence Report*, 90, 1998, p. 8, and 102, 2001, p. 39). These plots included plans to bomb buildings, banks, refineries, utilities, clinics and bridges; to assassinate politicians, judges, civil rights figures and others; to attack Army bases, National Guard armories, and a train; to rob banks, armored cars, and even other criminals; and to amass illegal machine guns, missiles and explosives.

In September 1995, for instance, Charles Ray Polk was indicted for plotting to blow up the Austin, Texas, state headquarters of the Internal Revenue Service, the federal tax agency. The next month, saboteurs signing themselves 'Sons of Gestapo' derailed a passenger train in Arizona, killing one person. In November, the leader of the Oklahoma Constitutional Militia and two others were arrested as they prepared to bomb targets including the Southern Poverty Law Center. In 1996, members of the so-called Aryan Republican Army were charged in connection with 22 bank robberies in the Midwest. The Atlanta Olympics were bombed, killing one person, and militia members plotted to blow up an FBI facility where 1,000 people worked. In 1997, three radicals were arrested in a bombing plot that authorities said could have killed more than 10,000 Texans. A heavily armed militiaman was arrested as he prepared to attack an Army base where he thought foreign troops trained.

The list goes on. In 1998, a small revolutionary gang from the Pacific Northwest, plotting to create a whites-only Aryan People's Republic, engaged in a nationally televised shoot-out with police and murdered an entire Arkansas family, including an eight-year-old girl. A police officer guarding an abortion clinic died when a terrorist watching from his truck set off a remote-controlled bomb. Three members of the North American Militia of Southwestern Michigan were arrested in a plot to bomb federal buildings, assassinate a radio show host and kill federal agents.

The movement cools

By the end of the 1990s, the terror seemed to be slackening somewhat. Partly, that was almost certainly due to aggressive law enforcement. Paranoia was rife in the movement, and militia and other extremists seemed to spend as much time accusing each other of working for the government as they did attacking those they saw as their real enemies. An unending stream of arrests was also convincing many of the dangers of launching actions. But the decline in violence also reflected the declining fortunes of the militia movement as a whole. From a high of 858 groups in 1996, the SPLC found that the number of such groups dropped to 523 in 1997; 435 in 1998; 217 in 1999; 194 in 2000, and just 158 in 2001. Certainly, this count is only one way of measuring the movement's strength, and some argue that it underestimates the level of activity by unaffiliated Patriots and those who have gone underground. But an obvious drop-off in attendance at meetings, a major circulation fall in Patriot publications and other evidence also underlined the decline.

Why has the militia movement – that particular expression of the American radical right – lost so much steam? There are a number of reasons, not the least of which is that white-hot social movements like this one cannot last forever. The human energy that drives them simply is unable to sustain itself for very long, rarely more than a decade or so. That was true of the civil rights movement, which was winding down even before Martin Luther King Jr. was assassinated. It was also true of the radical right in the 1980s, when the anti-Semitic Posse Comitatus raged through the Midwest organizing distressed farmers but petered out by decade's end.

There were, however, more specific reasons for the decline of the militia movement. Thousands of militiamen went home in the late 1990s, disillusioned and tired of waiting for the revolution (or attack by the New World Order) that never seemed to come. Others joined harder-line hate groups that seemed to promise more action. And still others, even those who saw Oklahoma as the work of the government, were frightened off by the many criminal conspiracies that the movement produced.

Crackdowns on 'common-law' tactics were important. At least 30 states passed new laws or strengthened old ones in the 1990s that punished such things as impersonating public officials, simulating legal process, and filing court liens against the property of enemies – the 'paper terrorism' tactics that became immensely popular with Patriots in the 1990s. As a result, hundreds, if not thousands, of people were arrested and often handed substantial prison terms. In addition, many were imprisoned on illegal weapons charges. Still others, engaging in the various scams that sprang up in the Patriot world, went to prison on theft or fraud charges. There was widespread fear, too, of government informants inside the movement.

At the same time, the Patriots had partly won some of their most important battles. Despite Clinton's gun control laws, most commentators agree that serious attempts to regulate guns ultimately failed. Although this was due to the votes of conservative Democrats and pro-gun Republicans, the coalition's members seem to have been influenced by the militias and 'mainstream' allies such as the NRA. By the end of the decade, after congressional hearings on abuses of the Internal Revenue Service, tax enforcement – another *bête noire* of the Patriots, who included many tax protesters – was essentially gutted by lawmakers who slashed IRS funding. Some of the key Patriot issues, in other words, were being resolved through the political process – even if it was not Patriots who were resolving them.

The capper came with the millennial date change. As January 1, 2000, approached, major sectors of the American radical right went into a frenzy. Some, with a more religious bent, predicted the world's end or some kind of apocalyptic final battle. Others, more secular, expected President Clinton or perhaps the United Nations to take advantage of the much-feared 'Y2K' computer problem to impose martial law or launch an invasion of the United States (*Intelligence Report*, 92, 1998, p. 6). Racists predicted that starving inner-city blacks, deprived of their welfare checks by computer shutdowns, would storm into the countryside to plunder the whites. Across the country, people built bunkers, bought generators, stored food and water and waited fearfully. In the event, January 1 dawned sunny and bright, with no apocalypse or social collapse in sight. Within days, large numbers of Patriots, hammered by their leaders for years with Y2K fears, reacted angrily. One wrote to *Media Bypass*, a publication popular in the militia movement: 'What am I to do with the thousands of dollars I was tricked into spending on preparing for the Y2K bug? The community of patriots were the loudest in proclaiming that the world would come to an end when the clock struck 12. Well, it struck. And time marched on. Thanks a lot.'

What remained of the militia scene was generally harder core, with an increasing number of groups influenced by the racist and anti-Semitic Christian Identity theology favored by some American neo-Nazi groups. Many others have embraced another radical theology, Christian Reconstuctionism, whose proponents seek to impose draconian Old Testament law on the United States. Typical of declining movements, the militia world increasingly came to be dominated by profiteers – men and women who played on the conspiracy theories that characterize Patriot thinking to rip off their supposed brethren in the movement. As the decade wound down, the government seemed to turn most of its attention elsewhere.

The rise of race-based hate groups

A remarkable thing occurred while America's militias rose and fell. Even as this very public phenomenon captured the attention of citizens and the press alike, hate groups – Klan, neo-Nazi and other organizations whose primary ideology is based on racial or other forms of group hatred – rose steadily. White nationalists, now describing themselves as separatists rather than supremacists, offered a racial analysis of the world that seemed to win increasing acceptance. By 2001, the latest figure available, the SPLC was tracking 676 hate groups, the largest number since the Center began monitoring extremism in the early 1980s.[9] Indeed, exclusionary ethnic nationalisms had been growing in places from the deep South, where the so-called 'neo-Confederate' movement took off in the late 1990s, to the nation's inner cities, where black supremacism took on new life.

There were many reasons for this very significant increase. They included the power of new communications technologies, the use of white power music to recruit youth, the falling proportion of whites in the US population, and rising Hispanic immigration. Hate groups saw the government as not merely failing to address these problems, but as actually being secretly run by Satanic Jews. At the same time, sharp economic pressures were coming to bear on young white workers, the middle class, farmers and workers in heavy industry. Finally, globalization and other rapid social and economic changes – accompanied by the rise of multicultural orthodoxy – have ignited an angry reaction among many who feel they are losing their heritage. One Southern group said in a typical comment on the plight of whites: 'In this so-called "multicultural" society, it has become increasingly obvious that there exists one culture that must die while all others are allowed and encouraged to flourish. Much energy is being expended to complete the eradication of the last vestiges of Southern culture.'

Jared Taylor, editor of the racist *American Renaissance* magazine, offers what is probably the most cogent critique of mainstream, 'politically correct' views – a critique that seems to have found great sympathy among many Americans:

> Some think that it's virtuous of the United States, after having been founded and built by Europeans, according to European institutions, to reinvent itself or transform itself into a non-white country with a Third World population. I think that's a kind of cultural and racial suicide. ... We're all now more or less obliged to say, "Oh! Diversity is a wonderful thing for the country," whereas, practically every example of tension, bloodletting, civil unrest around the world is due precisely to the kind of thing we're importing – diversity. (Cited in Swain 2002, p. 18)

Together, these factors created a situation that was ripe for organizers of the radical right. It may be instructive to examine each of them in more detail.

The radical right in America was very quick to take up new technologies (e.g. Marks 1996, pp. 147–54). In 1984, Tom Metzger of the neo-Nazi White Aryan Resistance led the right's foray into cable television, taking advantage of rules that required cable outlets to air different views from local citizens as a condition of their local monopolies. Metzger's show, 'Race and Reason', would peak in 1992, when it was airing in 62 cities in 21 states. Other white supremacists got into computers early on, setting up 'bulletin boards' for communications and propaganda in the 1980s. And in 1995, a former Klansman named Don Black set up Stormfront, the first major hate site on the Internet.

The radical right had extremely high hopes for the Internet, seeing it as a way to bypass the mainstream media and as a primary recruiting tool (e.g. Eatwell 1996). But they do not seem to have entirely panned out, in the sense that Web pages do not appear to have been very successful at recruiting (*Intelligence Report*, 101, 2001, p. 44, and 102, 2001, p. 54). Still, the Internet clearly aided the movement in other ways. Formerly isolated radical racists discovered like-minded people all over the country, and came to feel that they were part of a real movement – not simply social outcasts. Millions of people were exposed to the movement's ideas, and at least a few of them ended making contact with groups and even joining up. Ideas, plans, meetings and other information were communicated instantaneously.

White power music, which originated in Britain in the late 1970s, developed significant distribution networks in the 1990s in both Europe and the United States, growing from a cottage industry to a multimillion-dollar business in the space of a decade (*Intelligence Report*, 103, 2001, p. 24; Lööw 1998). In 1999, America's leading neo-Nazi – the late William Pierce, head of the National Alliance – paid some $250,000 to acquire Resistance Records, an early white power label. Pierce quickly built it up into the leading racist music distributor, and it now brings several hundred thousand dollars a year into the Alliance. Enterprises like Resistance Records are doing more than pouring money into the coffers of the radical right. The music they sell is also highly effective, according to a large number of people who have renounced the radical right, at bringing young people into the movement. Part of the attraction is the subculture that accompanies the music – concerts, parties, and the rest of the social milieu of skinhead youths. A great deal of recruiting occurs at increasingly common white power concerts. This business has become particularly active in the United States, where 'hatecore' music is protected as free speech by the Constitution's First Amendment. America now produces music and propaganda for the racist right worldwide.

Although the United States has always been a multiracial country, many whites view it as having been created by, and for, Christian whites. Beginning in 1965, when racial immigration quotas were abolished, large numbers of immigrants – particularly Hispanics – entered the country at the same time that birth rates of native-born whites were falling precipitously. As darker-skinned immigrants arrived in places that had only rarely seen such newcomers, many whites reacted with fear and anger. This has been greatly exacerbated by the US Census Bureau's prediction that whites will lose their majority in America shortly after 2050 – a fact that many white supremacist ideologues have harped upon relentlessly. The news in 2000 that California had lost its white majority fueled these fears even further. As other states follow suit in coming years, more whites may well resort to extremism. Many whites see the federal government, along with the nation's business elites, as specifically responsible for the failure to curb non-white immigration. On the radical right, the government is seen as plotting to destroy the white race.

The rise of neo-Pagan religions, in particular racist forms of pre-Christian Scandinavian theologies like Odinism, seems to have attracted a new kind of recruit – bright, typically college-educated young people, who have come to reject Judeo-Christian values (*Intelligence Report*, 101, 2001, p. 56). This development, increasingly marked over the 1990s, comes as more and more racists reject Christianity, which is seen as overly soft. The 'might is right' mentality of racist Odinism is viewed by these youths as far more attractive. Although numbers are hard to come by, one scholar suggests that half of new racist recruits now consider themselves pagans (Gardell, 2003). In addition, a number of racist Odinists are running energetic prison ministries with the aim of finding new recruits (*Intelligence Report*, 98, 2000, p. 25).

Globalization and the economy

At the same time as these factors helped boost the radical right, large numbers of Americans found themselves increasingly facing hard economic times. It is not clear precisely how such economic developments affected the growth of the radical right, although it seems certain that any correlation is not a simple one – people who lose their jobs do not rush out to join radical groups without further ado. What seems more likely is that difficult economic times, particularly when they affect people not accustomed to seeing their prospects shrinking, give the radical right an opening. It is at such moments that the sometimes convoluted explanations of the world offered by radical ideologues get more of a hearing than they otherwise would have.

Whatever the effect, things were not easy for many people. Farmers who survived the agricultural crisis of the 1980s continued to lose their land and their livelihoods. Industrial workers, especially in the auto and steel industries, lost jobs as their work increasingly moved abroad to cheaper labor markets. Overall, the bottom three-fifths of Americans experienced falling real wages between 1991 and the end of the decade – a stunning figure for a nation accustomed to prosperity. These kinds of changes hit young people – particularly those living in the aging inner-ring suburbs known as 'edge cities' – especially hard. For those with less education, the situation was becoming even more difficult with every year. A long-term downward trend for workers, in particular, was evident. Average hourly wages for workers aged 20–29, for instance, declined 21.7 per cent in real dollars between 1973 and 1996 (from $10.67 to $8.35 in constant 1996 dollars).

These figures support the remarkable findings of the four sociologists and statisticians in Bernhardt *et al.* (2001). Comparing two generations of young, white workers – one that entered the labor market in the late 1960s, and one that started work in the early 1980s – the study finds that 90 per cent of the latter generation will have lower lifetime wage growth. This change represents 'a massive downshift in earning standards'. Because of downsizing, the decline of unions and a stagnant minimum wage, the study concludes that most white men 'can no longer expect stable careers that lead to a solid, family-sustaining wage'.

Such changes provided a clear opening to the radical right. 'The whole climate for our revolution has shifted toward more favorable conditions', neo-Nazi leader William Pierce wrote in the *National Alliance Bulletin* (December 1999), an internal newsletter, seeking to explain his group's soaring growth rate. 'I believe that the conditions which have made our people angry enough in 1999 to overcome their fear will continue and intensify in 2000 and the years ahead. We are long way from exhausting our pool of potential recruits'.

Some of these changes are related, of course, to economic globalization, particularly the transfer of many industrial jobs abroad and the spread of neo-liberal approaches to economic problems. But globalization has also contributed to the loss of some national sovereignty, the spread of multi-culturalism and multiracialism, and pressures on local cultures to assimilate into a kind of Western world culture. To many, globalization means the steamrolling of their own national cultures in favor of a drab American monoculture of strip malls and fast-food restaurants. And to some, the only possible defense against this homogenizing juggernaut is what is seen as the 'organic' nation – a nation that is based on race, a community of blood.

The rise of the neo-Confederates

Few cases in the United States illustrate that better than the rise of the so-called neo-Confederate movement, which appeared in the mid-1990s and sought to defend white 'Southern' culture from the 'politically correct' elites. Partisans of this movement described the South as fundamentally 'Anglo-Celtic', and pushed the idea of a second Southern secession. But most remarkable was the way that racism – a visceral dislike for black people – came to characterize the movement (*Intelligence Report*, 99, 2000).

Certainly, this movement was not the first time in recent history that reactionary groups had arisen to defend the Southern cause. In the 1950s and 1960s, racist White Citizens Councils were formed to defend segregation. In the 1980s, a group that descended from those councils arose to espouse similar beliefs. But the contemporary movement did not really take off until the League of the South, a group led mainly by a group of Southern university professors, was formed in 1994. Both the League and the larger neo-Confederate movement grew ever more radical as they fought attempts by black activists to do away with the old Confederate battle flag, which to most black Americans is a potent symbol of racist hate. This conflict was especially acute in South Carolina, where the state finally removed the flag from atop the Statehouse, where it had flown since the civil rights movement.

The league, which opposes interracial marriage, mixes anger at the multicultural 'New World Order' with defenses of segregation and even 'biblical' slavery. It rejects the 'Jacobin' ideology of egalitarianism and the 'materialism' of the North. 'They certainly want the revival of the principles of the Confederacy', Arizona State University historian Brooks Simpson said of such groups, 'and one of those principles would in fact be white supremacy, unquestioned and explicit. The racism that's woven into their comments is often quite astonishing' (*Intelligence Report*, 99, 2000).

The League, in particular, took off. Within four years of its creation, it had 4,000 members. By 2000, two years later, it counted approximately 9,000. The League's academic veneer provided a home for thousands of Southerners with racist feelings who nonetheless sought the cover of an allegedly 'mainstream' group. And it got involved in politics, claiming credit for the 1996 ouster of South Carolina Governor David Beasley, a Republican who had spoken out against the Confederate flag.

The league also rejects the separation of church and state, seeking a government based on 'Christian principles' instead. And it specifically endorses all kinds of separatist movements – 'devolutionist' movements that it sees as rejecting the multiculturalism of the US-led 'New World Order'. In fact, in an essay entitled 'Merle vs. Madonna', League leader Michael Hill described the United States as two fundamentally different countries – the land whose culture is that of country western singer Merle Haggard, and the risqué, racially mixed world of pop star Madonna. Hill's description of a two-country nation made sense to many who read it. It seemed to reflect almost exactly the division between the states voting in the 2000 presidential contest between George W. Bush and Al Gore – the red- and the blue-colored states that became familiar to millions of television viewers.

The whites of the neo-Confederate movement weren't the only expression of burgeoning ethnic nationalism in the United States. Black nationalism, too, seemed to be clearly growing – and to have taken on a hard, anti-white edge. This was seen not only in the power of major groups like the Nation of Islam, but in the rise of new ones like the Black Panther Party (*Intelligence Report*, 100, 2000, p. 16).[10] Unlike the original Panthers of the 1960s and 1970s, the new Panthers did not form alliances with non-black groups and activists. Instead, they embraced an anti-white, anti-Semitic and homophobic ideology.

Looking forward

As the 1990s came to a close, it became obvious that the ideology of the American radical right – or rather, the ideologies of the various sectors of the extreme right – was changing. One of the most remarkable developments has been the shift, in large parts of the radical right, from seeing blacks as the primary enemy to focusing on Jews. And Jews are seen as equal to the government – they are the ones secretly ruining the world. Thirty years ago, the average Klansman's father had fought the German Nazis, and had no sympathy for them at all. With the advance of Holocaust denial and fading memories of historical Nazism, that same Klansman is today far more likely to agree with the original National Socialists. Also contributing to this change have been contacts with European neo-Nazis (see Kaplan and Weinberg 1998) and the theology of Christian Identity (see Barkun 1994), which helped spread anti-Semitism across the radical right.

Since the 1960s, Christian Identity – which says whites are the real Hebrews of the Bible, God created blacks as soulless 'beasts of the field', and Jews are the biological descendants of Satan – had increasingly come to dominate the radical right, even invading Klan organizations that had long held to mainstream strands of Christianity. Identity's identification of Jews as the underlying enemy, formulated in religious terms that were appealing to many Americans, was also adopted by a large number of American neo-Nazi organizations. In the 1990s, however, there were the first clear signs of the decline of Identity as a major force. For one thing, half a dozen key Identity leaders died toward the end of the 1990s, and attendance at a number of Identity events around the country was down markedly. For another, the theology, as heretical as it is, is tied inextricably to Christian doctrine – a fact that is a turn-off for growing numbers of radical youths, who are instead turning to racist variants of Odinism and other neo-Pagan religions, or who reject religion altogether.

In addition to these influences, the whole notion of 'the international Jew' – a person whose first loyalty is supposedly to his 'race', rather than to his nation – fits the radical right's conception of globalizing capitalists almost perfectly. Both groups are seen as self-serving materialists, contemptuous of neighbors and countrymen.

As the new millennium dawned, it appeared that the American radical right was changing in other ways as well. During the 1990s, radical groups keyed in on such issues as race, guns, immigration, abortion, homosexuality and the power of the federal government. In the new century, at least some sectors of the extreme right are focusing on issues that also are of interest to the traditional left: the environment, animal rights and, above all, the specter of growing economic globalism (*Intelligence Report*, 97, 2000, p. 40). Both far left and far right see the federal government as their primary enemy. Although this has yet to produce any alliance, it has prompted new thinking on the right.

'The New American Patriot will be neither left nor right, just a freeman fighting for liberty', is the way that Louis Beam, a key white supremacist ideologue, put it in 2000, following sometimes violent protests against the World Trade Organization in Seattle. 'New alliances will form between those who have in the past thought of themselves as "right-wingers," conservatives and patriots, with those who have thought of themselves as "left-wingers," progressives, or just "liberal"'.[11]

Indeed, growing numbers of right-wing radicals are embracing Third World struggles against the US government, which is seen as increasingly in the hands of the Jews and is often described as 'ZOG', for Zionist Occupation Government. To them, the government has become the world spearhead of multiracialism. The fact that many of these radicals have traditionally attacked dark-skinned Third Worlders as 'mud people' is an irony that does not seem to have affected their analysis. To them, anyone opposed to the United States is a potential ally in the struggle.

In many ways, the American radical right today represents an alienated and distrustful response to a rapidly changing world – a rejection of the vision of the post-Communist world that was summarized in President Bush Sr.'s 'New World Order' speech in 1990. In the heartland, Americans have not been so quick as their country's elites to endorse the drawing together of economies, races and cultures that globalism represents. Instead, they have increasingly come to see globalism as robbing America of its independence, culture, and economic health (e.g. Rupert 2000).

For the radical right, these developments have opened the door to racial explanations – and the market for them – in a way not seen in decades. Sam Francis, a white nationalist and former columnist for the arch-conservative *Washington Times*, put it like this at an *American Renaissance* conference: 'What we as whites must do is reassert our identity and our solidarity, and we must do so in explicitly racial terms through the articulation of a racial consciousness as whites' (cited in D'Souza 1995, p. 396).

It is not clear where all these developments will ultimately lead. That the American radical right has grown more revolutionary seems plain, especially when its reaction to the September 11 terrorist attacks is considered (although it is true that a few softer-line militia groups instead rallied behind the federal government). That the factors that helped the extreme right grow are still in place also appears difficult to dispute – although the government actions at Ruby Ridge and Waco, so critical to the early growth of the militia movement, are fading from Americans' collective memory. The US radical right is displaying a growing confidence and swagger, and some attempts to unify its often warring elements marked the start of the new millennium. If the US economy worsens in the years to come, and if radical right ideologues continue to tailor their message to the fearful and those who are losing out, it seems plausible that their movement will continue to expand.

Notes

1 This comment was made on a private National Alliance e-mail list on September 11, 2001. It was captured and publicized by the Southern Poverty Law Center (SPLC).
2 The idea that certain shadowy groups – Communists, Jews or internationally oriented groups like the Council on Foreign Relations – are engaged in a plot to form a socialistic global government goes back to the formation of the United Nations in 1948 and even before. But President Bush's speech gave this global government a name, the 'New World Order', that was quickly accepted by almost all extreme-right groups.
3 Officials of the SPLC made this argument in the mid-1990s. Others, such as historian Mark Pitcavage (1998, p. 28), have argued that this is unlikely 'even though there was some talk of paramilitary groups at the conference, because few of the attendees would eventually be directly involved in the militia movement, and those who did become so involved ... did not create any groups for some time...'

4 The first film, 'Waco: The Rules of Engagement', was actually nominated for a best-documentary Academy Award.
5 Although these numbers are very speculative, they are in line with estimates from leading watchdog groups including the SPLC and the Anti-Defamation League.
6 Although Aho's work predates the modern militia movement by several years, it seems clear that his subjects were essentially the same people who would later join militias. In addition, anecdotal accounts by journalists and others who have worked in the field, including this author, support this conclusion.
7 Nichols, who at one point renounced his US citizenship, was particularly involved in radical right theories about credit and money, among other things – theories that derived directly from the anti-Semitic Posse Comitatus of the 1970s and 1980s. McVeigh also adopted many key militia beliefs and at one point spoke of forming a militia. By his own account, he also attended some 80 gun shows, key venues for militia propaganda.
8 This was the first year SPLC carried out such a 'Patriot' count. Previously, the Center had only counted explicitly race-based 'hate groups'.
9 Due to changes in counting methods, the SPLC's hate group counts cannot be compared directly over the course of the 1980s and 1990s. Starting in the late 1990s, the Center began to count all chapters of national hate groups (the earlier method had not included some chapters).
10 Another interesting case is that of the United Nuwaubian Nation of Moors, another black supremacist group that also has many characteristics of a cult of personality, which is profiled in '"Savior" in a Strange Land,' *Intelligence Report*, Southern Poverty Law Center, 2002, Issue 107, p. 8.
11 "The Battle in Seattle: Americans Face Off the Police State," downloaded September 16, 2002, from http://www.louisbeam.com/seattle.htm.

Bibliography

Aho, J. (1990) *The Politics of Righteousness: Idaho Christian Patriotism*, Seattle: University of Washington Press.
Barkun, M. (1994) *Religion and the Racist Right. The Origins of the Christian Identity Movement*, Chapel Hill: University of North Carolina Press.
Bernhardt, A., Morris, M., Handcock, M.S. and Scott, M.A. (2001) *Divergent Paths: Economic Mobility in the New American Labor Market*, New York: Russell Sage Foundation.
D'Souza, D. (1995) *The End of Racism: Principles for a Multiracial Society*, New York: Free Press.
Eatwell, R. (1996) 'Surfing the great white wave: the internet, extremism and the problem of control', *Patterns of Prejudice* 30, 1: 61–71.
Gardell, M. (2003) *Gods of the Blood. The Pagan Revival and White Separatism*, Durham, NC: Duke University Press.
Gibson, J.W. (1994) *Warrior Dreams: Violence and Manhood in Post-Vietnam America*, New York: Hill and Wang.
Harding, S.F. (2000) *The Book of Jerry Falwell: Fundamentalist Language and Politics*, Princeton: Princeton University Press.
Hofstadter, R. (1967) *The Paranoid Style in American Politics and Other Essays*, New York: Vintage.
Intelligence Report(s), Montgomery, Southern Poverty Law Center.

Kaplan, J. (ed.) (2000) *Encyclopedia of White Power. A Sourcebook on the Radical Racist Right*, Walnut Creek: AltaMira.
Kaplan, J. and Weinberg, L. (1998) *The Emergence of a Euro-American Radical Right*, New Brunswick: Rutgers University Press.
Levitas, D. (2002) *The Terrorist Next Door: The Militia Movement and the Radical Right*, New York: Thomas Dunne.
Lööw, H. (1998) 'White-power rock 'n roll: a growing industry', in Kaplan, J. and Bjørgo, T. (eds) *Nation and Race. The Developing Euro-American Racist Subculture*, Boston: Northeastern University Press, pp. 126–147.
Marks, C. (1996) *The Faces of Right Wing Extremism*, Boston: Branden.
Michael, L. and Herbeck, D. (2001) *American Terrorist: Timothy McVeigh and the Oklahoma City Bombing*, New York: Regan.
Pitcavage, M. (1998) *The Investigator's and Prosecutor's Guide to Common Terms Used by Antigovernment Extremists*, Tallahassee: Institute for Intergovernmental Research.
Public Citizen. 2001. *NAFTA Chapter 11 Investor-to-State Cases: Bankrupting Democracy*. <http://www.publiccitizen.org/documents/ACF186.PDF>
Robertson, P. (1991) *New World Order*, Dallas: Word.
Rupert, M. (2000) *Ideologies of Globalization. Contending Visions of a New World Order*, London: Routledge.
Snow, R.L. (1999) *The Militia Threat: Terrorists Among Us*, Cambridge, MA: Perseus.
Swain, C.M. (2002) *The New White Nationalism in America: Its Challenge to Immigration*, New York: Cambridge University Press.

3 The extreme right in Britain
The long road to 'modernization'

Roger Eatwell

Introduction

During the last 20 years, there has been a major growth in electoral support for the extreme right in many European countries. This has been true even in countries that have historically been immune to extremism, such as Denmark or Norway. Until recently, Britain was the most notable exception to this trend. However, during 2001–3 there have been growing signs that the British National Party (BNP) is in the process of becoming a significant force in a number of areas. Among the party's most prominent achievements have been: winning 16.4 per cent of the vote in Oldham West in the 2001 general election and over 11 per cent in Oldham East and Burnley; electing three councillors in Burnley and another in Blackburn in 2002; coming third in the 2002 Stoke Mayoral election, only narrowly behind the winner; and winning another hotly-contested council by-election seat in Calderdale in early 2003.[1] As a result of this growing support, the BNP put forward 221 candidates for the 2003 local elections, mainly in northern England, and gained its best ever set of results, including winning eight seats on Burnley council, making it the second largest party in the town.

During the 1930s, Sir Oswald Mosley's British Union of Fascists had failed dismally (Eatwell 1995; Thurlow, 1998). After 1945, most extreme right groups – with the brief exception of the National Front (NF) in the 1970s – fared no better in electoral terms. Various arguments have been proposed to explain this historic weakness of the British extreme right. Many stress structuralist factors, for example the claim that Britain has been less affected than some European neighbours by sudden socio-economic changes, such as major depression. Another common approach is to focus on political culture, stressing factors like the prophylactic powers of deep-rooted democratic values and the association of Britishness with anti-fascism. Political science 'institutionalists' stress more the importance of First Past the Post (FPTP) elections to party system stability (Eatwell 2000; for a broader discussion of theories of extreme right support see Eatwell, 2003). However, the general conclusion was the same – namely, that the British extreme right was doomed electorally.

This chapter highlights the nature of 'extremist' parties themselves as an explanatory factor. In particular, it looks at the way in which the BNP has 'modernized' itself since 1999 when Nick Griffin, an articulate and relatively young Cambridge graduate, took over as leader. This has involved dropping or watering down many of the party's more extreme policies, and often concentrating on 'community politics' that exploit local concerns. As courting electoral allies is of less importance than in most European Proportional Representation (PR) systems, the main purpose of this change is twofold. First, the BNP seeks to attract activists from mainstream parties, especially the troubled Conservatives, and it hopes these changes will make the party more appealing to a broad swathe of voters. Moreover, modernization in the form of 'charismatic' leaders espousing populist policies maximizes the chance of attracting local and national media coverage, thus further disseminating news of the party's new policies and rising support.

However, the BNP faces a variety of problems in its quest for respectability. Although membership has increased notably since 2001, the party is short of talent to stand in local elections. Election victories can even turn sour if the winning candidates are not up to the job, or more generally fail to fulfil aspirations. The continued existence of non-modernized extreme right groups, such as the National Front, poses further image problems, as their supporters often mix with the more traditional members of the BNP. Moreover, modernization poses problems for hard-core members. Party literature since 2000 has at times contained 'coded' messages, which seem aimed at reassuring the 'traditionalists' that the party has not lost its extremist soul. Nevertheless, the BNP faces the classic 'adaptation dilemma' (see Chapter 1) – that is, the delicate balancing act of seeking democratic popular legitimacy without provoking a major internal split. The situation has been compounded since the Al-Qaeda attacks on 11 September 2001 by the leadership's attempts to collaborate with British Sikhs and other ethnic minorities in the struggle against Islam. This is anathema for activists weaned on a diet of compulsory 'repatriation' of all non-whites – the most prominent plank in the programmes of various British extreme right parties since the 1960s.

From the National Front to the BNP

John Tyndall formed the British National Party in April 1982. Tyndall had been active since the late 1950s in a variety of overtly neo-Nazi groups. However, the paramilitary group Spearhead, which he formed with Colin Jordan, was banned under the 1936 Public Order Act, and, after 1965, crude forms of racism risked prosecution under Britain's first Race Relations Act. Moreover, during the mid-1960s Tyndall decided that open Nazism could never provide the basis for a major political movement in Britain (Tyndall, 1970). As a result, his Greater Britain Movement was admitted into the newly formed National Front in 1968, which emerged mainly out of renegade Conservative Empire loyalist and anti-immigrant groups.

By the early 1970s, Tyndall had replaced the ageing A.K. Chesterton as leader of the NF (on the latter see Baker, 1996). During this decade, party membership peaked at around 17,500 and it enjoyed two mini-peaks of support, which followed the much-publicized arrivals of small new waves of expelled 'Asians' from Uganda and Malawi (in general, immigration had dropped notably after the introduction of the first Commonwealth Immigration Act in 1962, which was partly designed to dampen rising anti-immigrant politics). Influenced by the popularity of Conservative MP Enoch Powell's notorious 1968 'river of blood' speech, the NF had always focused on a policy of compulsory repatriation of 'immigrants'. In parts of troubled urban areas, such as Bradford and Leicester, the NF captured over 10–20 per cent of the vote, while in the 1977 Greater London Council elections it won 120,000 votes. However, when, in the 1979 general election, the NF put up 303 candidates – a post-war record for an insurgent party – they went down to humiliating defeat, averaging just 1.4 per cent of the vote (Billig, 1978; Husbands, 1983; Taylor, 1982).

The NF failed for three specific reasons. First, as well as contesting elections, the party engaged in provocative marches and rallies in immigrant areas, which advertised its extremism. It also attracted a youth – especially football hooligan – wing with a notable taste for much-publicized violence. Second, the NF was increasingly tagged as 'Nazi' by opponents, a task helped not just by the past views of some of its leaders but also by the fact that the party openly sold Holocaust Denial propaganda. Arguably, the most important opposition came from the mainstream parties and the media, although the radical left, in the guise of the Anti-Nazi League, also led street-protests against the Front, which led to further violence. Third, after 1977, key figures in the Conservative opposition specifically courted the NF vote: Margaret Thatcher even openly spoke of British fears of swamping by alien cultures. This reinforced the view among much of the electorate, dating back to the 1960s, that they were the main anti-immigrant party.

David Irving, a prominent 'historian' with extreme right tendencies, analysed the key problem in somewhat different terms.[2] Irving saw the NF as a rank and file in need of an officer class. The majority of its 'corporals' were relatively inarticulate members of the working class, and its leadership was hardly any more impressive. Moreover, he believed that the NF was too much of a single-issue party. Irving sought to break out of this ghetto by establishing, during 1979–80, the Clarendon Club, a dining and speaking coterie that sought to bring together conservatives and fascists, and a small Focus Group of like-minded thinkers, which sought to prepare the way intellectually for a new party.

Two specific 1970s' developments seem to have encouraged this strategy. The first was the rise of the New Right in the USA, which had been helped by syndicated columnists such as William Buckley, and by the new technology of computer-aided direct mailing. The second was Alain de Benoist, who addressed a small private meeting organized in London by Irving in 1980 (*Focal Point*, 31 January 1983). De Benoist was the key theorist of the French *Nouvelle Droite,* whose views would be more accurately termed 'Fortress Europe' – 'Third Way' (neither capitalism nor communism) than 'New Right' in the American globalized, free market sense. His strategy was to package key themes in a more acceptable way. For example, instead of proclaiming that there was a hierarchy of races, de Benoist advocated 'differencialism' – namely, the claim that all races had the right to their own identity, their own living space and respect (Sunic, 1990; Taguieff, 1994).

However, Irving was backed by no British equivalent of the intellectuals and journalists who had helped spread the American New Right cause (and after the late 1980s he increasingly lost much of his access to the mainstream media as he openly espoused the Holocaust Denial cause). Nor was there a British equivalent of the strong minority strand in French political culture, stemming back to the counter-Revolution, which legitimized the right. Finally, Irving's views on two issues were anathema to many on the extreme right. One concerned Irving's decision to adopt a policy of 'benevolent voluntary' rather than compulsory repatriation of immigrants. Irving believed that this would be much more acceptable to voters, but even some in the Focus Group objected. A second problem was highlighted in a letter from Tyndall, which appeared in the 5 June 1982 issue of *Focal Point*. This criticized Irving's 'sneering references to ... [the] "tattered flags of the past"', and support for greater European understanding. The vast majority of both British extreme right leaders and voters were isolationist-nationalists.

Tyndall, during 1981–2, was in the process of setting up the BNP, and seems to have feared that Irving might succeed in attracting the dreamed-of officer class. After the 1979 general election, the NF had broken up into warring factions, based on personality and ideology (Eatwell, 1996). The more-Conservative leaders believed that fascist influences had harmed the party's appeal. Others drew the opposite conclusion. Influenced especially by the thought of Julius Evola, a faction of young members believed that it was necessary to create an ascetic elite of 'political soldiers' who would prepare the way for the revolution. This faction was strongly anti-American (and Israeli), which led to *National Front News*' proclaiming on its cover in March 1988 'The New Alliance' between Libya's Colonel Khadaffi, Iran's Ayatollah Khomeini, the American black Muslim Louis Farrakhan, and the NF!

In spite of the near collapse of the NF, Tyndall and the BNP faced serious problems in terms of building a new electoral force. One concerned the fact that from April–June 1982, Britain fought a successful war over the Falkland Isles, which further reinforced Margaret Thatcher's 'Iron Lady'-nationalist credentials. The strength of Conservatism generally throughout the 1980s was a serious problem, as Tyndall's electoral strategy had always been based on the belief that splits within the Conservatives would open the way forward. A second problem concerned the generally unimpressive nature of the party's personnel, as it failed to pick up dissident Conservatives in the way that the NF had after Enoch Powell's sacking from the Shadow Cabinet in 1968. The presence around the fringes of skinhead and other violent alienated sub-cultures, such as racist music, posed further problems (Husbands, 1989). In 1983, Tyndall sought to break out of the impasse by putting up over 50 candidates in the general election, which guaranteed a free party broadcast (*Members Bulletin*, February 1984). However, the lost deposits were expensive for a small party and few long-term activists were recruited. The party therefore found itself with only around 2,000–3,000 members, many of whom played no significant part in the party's occasional rallies or forays into local and national elections.

In 1987, the party put up just two candidates in the general election. By the turn of the 1990s, its main activities centred on occasional meetings, sometimes provocatively arranged in ethnic minority areas, and the publication of small circulation journals and leaflets. Typical fare included an article in the October 1991 edition of *Spearhead* entitled 'Why South African Whites Must Fight', while the April 1992 issue's editorial claimed that political parties do not really represent the people, rather: 'real decision, lie with the oligarchies of financial power which interlock in common interest and which are best understood under the umbrella term of "New World Order"'. *Spearhead*'s book section regularly offered works relating to the Holocaust Denial, including *Did Six Million Really Die?*, which was written by a leading member of the 1970s' NF (see also Tyndall, 1988).

The first glimmer of hope for the BNP came when it won a much-publicized local election victory in Millwall in 1993 (Copsey, 1996; Eatwell, 1998a, 1998b; Holmes, 2000; Kushner, 1994). Millwall is part of London's East End, a relatively deprived area with a strong sense of white community, which felt increasingly threatened by both yuppie and immigrant incursions. However, these factors were also true of other areas where the BNP failed to make any significant electoral headway. Its electoral victory, therefore, owed much to political factors. Of particular importance were the activities of the local BNP itself, which often operated in the early 1990s under the name 'Rights for Whites', focusing on specific local grievances, such as the apparently racially motivated killing of a white youth. This helped it to extend its support within the local community, and even gain non-hostile coverage by the two local newspapers. This culminated in the BNP narrowly winning a seat with 34 per cent of the vote – probably helped by a last minute Labour publicity stunt, which released canvass returns showing that the BNP could win, in an attempt to squeeze the vote of other parties in Labour's favour.

The BNP's victor, Derek Beackon, was an inarticulate local activist who lost the seat the following year in the face of a major anti-fascist campaign. All the main parties joined in the attack, often helping ethnic minority voters to register (a notable change from the past, when both Labour and the Liberal Democrats had at times pandered to local racist sentiment). The local press now came out firmly against the BNP, as did the national media: for example, the mass-circulation *Daily Mirror* on 18 September 1993 greeted the victory with the headline: 'SIEG HEIL ... and Now He's a British Councillor'. Local opinion leaders, including churches and doctors, also joined the fray and almost certainly exerted more local influence than the usual array of left-wingers who typically make up 'anti-fascist' street protests.

Millwall did not prove a turning point in the BNP's fortunes. Campaigning during 1991–3 had very much been a local initiative, and most of the party's leading members placed little emphasis on 'community politics' and local elections. Growing anti-fascist street activity – often organized by the militant Anti Fascist Action – also raised the media profile of the BNP's more violent wing, which was only too happy to be provoked. Moreover, after 1993 the party was troubled by splits, and even violent attacks on members by Combat 18 (C18), which took its name from the first and eighth letters of the alphabet: A(dolf) and H(itler) – although C18's strategy owed more to contemporary American sources, especially the commitment to use violence to promote racial tensions, which were designed to radicalize complacent whites (Gable, 1995; Lowles, 2001). There is some evidence that the forces of 'law and order' penetrated C18. But this was probably intended to elicit information on activities such as white drug dealing rather than to halt the rise of the BNP, which was incapable of mounting a serious election challenge outside of a small number of areas.

In the 1997 general election, the BNP again put up over 50 candidates in order to qualify for a free electoral broadcast, with its best results coming in London's East End. It won 7.5 per cent of the vote in Bethnal Green and Bow, while Tyndall gained 7.3 per cent in Poplar and Canning Town. However, in many areas the BNP did not mount any form of campaign, and its average vote was only just over 1 per cent of the poll. Added to its usual problems was the entry into the electoral fray of the Referendum Party, formed by the millionaire Sir James Goldsmith. Although this party in general performed badly, it siphoned off some of the hard-core anti-EU vote which otherwise might have gone to the BNP. In the 1999 European Parliament elections, the BNP again put up enough candidates to gain free broadcasts in England and Scotland. But it faced an even more serious challenge from the UK Independence Party (UKIP), which – helped by the introduction of list PR for these elections – won 7 per cent of the national vote and three regional seats. The BNP again performed abysmally.

The BNP's leadership believed that the mainstream media, which were regularly portrayed as dominated by Jews and/or totally opposed to its cause, were a crucial cause of the party's failure (BNP, 1993?). In 1998, the party launched a Media Monitoring Unit to vet content and supply suitable stories. But the widespread media perception of the party as 'extreme', combined with lack of resources, meant that this attempt at agenda setting initially had little effect. There was also a growing BNP presence on the Internet, which was described in the October 1995 issue of *Spearhead* as the most important media development since television. However, Tyndall personally had little interest in the Net: as a result, the site was not always kept up-to-date, and was of low graphical sophistication.

In spite of the generally poor BNP performance, there were some grounds for thinking that a different form of radical British nationalist party might perform much better. For example, an opinion poll published in the *Daily Express* on 8 August 1995 indicated that 9 per cent of respondents would vote for a Jean-Marie Le Pen type Front National, and another 17 per cent said they would seriously consider doing so – results that were much-trumpeted on the BNP website. These, together with Le Pen's 15 per cent of the vote in the 1995 Presidential elections and the Front National subsequently winning control of four municipalities, further aroused interest in 'extremist' developments in continental Europe.

One lesson drawn concerned economic policy, with Tyndall increasingly turning away from his support for fascist-corporatist style economics towards a more Le Pen-like balance between free market and statist views. By 1999, Tyndall was coming under increasing pressure from leading party members, such as Eddie Butler, Tony Lecomber and Michael Newland, to make an even more dramatic change – namely, to alter the long-standing commitment to the compulsory repatriation of immigrants to one of voluntary repatriation. Tyndall agreed. But it was not enough to divert wider criticism of his leadership, including his inability to match Le Pen's 'charisma' – which some in the BNP saw as a crucial factor in Le Pen's ability to obtain mainstream media coverage.

Nick Griffin and the modernized BNP

As a result of growing discontent, Nick Griffin replaced Tyndall as leader at the October 1999 BNP conference. Griffin had been active in the NF since his student days, and during the 1980s he had been a leading member of the 'political soldier' faction, which brought him into contact with various forms of Europeanist extremist thinking, including de Benoist as well as Evola. However, by the early 1990s, the NF was clearly a spent force. Griffin turned to the International Third Position movement, a small extreme right coterie. He also dabbled in other extremist activities, including stewarding one of Irving's public Holocaust Denial meetings, and producing a journal called *The Rune*, which led to his prosecution for publishing material likely to incite racial hatred.

During 1996, Griffin joined the BNP, becoming the paid editor of *Spearhead*. Initially, his position seemed close to that of Tyndall (who was the proprietor of *Spearhead*). In *The Rune* Griffin had written that: 'the electors of Millwall did not back a post modernist rightist party, but what they perceived to be a strong, disciplined organisation with the ability to back up its slogan "Defend Rights for Whites" with well-directed boots and fists.'[3] He was also critical of those who sought to focus more on fighting local elections, especially on 'populist' platforms, arguing that a split in the Conservatives could open the way for broad-based gains (*Spearhead*, January 1997). Moreover, he shared Tyndall's concern with alleged Jewish power and helped to write a pamphlet entitled *Who Are the Mind-Benders?*, which purported to show that important sections of the media were controlled by Jews (BNP 1998?).

However, having become leader, Griffin quickly set about 'modernizing' the party. Griffin was helped by the fact that some changes were taking place within the BNP even before he became leader. Indeed, after 1999 there was some friction within the party, including resignations, which stemmed largely from Griffin seeking to take the credit for modernization. He was also helped by the fact that the NF remained weak, contesting only five seats in the 2001 general election, with a best performance of 2.2 per cent in Birmingham Erdington. In part, this weakness stemmed from a continued predilection for street activism. Symptomatically, its *White Nationalist Report* on 25 August 2000 stated: 'The NF WILL confront the enemy at every opportunity ... When the NF controls the streets, it controls the towns and the cities – we call on all past members – REJOIN!'[4] Nevertheless, Griffin was unquestionably an important factor in the subsequent rise of the BNP.

In its national propaganda, the BNP stressed the new line on voluntary repatriation. It also adopted a differencialist line on race. Its monthly newspaper, *The Voice of Freedom*, stated in February 2001 that: 'The BNP does not claim that any one race is superior to any other, simply that they are different'. The party also sought to distance itself from the fascist tradition. Its journal *Identity*, in June 2002, pointed to various unattractive aspects of Nazism, including the: 'corporate state, a mixture of big capitalism and state control'. It added that: 'British nationalists follow the Distributionist tradition established by home-grown thinkers like GK Chesterton and Hilaire Belloc and so we favour small, privately owned business.' Taking the offensive, it even accused New Labour of being fascist, not least through its attempts to control the media.

During 2000, Griffin sought to extend the BNP's appeal by targeting specific groups. One group initially courted was lorry drivers, who were engaged in mass protests against 'stealth tax' rises in fuel prices. Another group targeted was poorer farmers (Griffin runs a smallholding in Wales), although this expanded into a more general concern with countryside issues such as conservation and hunting. By the time of the mass-countryside march in London during September 2002, which protested against New Labour's alleged hostility to rural interests, the BNP had a special journal devoted to rural matters, the *Countrysider*. Although this has subsequently not appeared regularly, it reflects the growing BNP targeting of specific audiences. These include students, and for the first time the BNP has begun to attract some young educated members, including the youth organiser of the BNP, who was at Leeds University.

The BNP has also begun to pay more attention to local issues. There had been growing support for such a tactic after Millwall. A localist strategy was also encouraged by the fact that, for the 2001 general election, parties were expected to put up a minimum of 100 candidates to qualify for a free national broadcast. Given that the constituency deposit was £1,000 (returned if a party receives over 5 per cent of the vote), the BNP would have needed extensive funds to focus again on a general election. Latching on to local campaign issues provided a cheaper – and 'democratic' – route forward.

At the same time, the BNP improved its organization and propaganda. Far more attention was paid to the website. *Identity* and *The Voice of Freedom* have regularly appeared since 2000. Both have contained features on targeted areas: *Freedom* probably has a circulation of about 25,000, which is rising – although some copies are given away during campaigning. Although the party lacks a formal national HQ, by 2002 it was employing 30 full time-officials compared with five two years before *(Identity*, July 2002). This gives some credence to Griffin's claims that the party has begun to attract some relatively wealthy people – although funds have almost certainly come through the American Friends of the BNP.[5] By 2002, membership was almost double its 2000 level, although it appears still to be under 5,000. New members seem to have come mainly from the previously apolitical and ex-Conservatives, with some of the latter possibly stemming from the purge of extremists which Ian Duncan Smith promised after becoming Conservative leader in 2001 (during the leadership campaign, Griffin's father was expelled after 50 year's membership).

However, the main issue which seems to have hit home with voters was growing concern about the rising number of asylum seekers – a trend which by 2002 was to make Britain the main target of such migrants within the European Union. Discussion of the issue by the mainstream parties, including New Labour, which clearly saw a threat to its eroding working class base, and the popular press was hardly calming. Typically, the *Daily Mail*'s front page headline on 1 February 2001 proclaimed: 'ASYLUM: YES, BRITAIN IS A SOFT TOUCH!' The BNP added its own fuel to the fire, with the June 2001 issue of *The Voice of Freedom* claiming that 'every single "asylum-seeker" will be getting far bigger handouts' than millions of British pensioners and unemployed, and the nearly one-in-five British children who live below the poverty line.

The BNP also saw the potential for stirring up hostility against long-standing ethnic minorities, especially Muslims. Even before the terrorist attacks on the World Trade Center in September 2001, the BNP was increasingly targeting Muslims. *The Voice of Freedom* in February 2001 claimed that Islamic extremists were recruiting young Muslims for war against the West. In the August 2001 issue of *Identity* Griffin claimed that radical Muslim clerics like Abu Hamsa want: 'militant Muslims to take over British cities with AK-47 rifles'. After 11 September 2001, the BNP website and print propaganda attacked Islam, which was portrayed as meaning: 'Intolerance, Slaughter, Looting, Arson and Molestation of Women.' The BNP claimed that Islam was Britain's fastest growing religion, with an estimated 2.5 million believers.

Interestingly, some BNP leaders sought to forge links with Hindus and others in an anti-Islamic alliance. Even before 11 Spetember there had been a growing tendency to use the word 'Muslim' rather than 'Asian'. Griffin, when interviewed on the BBC television programme *Newsnight* on 26 June 2001, specifically noted than Hindus had often been a target as well as whites in the 'Muslim' rioting in 2001. Although the Ethnic Liaison Committee which BNP set up to encourage contacts was largely spurned by non-Muslim ethnic minorities, the strategy did result in a 'Rajinder Singh' column in *Freedom*, which was headed by a picture of a turbaned Sikh! Predictably, this line caused considerable tensions within the largely unreconstructed rank and file.

The BNP supported the launching of the post-11 September war in Afghanistan. Unlike some groups in Europe and the USA, which expressed solidarity with Islamicism on account of its hostility to Israel, Griffin specifically rejected this line. However, as war with Iraq approached, the BNP revealed increasing opposition to US policy. In February 2003 its website supported anti-war demonstrations.[6] The BNP argued that the war had nothing to do with Britain, that it would cost a fortune, and (somewhat disingenuously as it stood to benefit from this) result in growing ethnic tensions within British cities. In addition, the BNP argued that a second Gulf War would be about US interests, encouraged by the power of Jewish lobbies.

There had always been an ambivalence in BNP attitudes to 11 September and its aftermath even at the leadership level. In the December 2001 issue of *Identity*, Griffin argued that the main target on 11 September was: 'a Twin Tower of Babel – part of the power structure of global capitalism which has no loyalty to our ethnic group'. There were frequent critical references in BNP journals to alleged Israeli and American plans for world domination, which were typically referred to as the 'New World Order' (for instance, *Identity*, October 2002). This term had first been used by

72   *Roger Eatwell*

George Bush Sr. to describe post-Cold War global politics, but it has been increasingly picked up by the American extreme right as a synonym for American/Israeli world dominance (see Chapter 2).

Since 2000, the BNP propaganda has regularly used issues and phrases in ways that seem designed to keep the party's hard-core happy. An interesting, although relatively guarded, example can be found in the April 2002 issue of *Identity*. In this, Griffin argued that for 'radical nationalists', the ideological divide which 'separated us from conservatives was marked primarily by attitudes to capitalism'. Whereas 'Reactionaries' supported it, 'We' opposed it. Griffin added even more revealingly: 'Neither Red Front, nor Reaction' ran one old slogan which summed it all up. This was an old Nazi slogan, and Third Way thinking was central to pre-1945 fascist ideology (Eatwell, 1992, 1995) Griffin also talked of a 'Western, Faustian spirit', a term common in Mosley's writings after 1945.

Even more remarkably, *The Voice of Freedom* in April 2001 reported that the Croydon branch of the BNP (in which Griffin had been active) had entertained Günter Deckert, a leader of the German National Democratic Party (NPD). Within the NPD, Holocaust Denial and Nazi nostalgia was common – traits that were to lead the German government to seek to ban it (a move which failed in 2003). The September 2002 issue of *Identity* noted that Griffin had recently been to the annual rally of the NPD, and featured a picture of Griffin with Horst Mahler. Mahler is a leading theorist of the NPD, who has moved from radical left to extreme right and who argues that the consistency in his position lies in his hostility to the US and to bourgeois democracy!

BNP community politics in action

A case study of the BNP in Oldham illustrates the importance of factors such as chance, local and national media coverage, together with Griffin's media skills. Burnley provides a better example of how local hard work, combined with the new 'community politics', which sought especially to exploit a sense of white resentment about alleged preferential treatment of ethnic minorities, could bring results. Oldham and Burnley also point to the increasing difficulties of old-style anti-fascist campaigns, typically based on a left that had little if any real contact with potential BNP voters and which remains obsessed with portraying the party as 'Nazi' and its leaders as criminals. Appeals from mainstream political leaders to shun the BNP also seem to be losing their power. These last points seem confirmed by BNP progress in Stoke, Blackburn and Calderdale during 2002–3.

The BNP's website 'Oldham in Harmony' gave a clear indication of why this town was a prime target in the 2001 general election. Its welcome page's masthead claimed that 'multi-racial fanatics' had 'turned a decent, proud, working class community into a mini Bosnia.'[7] The ghettoized and tense nature of some inner-cities was later stressed in more restrained language by a government report into the violence that erupted in northern cities, especially Oldham, Burnley and Bradford, over the summer of 2001. This noted: 'Whilst the physical segregation of housing estates and inner city areas came as no surprise, the team was particularly struck by the depth of polarisation of our towns and cities.'[8] However, there were similar urban areas across Britain in which the BNP performed much worse than in Burnley and Oldham. For example, it won only 4.6 per cent of the vote in Bradford North in the 2001 general election.

A similar point applies to three general political arguments which have been used to explain the BNP's leap forward. Although difficult to research, there seems to be no clear correlation between the demise of the Labour grass roots' organization and the rise of the BNP. Turning to the Conservatives, from the outset they were clearly going to lose the 2001 election, which encouraged protest voting (Mudde, 2002). Perceptions of weak leadership both before and after the 2001 general election, and arguably a decline in 'ownership' of the immigration issue in the face of New Labour and BNP propaganda, also probably harmed the Conservatives. However, such factors do not explain why the BNP did well in specific localities, such as Oldham.

Since 1999, BNP propaganda had increasingly reported on racial attacks on whites in this town, a theme mirrored in the local press. In early 2001, the trend appeared to be confirmed when the police published statistics showing that racial attacks on whites were more common than vice versa. The BNP was further helped in April 2001 by a BBC national radio report, picked up widely in the media, that there were racial 'no go' areas in the town. Shortly afterwards, a brutal attack on a white war-veteran pensioner was widely reported in both the local and national media as racially inspired. Griffin's announcement, on St. George's Day, that he was to stand in Oldham in the general election received yet more publicity – much of it uncritical. Subsequently, Griffin demonstrated in the national media, and especially the local media, that he was a far more skilled performer than the bombastic and pompous Tyndall.

After the pensioner-attack, Oldham's 'Fine Young Casuals' football gang, together with hooligans from other clubs, marched through Asian areas of the town on 28 April. Predictably, this provoked a response, and serious fighting broke out as fans returned after the match through the Asian area. These 'riots' brought other extremists into the area, including representatives of C18 and the NF who sought to foment further troubles. Although the earlier violence in Oldham undoubtedly helped the BNP's cause, such openly provocative activity could have backfired. Its leadership, therefore, specifically stated that: 'the BNP prefers to avoid confrontation and to concentrate on serious grassroots work to build a political voice for the people ... most BNP members regard the NF as being politically immature, irresponsible, and too extreme.'[9]

In practice, links remained between the BNP and members of other extremist groups. Covert film taken for a BBC *Panorama* television programme, broadcast on 25 November 2001, even depicted 'star' performances by leading members of the racial music scene at the BNP's national Red, White and Blue party festival (copied from the much larger French Front National event), and showed people present singing Nazi favourites. Predictably, such links have encouraged anti-fascist groups to continue to stress charges of Nazism, or the criminal nature of BNP members. For example, *Searchlight* magazine in March 2002 listed the following among the small band of Oldham activists: Mick Treacy (2001 Parliamentary candidate) 'five convictions for violence, theft and handling stolen goods'; Dave Probert 'conviction for sending excreta through the post'; John Shearer 'convicted drug dealer'; Kevin Gough 'Convicted football hooligan and C18 nazi thug.' Nevertheless, the five BNP candidates in the 2002 elections still managed to win between 22.9 and 35.0 per cent of the vote, coming second in four wards in multi-cornered fights!

In the 1999 European Parliament elections, the BNP won 3.7 per cent of the vote in Burnley – slightly higher than in Oldham West. However, Burnley after 1999 became a hive of BNP activity. Steve Smith, who was to fight the parliamentary seat in 2001, was a good quality local candidate who built the local party up from just two paid-up members in 1999, using mainly traditional door-to-door methods to discover potential support and distribute propaganda. The new activists were also willing to put in hard, traditional political work: most houses seem to have been leafleted in the 18 months before the 2001 election (*The Voice of Freedom* July 2002). Moreover, in the 2000 local elections, BNP candidates polled 21.5 and 5.9 per cent of the vote in the two wards contested: the higher figure gave the party a notable boost in confidence and pulled in new recruits.

Burnley BNP showed a particular talent for obtaining publicity in the local media. One tactic was to send in letters to the local press, usually not directly attributed to the BNP, which picked up issues of local concern, such as racial attacks. The BNP also used various stunts to attract publicity. For example, in May 2001, *The Voice of Freedom* noted that a huge 'Vote BNP' banner had been hanging on a mill chimney by a busy main road: 'Local council Jobsworths tried to get it taken down but failed, leading to more useful media coverage about the "BNP victory"'.

Interestingly, the June edition of *Identity* concluded that the Burnley result was 'arguably the best natural vote of the election.' Although Griffin's 16.4 per cent in Oldham was notably higher than Smith's 11.3 per cent in Burnley, he had benefited from a variety of special factors, including the BNP bringing in activists from outside. The party in Burnley fought essentially on its own resources, and its local publicity coups were more of its own making.

The ethnic 'riots' in Burnley over the summer almost certainly helped the BNP in local by-elections in November 2001, when it polled 23.5 per cent, 19.2 and 19.0 per cent of the vote in the three wards contested. On this occasion the BNP faced a full-scale onslaught from the mainstream parties. This included: the presence of full-time Labour organizers, glossy leaflets, the appearance of national personalities, local media hostility and the actions of the Liberal Democrats, who withdrew their own candidates.

Similarly, in the 2002 local elections, the BNP faced a strong campaign locally both from opposing parties and anti-fascists. It also faced notable national media hostility, including a front page headline of the *Daily Express* on 2 May, polling day, which showed pictures of 20 BNP national candidates around the headline 'VOTE THESE NAZIS OUT'. Burnley's voters responded by electing three BNP candidates, two coming in second place and one finishing third in multi-candidate contests (as the whole council was up for election, a seat could be won by coming third as there were three councillors per ward).

The Voice of Freedom gloated, after the elections, that victory had come despite: 'The *Daily Mirror* and the pornographer's favourite – *The Express*, a stablemate of *Asian Babes* and *Fantasy Filth*' both doing 'their lying best to cheat, slander, demonise, lie, distort and pervert both the truth and the democratic process' (May 2002). This attack reflected not simply a long-standing animosity to the national media, but also a growing tendency to answer anti-fascist charges about BNP criminality with counter-claims. Opponents at the local level were frequently accused of having criminal records and – a particular favourite – engaging in various forms of paedophilia (a charge which was linked to anti-paedophile campaigns in some localities).

Further electoral progress came in Stoke during the autumn of 2002, when a BNP candidate of no personal merit came a close third with 19 per cent of the vote in a new-style Mayoral contest. In October, *The Voice of Freedom* contained a special feature on Stoke (next to the article was another on a Liberal Democrat 'pervert' on Stockport council). A special Stoke section was added to the party's website, which picked up local concerns, including ones related to relative economic decline and asylum seekers. The main overt opposition came from anti-fascists, though it is far from clear that this helped. A report written by a professional community artist at the time concluded that the anti-fascist opposition was 'dangerously out of touch', arguing that: 'they are not even seeking to demolish the BNP's policies and arguments through rational debate. All they seem to offer is empty rhetorical posturing.'[10] A BBC Radio Stoke straw poll, which asked whether people would 'vote for a fascist' (changed on publication to 'BNP member'), revealed that 52 per cent said 'yes'.

During late 2002-early 2003 the BNP won further local by-election victories in Blackburn and Calderdale. In Blackburn, the BNP faced a strong campaign by the mainstream parties, trade unions, and anti-fascist groups. Moreover, the local *Lancashire Evening Telegraph* campaigned strongly, and on 20 November, the day before polling, ran a front page picture of

Tony Blair with the headline plea: 'DON'T LET THEM IN – BLAIR' (the paper greeted the BNP's victory on 22 November with the headline 'SHAMEFUL'). The BNP countered by picking up doorstep issues, focusing on local concerns such as the possible siting of an immigrant hostel in the area. The result was the first victory of the modernized BNP in a FPTP contest, with the party taking 32 per cent of the vote in a four-cornered race.

In a relatively deprived Calderdale ward, the BNP won just over 29 per cent of the vote in a five-horse race. Here, extensive BNP canvassing was helped by bringing people in from other parts of Yorkshire and also Lancashire. A key theme was the way in which the election of BNP councillors had prevented the dispersal of refugees to Burnley and Blackburn. Other local issues which were picked up included the large expenses increase that councillors had recently voted themselves. The BNP also deployed new techniques, including leaflets designed for more working class and more middle class areas, and the distribution of a special video to what were seen as local opinion makers. After the BNP's victory, Griffin sarcastically thanked the 'far-left' anti-fascists for their help by extensive campaigning in the area! (*Identity*, February 2003). Griffin is hardly an independent judge of such opposition, but once again many of the anti-fascists lacked real links with the local community and mainly ran a knocking campaign against the BNP, which probably gave it further publicity. Certainly the anti-fascist magazine *Searchlight* accepted in March 2003 that: 'More thought needs to go into the literature produced by anti-fascists, with localising the material a priority.' It added: 'There has never been a more difficult time to be an anti-fascist. Yet there has never been such an important time to be an anti-fascist.'

Conclusions

It is important to stress that this chapter has not sought to analyse systematically who has voted for the BNP in recent years. Because of the limited nature of its campaigns, the evidence remains weak – although the party has undoubtedly not just won votes from disillusioned Labour supporters in deprived areas. Rather, this chapter has sought to point to a major political reason why the BNP has been more successful – namely, its modernization.

This is not to deny the importance of a broad set of factors, including: urban deprivation, new fears about immigration, the impact of ethnic urban disturbances, growing hostility to Islam (especially since 11 September 2001), the weakening links of the mainstream parties with civil society, institutional change, and the impact of the media, which manages to denounce the BNP while at times agenda-setting in a way that helps it. (In the case of some newspapers, the intention appears to be to favour the Conservatives, which helps explain this paradox.) Nevertheless, since

2000, the BNP has undoubtedly positioned itself more shrewdly within the democratic electoral market.

However, it is important not to overstate this success. The party remains small and some new members will quickly pass through the party. This will probably be the case for some councillors too, as they realize the demands made on them by office. So far, the party has largely failed to attract a significant number of what David Irving, at the beginning of the 1980s, called the 'respectable officer class'. Revealingly, Griffin warned in the June 2002 issue of *Identity* against the 'three Hs': 'Hard talk, Hobbyism and Hitler'. He stressed that the party needed to get things done to help people, not talk about violence, if it was to consolidate local electoral successes. Hobbyism referred not just to those who were unwilling to devote considerable time to party activity, but also to the heavy drinkers in the party (the January 2003 edition of *Identity* noted that thousands of pounds of local funds had disappeared 'literally down the throats of the beer faction'). On Hitler, Griffin remarkably concluded: 'let's face facts: Hitler was a disaster not just for Germany, but for the entire white race'.

In a quest for yet greater legitimacy, Griffin is pushing the party further away from its historic identity. The February 2003 issue of *The Voice of Freedom* contained an article on 'How Dare they Call Me a Racist and a Nazi' by Charlie Bickerstaffe, a BNP prospective candidate in Barrow, who was pictured proudly with his black son-in-law and grandchildren. On BBC television's *Politics Show* on 9 March 2003, Griffin moved towards a further line on repatriation, appearing to accept the ethnic minorities who were legally already in the country. As well as courting mainstream voters, Griffin appears to have an eye for the 2004 European elections. An agreement with the UKIP, which includes some former extremists, not to contest the same regions would notably increase the BNP's chances of winning a seat. Griffin also seems keen to forge some form of trans-European 'populist' alliance with parties like Le Pen's (such groupings within the European Parliament are necessary to receive various material benefits).

The BNP is still not accepted as a legitimate player by the mainstream parties in Britain – and also by some of the continental 'populist' ones. Nevertheless, there appear to be a growing number of voters for whom the BNP is now a credible alternative. Perhaps its major short-term problem is how to manage the classic adaptation dilemma – namely, continuing to moderate its appeal without provoking major splits, or losing a clear identity in the process. The lingering presence of hard-core extremists within its ranks makes the former difficult. Arguably, however, the Conservatives' 'ownership' of the immigration issue is weakening. Given the likely continued salience of this issue, the BNP's prospects have never been better.

Notes

1 I am grateful to the British Academy for awarding me a grant to study the 'modernization' of the British National Party, including local studies of northern cities (this followed three earlier grants to study the European extreme right). NB In virtually all cases, local activists refused to give information on an attributable basis. I am also grateful to Karen Thomson, one of my doctoral students, for providing me with the insights of her research.
2 Part of the information that follows is based on my reading of the David Irving diaries and papers from 1959–98, obtained under Discovery for the 2000 Irving versus Deborah Lipstadt and Penguin books libel trial in the British High Court. For legal reasons, they cannot be cited directly unless the material was used in open court.
3 http://news.bbc.co.uk./hi/english/static/1...s/2001/bnp_special/the_leader/beliefs.stm. Downloaded 27 November 2001.
4 http://www.natfront.com/wnr26.html. Downloaded 13 July 2001.
5 See the Southern Poverty Law Center's *Intelligence Report*, Fall 2001.
6 http://www.bnp.org.uk/ Downloaded 21 February 2003.
7 http://www.oldhamharmony,org/ Downloaded 13 July 2001.
8 http://www.homeoffice.gov.uk/reu/community_cohesion.pdf, p. 9. Downloaded 22 December 2001.
9 http://www.bnp. org.uk. Downloaded 1 June 2001.
10 http://www.peoplelikeyou.org.uk/ Downloaded 11 November 2002.

Bibliography

Baker, D. (1996) *A.K. Chesterton and British Fascism*, London: I.B. Tauris.
Billig, M. (1978) *Fascists*, London: Academic Press.
BNP (n.d. 1993?) *The Enemy within: How TV Brainwashes a Nation*, Welling: BNP.
BNP (n.d. 1998?) *Who Are the Mind-Benders?*, Welling: BNP.
Copsey, N. (1996) 'Contemporary fascism in the local arena: the British National Party and "Rights for Whites"', in Cronin, M. (ed.) *The Failure of British Fascism*, Basingstoke: Macmillan.
Eatwell, R. (1992) 'Towards a new model of generic fascism', *Journal of Theoretical Politics* 4, 2: 161–194.
Eatwell, R. (1995) *Fascism. A History*, London: Chatto and Windus.
Eatwell, R. (1996) 'The esoteric ideology of the National Front in the 1980s', in Cronin, M. (ed.) *The Failure of British Fascism*, Basingstoke: Macmillan.
Eatwell, R. (1998a) 'The dynamics of extreme right electoral breakthrough', *Patterns of Prejudice* 32, 3: 3–31.
Eatwell, R. (1998b) '"The BNP', in Betz, H.-G. and Immerfall, S. (eds) *New Party Politics of the Right*, New York: St. Martin's Press.
Eatwell, R. (2000) 'The extreme right and British exceptionalism: the primacy of politics', in Hainsworth, P. (ed.) *The Politics of the Extreme Right*, London: Pinter.
Eatwell, R. (2003) 'Ten theories of the extreme right', in Merkl, P.H. and Weinberg, L. (eds) *The Extreme Right in the Twenty-First Century*, London: Frank Cass.
Gable, G. (1995) 'Britain's Nazi underground', in Cheles, L. *et al.* (eds) *The Far Right in Western and Eastern Europe*, Harlow: Longman.

Holmes, D.R. (2000) *Integral Europe. Fast Capitalism, Multiculturalism, Neofascism*, Princeton: Princeton University Press.

Husbands, C.T. (1983) *Racial Exclusionism and the City*, London, Allen and Unwin.

Husbands, C.T. (1989) 'Racial attacks: the persistence of racial vigilantism in British cities', in Kushner, T. and Lunn, K. (eds) *Traditions of Intolerance*, Manchester: Manchester University Press.

Lowles, N. (2001) *White Riot. The Violent Story of Combat 18*, Bury: Milo Books.

Kushner, T. (1994) 'The fascist as "other"? Racism and neo-Nazism in contemporary Britain', *Patterns of Prejudice* 28, 2: 27–45.

Mudde, C. (2002) '"England belongs to me": the extreme right in the UK parliamentary election of 2001', *Representation* 39, 1: 37–43.

Schoen, D. (1977) *Enoch Powell and the Powellites*, London: Macmillan.

Sunic, T. (1990) *Against Democracy and Equality. The European New Right*, New York: Peter Lang.

Taguieff, P.-A. (1994) *Sur La Nouvelle Droite*, Paris: Descartes and Cie.

Taylor, S. (1982) *The National Front in English Politics*, Basingstoke: Macmillan.

Thurlow, R.C. (1998) *Fascism in Britain*, London: I.B. Tauris.

Tyndall, J. (1970) *Six Principles of British Nationalism*, 2nd edn, London: Albion Press.

Tyndall, J. (1988) *The Eleventh Hour: a Call for British Rebirth*, London: Albion Press.

NB Some local material came from newspapers, especially the *Burnley Express*; *Lancaster Evening Telegraph* and *Oldham Chronicle*.

Part II
Democratic responses to right-wing extremism

4 Defence of democracy against the extreme right in inter-war Europe
A past still present?

Giovanni Capoccia

Introduction

How to deal with extremists has been one of the main problems of mass democracies, both historically, as many democracies had to cope with the emergence of totalitarian parties and movements, and recently as new forms of political radicalism have emerged to challenge the stability of both old and new democratic regimes. Constitutional lawyers and political theorists have dealt variously with the difficult dilemma of the 'tolerance for the intolerant' raised by the presence of radical political associations or parties in many democracies. In general, they have taken an intermediary position between the two poles of 'no freedom for the enemies of freedom' and 'real freedom is freedom to dissent' (e.g. Agnoli and Brueckner 1967; Lippincott 1965). As an international law scholar put it: 'to strike a reasonable balance between safeguarding the substance of the rights enunciated to the greatest extent possible, on the one hand, and forestalling any abuses, on the other, has become one of the most delicate issues in a liberal state' (Tomuschat 1992: 33).

Several examples can be proposed to underline the current relevance of the problem of how to cope with extremists. In Germany, the elaborate system of legal protection of the liberal democratic order against extremists has been recently re-activated against an important extreme right-wing party, the National Democratic Party of Germany (NPD). In the United Kingdom after the attacks of 11 September, the law seeking to hinder the activities of terrorists took on even more draconian form, leading to protests from civil rights groups. Moreover, many new democracies of Eastern Europe have included in their democratic constitutions rules limiting political pluralism with the goal of protecting the integrity and viability of the state: this is the case for Croatia, Poland, Lithuania, Romania, Slovenia and Bulgaria (Fox and Nolte 1995).

Despite its clear political importance and its eminently *political* nature, the problem of the *politics* of legal-institutional reactions to extremists has rarely been analysed with the tools of comparative political science.[1] Few comparative studies of the politics of institutional 'defence of democracy' exist, and the existing scattered literature deals primarily with a few important (and controversial) cases, in particular the *streitbare Demokratie* system in the Federal Republic of Germany and the anti-Communist legislation in the USA.

In other words, comparative politics is still a long way from achieving a systematic and cumulative knowledge of the problems connected to the determinants and consequences of institutional and political reactions to extremism in democratic systems. In general, it seems that the existing literature needs to be complemented in at least two respects. On the one hand, a systematic typology of anti-extremist reactions in general, and of special legislation in particular, needs to be elaborated. On the other hand, the analysis should be expanded beyond the narrow set of the most well-known cases to less-researched democratic regimes that present interesting features in this respect.

The aim of this chapter is to illustrate the political-institutional reactions of the democratic rulers against extremist parties in the European democracies between the wars. It identifies the main aspects of the problem of the relationship between democracy and extremism in that historical phase of the European political development. It describes the main strategies used against extremists in democracies in which the problem was particularly acute. In addition, it identifies the principal protagonists in the process of defence of democracy, those actors whose choices have the maximum influence on the outcome of the crisis. Finally, it draws conclusions on the dynamics of defence of democracy in inter-war Europe and reflects on the continuing importance of the legacy of that first encounter between mass democracy and mass extremism for the theory and practice of the relationship between democracy and extremism in Europe today.

The problem of reactions to extremism in inter-war Europe

In inter-war Europe, the encounter between extremism and democracy was a deadly fight, from which only one of the two contenders would emerge alive. While the term can be reconstructed at different levels of abstraction, by 'defence of democracy' I mean here the elaboration and enactment of *short-term* political strategies[2] that are explicitly aimed at reacting against those political forces that exploit the rights and guarantees of democracy in order to undermine its fundamental bases. Unlike in several of today's cases, the forms of political extremism that emerged in the 1920s and 1930s embodied totalitarian or authoritarian ideologies, which were incompatible with any form of political democracy. Thus, the stakes of 'defence of democracy' were in most cases extreme themselves, i.e. they consisted of the survival or breakdown of the democratic regime itself.

Reflecting the normative dilemma mentioned above, the most important characteristic of democratic defence is its delicate balance between two

Defence of democracy in inter-war Europe 85

opposing threats to democracy. On the one hand, the discrimination against a certain political actor for political or ideological reasons represents a serious restriction of civil and political rights, which, if pushed too far, can give rise to authoritarian tendencies. On the other hand, tolerating an anti-democratic (extremist) actor might lead the system to collapse in a time of crisis. This dilemma is particularly urgent when extremist actors have strong support. It is in cases such as these, when the defence of democracy is most needed, that it would be most difficult to achieve.

For this reason, after a general perusal of the successes and failures of democracies in inter-war Europe, I will concentrate attention exactly on the cases in which the democratic regime survived strong extremist challenges, and compare them with cases of breakdown. By so doing, I explore this phenomenon in the worst possible conditions, and show that, while there can be different paths to democratic persistence, defending a democratic system is indeed possible, although at the cost of restricting some rights and freedoms.

More specifically, what drives the selection of the cases for this analysis is the particular kind of *process* leading to the outcome of democratic breakdown or survival. In fact, if we want to explore the conditions and effects of politico-institutional reactions of democratic incumbents to anti-system forces arising in political society, it is imperative to choose cases in which the process of regime crisis was characterized by the political struggle between a democratic government and an extremist party (or parties) threatening to take over. Figure 4.1 classifies 22 European regimes that could be considered democratic around 1920, according to, on the one hand, the presence or absence of a struggle between democratic incumbents and extremist outsiders, and, on the other hand, the survival or the breakdown of the democratic system. What the typology highlights is that within the two sets of breakdowns and survivals there are important differences in the political processes leading to the respective regime outcomes.

In inter-war Europe, breakdown of democracy came about in two different ways. The model of 'legal revolution' (e.g. Bracher 1953) – by which aggressive anti-democratic parties exploit the rights and guarantees of democracy to participate in the political process with the ultimate aim of bringing democracy down – has often been used to describe the paradigmatic cases of the victory of Fascist and Nazi forces in Italy and Weimar Germany in the early 1920s and the early 1930s respectively. In these countries, extremists played the democratic game, and the government, despite the extremists' obviously cynical attitude to the rules of democracy, did not do enough to weaken the position of such dangerous players.

This, however, is not the way things went in most of the European countries in which democracy did not survive in the 1920s and 1930s. Leaving aside the particular case of Spain, where the increasingly harsh confrontation between the left and the right ended in a civil war, in several

86 *Giovanni Capoccia*

		Struggle between democratic incumbents and anti-system outsiders as main characteristics of the political process	
		Yes	No
Democrats prevail	Yes	**Challenged survivors:** Czechoslovakia, Finland, Belgium, (France)	**Non-challenged survivors:** The Netherlands, Norway, Sweden, Denmark, Switzerland, United Kingdom
	No	**Takeovers:** Germany, Italy	**'Suspension' (or pre-emptive coup):** Bulgaria, Portugal, Poland, Lithuania, Yugoslavia, Austria, Estonia, Latvia, Greece, Romania

Figure 4.1 Political processes and political outcomes in inter-war Europe.

other cases – either because large parts of the political establishment were not democratically oriented, or because the challenges were too strong to keep the system of democratic guarantees alive – democracy was 'killed from above', rather than 'taken over from below'. That is, either the government in charge indefinitely suspended democratic rights and guarantees, or there was a successful coup, and the regime was turned into a non-democratic one by the action of sectors of its institutional elites, not infrequently exactly against extremist 'outsiders' (see Capoccia 2004).

In sum, while commonalties exist between the 'takeover' and 'suspension' types of democratic breakdown, they can indeed be distinguished by a crucial trait in the political process that led to the regime outcome. In the two 'takeovers', a harsh struggle took place between the democratic incumbents and (at least) one anti-democratic political actor. To be sure, the latter attacked the citadel of democratic power also 'from outside', undermining the regime's effectiveness by using political violence.[3] At the beginning of this process, democratic forces held power, but failed to respond effectively to the anti-system challenges arising from political society. As a result, the democratic forces increasingly lost power, until an anti-system actor, thanks to a shrewd coalition strategy, took control of the levers of government, formally respecting the constitutional procedures, and established a non-democratic regime soon thereafter.

On the contrary, in the cases classifiable as '(indeterminate) suspensions of democracy', (the 'killing from above' of a democratic system), the process of crisis took one of the following two paths. In some countries, non-democratic factions within incumbents wrested power from the hands of the more democratic sections of the establishment, and created an authoritarian regime. In another set of countries, democratically elected leaders pre-empted the anti-system threat, preventing possible takeover and loss of power by abandoning democratic procedures altogether. In both sets of cases, the struggle that characterized the crisis process did not oppose democratic incumbents to anti-democratic outsiders. In 'suspension' cases, the main fight took place either among sections of the establishment, or between non-democratic incumbents (or incumbents disregarding *in toto* democratic procedures), and non-democratic outsiders.

Radically different political processes may also account for democratic survival. As in breakdown cases, the existence (or the absence) of a political struggle between democratic incumbents and anti-democratic outsiders marks the line of distinction between different types of survived democracies in inter-war Europe. The main indicator that reveals the presence of such a struggle in survival cases is the strength of anti-system political forces (Capoccia 2002a). In fact, if no relevant anti-system formation is present to challenge the persistence of the democratic system, the incumbents will not have to undertake any serious struggle to make the regime survive. On the contrary, a political struggle of the kind that I have singled out in 'takeovers' exists in those cases in which anti-system forces, formally playing by the rules of the democratic game with the more or less concealed intention to do away with democracy itself, reach a significant level of strength.

The strength of the challenge to a democratic regime can be operationalized as the highest percentage of seats held by parties that challenged either the fundamentals of pluralist democracy or the territorial unity of the state, or both, in the lower chamber of parliament. This basically restricts the field of such formations to Nazi, fascist or authoritarian parties, communist parties, and secessionist-irredentist parties (see Capoccia 2001a). Figure 4.2 ranks ten democracies that survived on the basis of the 'peak' percentage of seats reached by extremist parties in the Lower Chamber between 1919 and 1939. The peaks represent, therefore, moments of crisis, in which the democratic system underwent considerable strain and was in serious danger of breakdown.

The graph highlights that at least three of the countries where democracy survived had, in fact, to face very strong challenges. In Czechoslovakia after the 1935 elections, and in Finland in 1930–1, extremist parties had about one third of the parliamentary seats in the more important chamber, while in Belgium (1936–9) this percentage was slightly below a

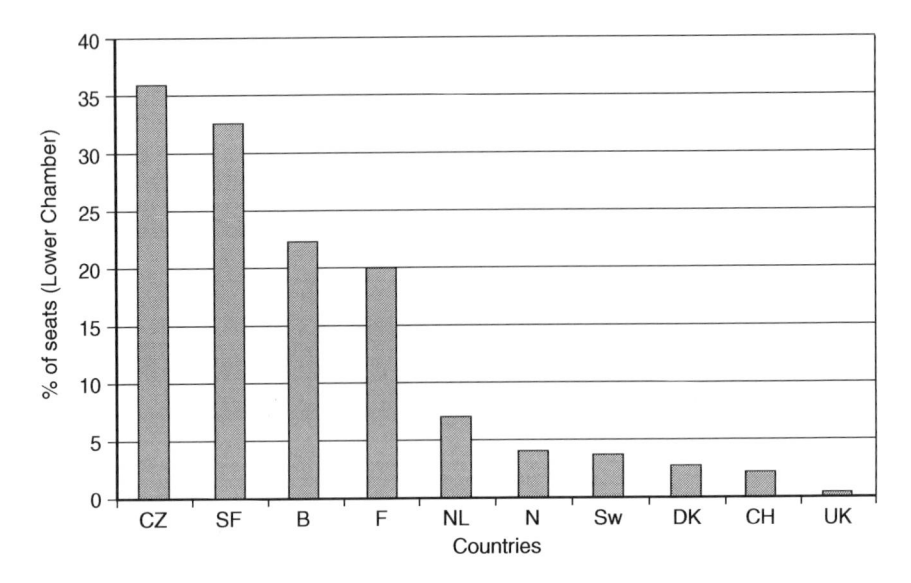

Figure 4.2 Peak results of extremist parties 1919–39.

quarter. These three cases therefore present themselves as critical ones for the assessment of the opportunity for enactment and possibilities of success of democratic defence strategies. In these countries, in fact, the parliamentary strength of anti-system forces rendered the political conditions for the coordination of democratic forces around a common strategy worse than in any other case of survival.

In what follows, I will briefly account for the historical developments in these three countries and compare the political crises there with those in Italy and Germany. Prior to analysing those cases, though, it is necessary to have a better look into the politics of democratic defence.

Actors and the process of democratic defence

The analysis of the inter-war European cases of problematic survival highlights the crucial importance of the government and the Head of State in the process of short-term defence of democracy. The crucial factor for a democratic government attempting to act effectively against extremists is the stability of the political coalition on which it is founded. In political systems where extremist parties are strong, as in the cases under analysis here, the crucial element for this stability is the political strategy of those components of the coalition that border ideologically with the extremists.

Sartori's analysis of polarized party systems shows that such systems have an in-built tendency to 'centrifugal competition', since extremist parties compete in such a way to force all others, and in particular those bordering with them along that space, towards extreme positions. Extremist parties, by using 'outbidding' propaganda tactics, attract electors from the centre and especially from the moderate wings, which here I call 'border' parties. The systemic propensities of the party competition, thus, push the border parties towards the extremes, in order to regain the electors that they have lost, thus nurturing the overall polarizing trend (Sartori 1976).

Sartori's model does not have any deterministic nature: although polarization and centrifugal competition push the system towards breakdown, they do not pre-constitute a specific regime outcome. Between the systemic propensities and the regime outcome are the political actors, who can stop or even counteract these propensities, and therefore have an impact on the final outcome (Sartori 1982). In general, depending on the historical and geographical context, various actors and as many strategies can successfully counteract the centrifugal tendencies of a polarized party system. In the cases analysed here, the decisive (re-)actions against extremists mainly came from the leadership of the border parties, the government and the Head of State.

Focusing first on the border parties and the government, it can be expected that the centrifugal tendencies give rise to 'defectionist' tendencies in the parliamentary arena (Figure 4.3). In polarized systems, the government is normally supported by a centre-based coalition. By definition, the stronger the parliamentary representation of extremists, the more likely it will be that the border parties will be part of the governmental majority, and possibly a numerically necessary part of it. A further

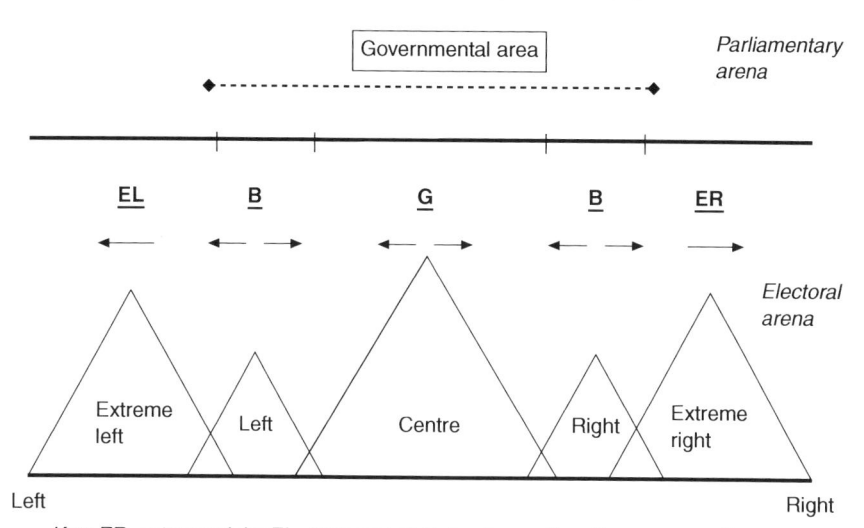

Key: ER, extreme right; EL, extreme left; B, border parties; G, government's core

Figure 4.3 Party system propensities in the electoral and parliamentary arena (adjusted from Sartori 1976).

consequence is that the government majority will also be heterogeneous, which on the one hand makes governmental paralysis likely, and, on the other, makes border parties uncomfortable.

In other words, we can say that border parties generally face a choice: either they abide by 'systemic' considerations, and make a common front against the extremist party, perceived as a common enemy; or they put their immediate electoral and political interests first, and defect from the governmental alliance. They might choose to defect from the centre either in order to reclaim the votes lost to the extremists, or to create the political conditions for a different and more rewarding governing majority. Border parties' decisions during times of crisis are the crucial factor in making democratic defence in the short-term possible or impossible in the face of the challenge of strong extremist parties.

This causal process unfolds as follows: the cooperation of the border parties, by stabilizing the governmental majority, gives the government the possibility to react against the extremists, which increases the probability of a decline in the latter's popular support. The defection of border parties, on the contrary, triggers the opposite causal process, leading to the increase of centrifugal tendencies in the party system and ultimately to democratic breakdown, either in the form of extremist takeover or of suspension of democratic rule by a government that can no longer count on a political majority.

The Head of State is a crucial actor in short-term democratic defence. While the effectiveness of the government in acting against extremists is largely conditioned by the strategies of border parties, the Head of State can generally operate with a greater degree of independence. This is certainly the case in systems in which the Head of State has a prominent position in the executive (such as in the semi-presidential systems of the Weimar Republic and Finland), but also when, although formally endowed with limited competencies, the Head of State enjoys a great personal prestige.

To be sure, in no case could they ignore the equilibrium between the political forces when making choices, especially in critical political junctures. But they can nonetheless be decisive in using personal prestige and political influence to channel the crisis towards a certain outcome. Generally speaking, the Head of State can intervene in all the intermediate steps of the causal process described above, by influencing the party interplay and the coalition-formation process, by supporting the government and its strategies in front of public opinion, and in some cases by exerting influence on the policy choices of the cabinet. Moreover, they can exert independent powers in exceptional situations, where the legal prerequisites for this exist.

The breakdowns

Table 4.1 shows the opposite patterns of survived and collapsed democracies in the strategies of border parties, the government and the Head of State. I will not waste too many words on the quite well-known stories of the breakdown in Italy and the Weimar Republic (Farneti 1978; Lepsius 1978). Generally speaking, one of the main factors precipitating the political crisis in both Italy and Germany was that border parties, or important sectors of these, defected from the political centre and pursued a different political alliance that, at one stage or another, would have foreseen the inclusion of the extremists. In pursuing this project, they were mainly driven by the (wrong) belief that in such alliance they would have the leading role.

The same contrasting patterns of behaviour between cases of survival and breakdown can be seen in the political strategies and actions of the Heads of State in critical moments. The actions of Finnish President Per Evind Svinhufvud in implementing emergency powers against the Lapua insurrection in 1932, the political activism of President Edvard Beneš in Czechoslovakia after 1935, and the determination of King Leopold III in Belgium in solving the political deadlock of a hyper-fragmented party system were decisive at key junctures of the political crises in the respective countries. By contrast, the decision of Victor Emmanuel III in Italy not to oppose the Fascist insurrection of 1922, and especially the decisions of Hindenburg and his advisors between 1930 and 1933 in Germany, were crucial in favouring an anti-democratic outcome of the crises (Dorpalen 1964).

The survivals

The three cases of 'difficult survival' of Finland, Belgium and Czechoslovakia are much less known, but are crucial to understanding the working of the politics of defence of democracy in countries where extremists are particularly strong in the party system.

Finland

Finnish inter-war democracy had to react to two opposed and consequent extremist challenges. In the 1920s, the government exerted strong repression against the Communist Party, resorting widely to police action and to the intelligence services. Many Communist militants and leaders were charged with treason or sedition, and the party's organization was repeatedly disbanded during those years (Mäkelä 1987; Hodgson 1967; Upton 1973). Although the object of continuous repression, and politically isolated – the Social Democratic Party constantly kept its distance from them – the Communists remained in the public sphere. Constantly changing

Table 4.1 Defensive actions of the Head of State and the Government

Country	Belgium	Finland	Czechoslovakia	Italy	Weimar
Challenge Actor	Rexists (1936–9)	Lapua Movement/ NC (1929–32)	SdP (1933–8)	PNF (1919–25)	NSDAP (1928–33)
Head of State	(Leopold III) Interventions on coalition-making process to solve deadlocks. Constant exclusion of Rex	(Svinhufvud) Orders military reaction against armed insurrection of Lapua. Outlaws movement afterwards	(Beneš) Appeals to public opinion; influence on governmental policies in favour of moderate German parties	(Victor Emmanuel III) Vetoes state of siege proposed by government against Fascist insurrection (Oct. 1922). Appoints Mussolini as PM thereafter	(Hindenburg) Suspends parliamentary rule after break of Grand Coalition in March 1930. Destabilizing influence on cabinet thereafter
Border Parties	(Catholic Party) No defection. Prompt reaction at organizational and propaganda levels	(Agrarian Party) Defection until early 1931. No defection afterwards	(Agrarian Party) Internal right wing defects consistently before 1935, and sporadically later countered by an alliance of rest of the party with Socialists and Presidency	Large sectors of the liberals prefer an alliance with the Fascists in 1921 and in 1924 to a centre-based alliance	Extremization of National Conservatives after 1928. Move to the right of centrist parties after 1930
Government (majority)	Administrative provisions against Rex. Some *ad hoc* legislation. Appeals to public opinion	Implementation of 'anti-Communist' legislation against Lapua	Policy concessions (to moderate German parties). Strong anti extremist legislation	Negotiations with Fascists to stop political violence fail	Scarcely autonomous from the Presidency after 1930 (presidential decrees)

organizational form, the party managed to stay in the political arena and to participate in elections until 1929.

The decisive factor for the eradication of Communism from Finland in the inter-war period was the emergence, at the end of 1929, of a strong extreme right-wing movement, the Lapua Movement, which itself turned into a danger for Finnish democracy. Backed by large and influential parts of the Finnish conservative establishment, this movement unleashed an unprecedented wave of political violence throughout the country and forced the parliament to pass a very elaborate apparatus of anti-extremist legislation and to implement it against the Communists, banning them from public life in 1930–1.

Shortly afterwards, the same legislation was used against the Lapua Movement. President Svinhufvud used the broad emergency powers that the new laws conferred on him to react against an armed uprising by Lapua in early 1932, and outlawed the movement. His prompt reaction (and the support given to it by the Chief of Staff Aarne Sihvo, who resisted strong pressure from within the army) was certainly of vital importance, but such a strategy was helped by the increasing political isolation of Lapua after 1931. While, in a first phase, large sectors of the bourgeois establishment gave their support to the Lapua Movement, after 1931 most bourgeois parties clearly distanced themselves from it. The political trajectory of the Agrarian Party, the most important centrist party in those years, is crucial in this respect. Once the Communist challenge had been eradicated, it was no longer necessary for the moderate parties to tolerate Lapua's outright political violence, as well as its increasingly authoritarian and anti-democratic positions (Rintala 1962).

Czechoslovakia

In the First Czechoslovak Republic (1920–38), the main challenge to the regime came from Sudeten German ethnic parties. The political expression of this ethnic cleavage – about one quarter of the population of Czechoslovakia was German-speaking and concentrated in the border regions – had a moderate and an extremist face. The former was that of the German bourgeois and Social Democratic parties, which decided quite early (1921–3) to cooperate with the newly born Czechoslovak State, and were fully integrated politically within a few years. The other face was both nationalist-secessionist and anti-democratic, and was represented by the German Nationalist Party and the German National Socialist Workers' Party. These two parties had little significance in the 1920s, when the regime was stable and they were politically entirely isolated. They became a reason for concern, however, after Hitler's rise to power in January 1933.[4]

The Czechoslovak government's first reaction was to ban these two parties in October 1933, and to reinforce anti-extremist legislation in several areas. In 1933–4 several special laws were passed limiting political propaganda, introducing the political screening of public employees, and allowing the ban of extremist parties (e.g. Sander 1935). Most members of the two dissolved parties, however, were absorbed by the newly founded Sudeten German Home Front (SHF), which would constitute the fifth column of Nazi Germany within democratic Czechoslovakia for the remaining years of the Republic.

Although the legal prerequisites for this existed, and the majority of the governing parties were in favour of banning the SHF before the 1935 elections, the government did not take this decision. Given the disagreement within the cabinet on this issue, Agrarian Prime Minister Jan Malypetr transferred the decision to President Thomas Masaryk. Although in principle favourable to the ban, he decided against the dissolution of the SHF in order not to endanger the stability of the government coalition, thinking that the party would be 'parliamentarized' after the elections, i.e. its entry in parliament would lead it to adopt more moderate positions. Then, if the need arose, the party could be dissolved anyway (Mamatey 1973). This decision was based on a gross miscalculation, but did not have easy alternatives when it was taken. The necessary counterweight to banning the SHF would have been making generous concessions to the German minority in general, which no Czech party was willing to do on the eve of the elections. Thus, the closer the elections, the feebler the position of the forces pushing for the party's dissolution, and so the scenario of a ban increasingly lost credibility.

In other words, the real reasons for this 'non-decision' were not a political mistake by Masaryk but rather the strategies of important political groups, notably the two Agrarian parties, who were members of the government coalition. In Czechoslovakia, as in other countries, the emergence of a new extremist actor had triggered plans for political re-aggregation, offering to some members of the democratic coalition the possibility of improving their political dividends.

At first, the German Agrarian Party (BdL), feeling threatened in their countryside strongholds by the dynamism of the SHF, tried to reach an agreement with them, with negotiations going on for most of 1934. Soon, the project of the BdL became part of a more comprehensive political plan of the internal right wing of the Czechoslovak Agrarians which, in order to increase their share of governmental power and to pursue their policy preferences (heavily constrained in a coalition in which the moderate working class parties played a major role), aimed at a general shift of the equilibrium of the national government towards the right.

More specifically, their project was to form a new coalition that excluded both the Czechoslovak and the Sudeten German Social Democrats and included the SHF along with the Czechoslovak conservatives and the tiny Fascist party. This would have enabled the election of a new President of the Republic, who would be more sensitive to their political orientations than Masaryk was. To this aim, the SHF hoped to form an electoral alliance with the BdL, in which the former would obtain 'fifteen or twenty seats', and reinforce the new majority (Brügel 1967).

The large electoral victory of the SHF, renamed as the Sudeten German Party (SdP) in the 1935 elections, rendered this project difficult to realize. The SdP turned out to be the strongest party in Czechoslovakia in terms of votes (about two thirds of the Sudeten Germans voted for it), and was only one seat smaller than the Czechoslovak Agrarian Party. In these conditions, it became obvious that the SdP was not easily amenable to play a subservient role in someone else's political plans. Thus, after 1935, the German Agrarians assumed a generally more confrontational attitude, while the right-wing circles of the Czechoslovak Agrarians still displayed, although less continuously, defectionist tendencies.

Crucial to defeating the project of the right-wing Agrarian circles, however, was the timely political alliance formed between Masaryk and Edvard Beneš (and the Social Democratic forces influenced by them), on the one hand, and the leader of the Slovak wing of the Czechoslovak Agrarian Party, Milan Hodza, on the other. Hodza, very influential within his party, was appointed Prime Minister after the 1935 elections. This alliance proved decisive in stabilizing the political situation on several occasions in which, also after 1935, the right-wing Agrarian circles defected from the majority.

The governing parties and the President of the Republic devised a three-pillar defensive strategy against the SdP in 1935–8. First, they gave a strong impulse to rearmament, and to the construction of military fortifications at the Western boundaries, which was undertaken at a tremendous pace (Hauner 1986). Second, they equipped the state with the legal means necessary to cope with internal and international emergencies. This was done by passing the 1936 law on the 'defence of the State', which gave the government the legal possibility to declare military rule and govern by decree in the whole national territory or large portions of it (e.g. (Sander 1937). Third and last, the executive pursued the nationality policy towards the German minority with a firmer hand, both by making important concessions to them in several areas, and by resorting to intense appeals to the public to support coexistence and fair cooperation between Czechs and Germans (see below). This articulate strategy managed to keep the SdP at bay, although obviously it could not avoid the dismemberment of Czechoslovakia, decided in Munich in 1938 by the European powers, and its subsequent military conquest by Germany in 1939.

Belgium

Belgian democracy faced a serious challenge in 1936–9, with the rise of the Rexist party, a right-wing Catholic party with authoritarian leanings. In the elections of May 1936, Rex, created only a few months earlier, obtained 11 per cent of the seats in parliament, while the Flemish nationalist and authoritarian Flemish National League (VNV), and the Communist Party also reported large victories and obtained a further 12 per cent in total.

The Rexist challenge, the most aggressive and dangerous of the three, was counteracted quickly and effectively thanks to the prompt reaction of the establishment. In particular, the strategy of the Catholic Party, which had been the biggest loser to Rex in 1936, deserves attention since it was decisive in allowing an effective defence.

The Rexist Party came from within the Catholic political area, and its young leader, Leon Degrelle, was director of a Catholic publishing house. After the constitution of Rex as an independent political party in February 1936, and Degrelle's strong propaganda attacks against the Catholic leaders, mainly by denouncing cases of corruption and politico-financial collusion, the Catholic Party reacted promptly. They officially severed all contacts with Rex and accelerated internal organizational reforms to make the party and its leadership less vulnerable to Rexist propaganda, in part by achieving stricter central control over the loosely connected peripheral Catholic political organizations (Beaufays 1973). In the campaign for the May 1936 elections, the new party leader Hubert Pierlot made specific moves aimed at capturing the vote of the younger generations of Catholics, who had been largely attracted by Degrelle's oratory; for example, by sponsoring and supporting the formation of new groups of young Catholics (Gérard 1985). This, however, was not enough to avoid the electoral defeat of the Catholic Party; virtually all of the Rexist Party's votes came from the ranks of the Catholic electorate.

After the elections, a situation emerged similar to Czechoslovakia after 1935, in which the main danger for Belgian democracy came not so much from the increasing popularity of Degrelle, but rather from the presence of a sector of the Catholic Party itself. One part was in favour of a political alliance with Rex in a *bloc d'ordre*, a project which would have made Rex's chances of taking power much higher. The Catholic Party was in disarray, and Pierlot's frantic attempts at fostering internal reforms encountered unconcealed internal opposition from various sectors of the party. Moreover, the Catholic Party also had to confront the challenge of the VNV in Flanders, where it had lost some 100,000 votes, mainly to the VNV (Rex had been more successful in Wallonia).

After the 1936 elections, several projects for regrouping Flemish Catholics in different coalitions emerged, and were discussed in an innumerable series of reserved meeting and public interventions by various personalities of the Catholic world (Gérard 1985). A further problem for the Catholic Party was the political alliance that Degrelle and the leader of the VNV, Staf De Clercq, signed in October 1936, in which a fusion between the Flemish sector of Rex and the VNV was foreseen. The leadership of the Catholic Party reacted to this difficult situation by changing its internal organization and giving more visibility to its Flemish component. In October 1936 it was established that the leading body of the party, a 'Directorium' endowed with full powers, should be divided into two separate wings – the Christian Social Party and the Catholic Flemish People's Party – which should be responsible for the activities of the party in Wallonie and Flanders respectively (Mabille 1986).

This change strengthened the position of the Flemish leaders of the Catholic Party: Alphonse-Pierre Verbist, the leader of the KVV, started negotiations with the VNV, which ended in an agreement of principle between the two parties in December 1936. Although this agreement did not lead to concrete developments, and actually met with the opposition of the Christian Labour Union and the bishops (Gérard 1985), it had the effect of providing a partial counter-force to the tendencies towards an inclusion of both Rex and the VNV in a right-wing catholic front. It must be kept in mind that these were very unfavourable times for the Catholic Party: the party was in crisis after the defeat, undergoing a process of internal restructuring, torn by centrifugal tendencies due to the political dynamism of Rex, and it was a senior partner in a government coalition whose members were attacking in their propaganda not only Rex, but also the VNV.

In these difficult conditions, the prospect of a split, or even disintegration, of the Catholic Party would not have been unlikely, had the projects for a broader right-wing alliance materialized (Gérard 1985). Despite these centrifugal tendencies, the leadership of the party managed to keep a firm route towards a centrist alliance with the Liberals and the Socialists, and to resist the various attempts of the internal traditionalist wing to move the whole party to the right. This gave the government the political strength to react effectively to Rex's challenge.

The Belgian King Leopold III was also important in channelling the political crisis towards a democratic solution, in particular by intervening actively in the coalition-forming process. After the 1936 elections, several attempts to form a government failed, and the country was left without a government for a month, during which big Communist-led strikes blocked several industrial sites, and Rex continued to ride the wave of its political success. After the resignation of several *formateurs*, Leopold III intervened directly, summoning the leaders of the internal factions of the three centrist parties (all politically necessary for a government) and asked them to give the go-ahead to a tripartite coalition. The decisiveness of this intervention is demonstrated by the fact that the new government, led by the Catholic-leaning technocrat Paul Van Zeeland, saw the light only two days later (Höjer 1946).

Once formed, the Van Zeeland government decided to react against the challenges from Degrelle and Rex: *inter alia*, it prohibited a Rexist mass demonstration in Brussels, it denied Degrelle access to the State radio for a propaganda speech, some Rexist journalists and militants were arrested, and the trials under way against Rexist members were sped up. The government also took up the most overt and symbolically loaded challenge that Rex put forward against the regime: a by-election, tactically provoked by Degrelle in April 1937, in which the Rexist leader would stand in person. The majority supporting the government responded by passing an *ad hoc* law forbidding 'frivolous' by-elections, and put forward the Prime Minister in person to stand against the Rexist leader. Van Zeeland, supported by all the traditional parties and even by the Communists, who decided not to put forward a candidate, defeated Degrelle heavily, marking the beginning of his decline and that of Rex (Étienne 1968).

The repressive strategies

What instruments did the democratic governments of Belgium, Czechoslovakia and Finland use to respond to extremism? First of all, reinforcing the legislative apparatus for repression of extremists was a strategy to which most European democracies resorted in the inter-war years in their responses to internal challenges, and it was also present, as mentioned, in the cases analysed here.

The special legislation against political extremism passed in European democracies during the inter-war years is very complex and covers a very broad area. Under the heading of 'anti-extremist legislation' one can find the special norms conferring on the cabinet or the Head of State extraordinary powers to face emergency situations; norms aimed at protecting the bureaucratic and military structures of the state from extremist influences; the special legislation enabling the government to ban or temporarily suspend parties or associations considered threatening to some fundamental feature of the system; legislation limiting political propaganda on certain issues; and legislation aimed at the protection of public order (see Capoccia 2001b).

The analysis of anti-extremist legislation in the inter-war European democracies reveals a mixed picture. On the one hand, Czechoslovakia and Finland, which survived the worst political crises, possessed the most elaborate systems of protection against extremism, with strong legislative restrictions in virtually all areas mentioned above. A large part of this legislation was a conscious reaction of the democratic elites to the rise of extremist actors (Capoccia 2004). Comparatively less important, although not irrelevant, was the role played by the reinforcement of *ad hoc* legislation in the overall defensive strategy of the Belgian democratic elites against the challenge of the Rexist Party.

On the other hand, special anti-extremist legislation was also present in the Weimar Republic, where a 'law for the protection of the Republic', introduced restrictions to extremists' activities in several areas. Furthermore, several presidential decrees in 1931–2 provided for severe legal restrictions, especially for the protection of public order and the limitation of extremist political propaganda (Jasper 1963). What differentiated Czechoslovakia and Finland from Germany was the persistence, during the crisis, of a democratic coalition that was sufficiently strong to devise and enact a coherent *political* strategy against extremists (see also Gusy 1991). Of such a strategy, the reinforcement of special legislation can be an important part, but the crucial factor is the *politics* of democratic defence.

The 'inclusive' mechanisms of democratic defence

As the Italian and the German cases show, inclusion of a totalitarian party might be dangerous, yet successful short-term reactions against political extremism are not confined to political exclusion and legal repression. On the contrary, they are normally accompanied by explicit attempts by the democratic establishment to include *specific sectors* of the extremist challenge. Apart from the attempts of border parties to appeal to the electors supporting the extremist formations, inclusive strategies can be developed and enacted by institutional actors too. In fact, the government and the Head of State can develop inclusive strategies aimed at 'integrating' the extremist rank and file, or sectors of the extremists' elites. Table 4.2 summarizes the use of these mechanisms in the three survival cases analysed here.

The resort to repressive provisions, particularly strong in Finland and Czechoslovakia, has already been analysed in the previous sections. The defensive strategies labelled as the 'integration of rank and file' aim at reducing the electoral appeal of the extremist party. Into this category fall the explicit appeals to the public against the extremists, a course of action to which both the Belgian and the Czechoslovak government resorted. Under the label of 'appeals to the public' I include the public speeches, meetings, conferences etc, held by important political figures (the Head of State, the Prime Minister, democratic leaders, etc) and explicitly aimed at alerting the electorate to the danger presented by a specific extremist challenge, and at enlarging the legitimacy of the system. More specifically, I only refer to those appeals explicitly conceived by their authors as part of a strategic reaction against the extremist challenge, as was the case in both the countries mentioned.

In Belgium, the Van Zeeland government decided to react without hesitation against Rex's increasingly aggressive propaganda, with the Prime Minister taking an active role. A programme of public meetings and speeches by the Prime Minister and several ministers and democratic leaders was planned, in which they warned the population, and in particular the Catholic electorate, about the danger represented by Rex.

In Czechoslovakia, the most active figure in addressing public opinion in order to undermine support for the extremists was President Beneš. In 1936–7 he travelled incessantly in the German-inhabited regions of Czechoslovakia, addressing the problem of national minorities and

Table 4.2 Mechanisms of democratic defence (Finland, Belgium, First Czechoslovak Republic)

Country	Extremist actor	Strategy		
		Repression (special legislation)	Integration	
			Rank and file	Sectors of the elite
Belgium	Rexists (1936–9)	Medium	• Appeals to the public • Sector organizations of the Catholic Party created for electoral appeal	No
Finland	Lapua Movement/NC (1929–2)	Strong	• Ban of Communist organizations to contain extreme right • Attempts to create a new organization	Attempts to create a new organization
Czechoslovakia	SdP (1933–8)	Strong	• Appeals to the public • Strategic policy concessions to German moderate parties	(Sterile) contacts with SdP

highlighting the government's willingness to meet all reasonable requests for equal treatment for all citizens (see Brügel 1967, Beneš 1937). He instructed several cabinet ministries to allocate their budgets to German-inhabited areas in proportion to their population. The government independently followed the same line, both in allocating public expenditure and in accepting the requests of the German moderate parties, which needed support to restore their credibility with the Sudeten community after the landslide victory of the SdP.

Ad hoc inclusive strategies can also be directed at the extremist elite with the aim of integrating at least its more moderate sectors into the democratic process by meeting some of their demands without however questioning the fundamentals of the democratic regime. An attempt to integrate both the rank and file and part of the extremist elite was made by Finnish President Svinhufvud after outlawing the Lapua Movement. He tried to recreate an all-inclusive, new right-wing movement under his control, which would continue the work of the Lapua Movement without endangering public order. Emphasis was to be put, in his opinion, on educational means: 'even though they take more time, they will certainly lead in the end to definite results' (quoted in Rintala 1962, p. 221). These were the ideals that were originally at the base of the People's Patriotic Movement (IKL). However, this attempt failed and less than one month after the founding convention, held in April 1932, Svinhufvud's collaborators found themselves sidetracked and outnumbered. Having completely lost control of their 'creature', they left the IKL shortly afterwards.

In Czechoslovakia, the Hodza government sought an agreement with the moderate Sudeten German parties, but also had repeated contacts with SdP leader Henlein. Although these never evolved into an articulate negotiation, and probably came too late to attract part of the SdP elite towards more moderate positions, their existence shows that the attitude of the Czechoslovak government, although certainly uncompromising, was not of total closure towards the Sudeten German nationalists.

Whether the inclusive strategies were successful or not, their presence in the toolbox of short-term regime defence shows that democratic elites clearly thought that mere repression was insufficient to respond effectively to a serious extremist challenge. Repression was deemed necessary, but trying to regain as much systemic loyalty from the extremists as possible was also crucial, as this reduced the costs of democratic defence and the risk of authoritarian involvement.

In conclusion, not all strong extremist challenges to democracy in inter-war Europe led to democratic breakdown, as in Italy and Weimar Germany. In Belgium, Czechoslovakia and Finland the political elite managed to react effectively against dangerous anti-democratic threats by politically isolating the extremists and using both repressive and inclusive strategies. The high degree of political intolerance against the extremists generally reached in these democracies was in fact accompanied by attempts to convert extremists to systemic support. The analysis of the centrifugal propensities of electoral competition in systems where relevant extremist actors are present highlights simultaneously the non-obvious nature and the political importance of the political choices of the 'democratic defenders' in Belgium, Czechoslovakia and Finland. On these bases, maintaining that different decisions of those same actors at crucial moments would both have been possible and have led those democratic systems much closer to breakdown seems to be plausible (on this, see Fearon 1991 and Tetlock and Belkin 1996).

The inter-war years and defence of democracy in contemporary Europe

The issue to be addressed in this concluding section is what we can learn from the analysis of the defence of democracy in inter-war Europe, for the contemporary relationship between democracy and extremism. The analysis of inter-war Europe is important at several levels.

First, at a more general level, the study of reactions to extremism in democracies is an almost unexplored field in comparative politics, and the analysis of extremist challenges and defensive reactions in Belgium, Czechoslovakia, and Finland (as well as Italy and Germany) between the wars can usefully complement the existing knowledge about this kind of political process. More specifically, by analysing cases in which extremist forces reached a substantial strength and entered *en masse* the representative institutions, a useful perspective is added to the scattered existing studies on this phenomenon, which focus on countries and periods in which extremists were relatively weak (the US and the Federal Republic of Germany first of all). This analysis warns, therefore, against too hasty generalizations about the viability and effects of such measures – and in particular the conventional wisdom according to which these are 'viable only if extremists are weak, and not otherwise' which, focusing only on the best-known cases, ultimately suffers from selection bias.

Second, the focus on 'difficult' democracies, a category that includes most of the recent democratization cases, in which extremist forces are relevant players in the transition or the post-transition phase, yields interesting insights. The analysis shows the importance of the maintenance of a cohesive democratic coalition for the viability of politico-institutional reactions, which would otherwise be impossible. That is, a strategy of institutional reactions against strong extremist parties is only possible if a parliamentary majority supports it, and is able to remain a majority to counteract the centrifugal tendencies that may destabilize it.

The analysis shows that a crucial factor for the stability of the parliamentary majority is the expectations of some sectors of the elites, in particular the leaders of the border parties. In this respect, border parties constitute a special case of what Nancy Bermeo (1999) has called 'pivotal elites', whose expectations of the future performance of extremists drive their decisions in critical moments, and therefore constitute a key factor in conditioning the outcome of a democratic transition.

A third interesting aspect is the composite nature of anti-extremist strategies, and the importance of the mix of repression. In the inter-war European democracies analysed here, both repression and inclusion had an important place in the overall strategy of reactions to extremism: strategies such as policy concessions and targeted appeals to the public were intensively used in crucial moments. Such strategies pose fewer normative problems than legal repression, but it is difficult to imagine how the former could have been successful without the actual and deterrent effects of the latter.

A further area of contribution is the reflection on the connections between the experience of inter-war Europe and the situation of contemporary Europe. Is there a direct legacy of the inter-war years on the strategies that European democracies today adopt to react to extremists? And how important is it? While an exhaustive answer to this complex question is obviously impossible here, a general answer is that, while some things have obviously changed in both the nature of the extremist challenge and the democratic response, the legacy of the inter-war years in this respect still seems to be very important indeed.

While the relationship between extremism and democracy in Europe today is certainly more complex and multifaceted than it was in the inter-war years, I will briefly focus on one of the many important differences between that period and now: the changing nature of political extremism in Europe, and the wide-ranging implications that this has for defence and the very conception of democracy. More specifically, this change influences the limits and possibilities of responses to extremism in democracies, but these changes do not mean that the 1920s and 1930s have left no legacy.

Back in the 1920s and the 1930s, European democratic regimes were confronted with the fully-fledged totalitarian and authoritarian ideologies of Nazi, Communist and Fascist parties. In contemporary Europe, extreme left parties have either changed radically and become fully integrated in the social democratic tradition, or (with few significant exceptions) have been reduced at the role of marginal forces. Many analysts have stressed the emergence of many extreme-right wing or populist parties in several European countries. In several cases, however, these parties present significant differences from traditional Fascism and Nazism (e.g. Eatwell 2000; Ignazi 1992, 1994). Whether their views and policies are 'law-and-order' oriented, 'welfare-chauvinist', anti-immigration, anti-EU, or all of these together, the incompatibility of these positions with democratic rights and guarantees requires a more elaborate conception of democracy, which might not perfectly fit all European states (Capoccia 2002a).

Yet it seems that despite these differences, the general way in which European democrats think of the relationship between 'their' democracies and these 'new' extremist challenges is still informed by the legacy of the inter-war years, when the clash was between radically different visions of the world. Although the mobilization of civil society has played an important role in some cases, the role played by state repression (or deterrence) via special legislation still seems to be key. I have already mentioned the trial against the German NPD pending before the Federal Constitutional Court, and the various norms of restriction to political pluralism included in the constitutions of many East European democracies. The most recent example comes from Spain, where the Parliament has just passed a new organic law on political parties (Ley Organica 6/2002, BOE num 154, 27 June 2002) that prohibits parties that attack the democratic regime, promote racism or xenophobia, or support terrorist organizations. Similar provisions are in force in virtually all European democracies.

Are all European democracies becoming 'militant', at least to some extent (Fink 2001)? While a fully satisfactory answer to this question will have to be left to future research, a simple perusal of the constitutions and statute books of European democracies shows that this seems to be the direction in which many countries are going. The paradox is that, as said before, this is happening in a situation in which the 'old' totalitarian ideologies have waned, and the organizations abiding by them ceased to be dangerous for the survival of democracy.

Notes

1 The comparative study by Van Donselaar (1995), although of great interest, does not make use of the theoretical tools of comparative politics (the author is an anthropologist) and is virtually ignored in the debate.
2 In principle, democracy can be also 'defended' by strategies with long-term goals, such as those aiming at promoting a democratic culture through education, or democratic propaganda etc. These strategies are very important, for example, in the present context of the 'protection and promotion' of democracy in newly democratizing states, but this is not considered in the present analysis (Schmitter & Brouwer 1999). For a general typology of defensive strategies against extremists, see Capoccia (2001b).
3 As has been rightly argued, political violence was important not so much in the takeover itself, but rather before it, in limiting the efficacy of the democratic government in keeping public order and thereby creating a power vacuum that made the 'legal' takeover easier (Linz 1978, p. 56).
4 The Sudeten German nationalists were not the only extremist challenge that the new Czechoslovak Republic had to confront. Apart from the Communists and the relatively weaker Fascists, a serious threat for the Republic also came from the Slovak autonomists of the Slovak People's Party (HSL'S). These other challenges constituted further constraints on the action of the democratic forces in defence of the regime.

Bibliography

Agnoli, J. and Brueckner, P. (1967) *Die Transformation der Demokratie*. Berlin: Voltaire.
Beneš, E. (1937) *Gedanken und Tat. Aus den Schriften und Reden von E. Beneš*. Prague.
Bermeo, N. (1999) 'Myths of moderation: confrontation and conflict during democratic transitions', in Anderson, L. (ed.) *Transitions to Democracy*. New York, Columbia University Press, pp. 136–157.
Bracher, K.-D. (1953) *Die Auflösung der Weimarer Republik*. Villingen: Ring.
Brügel, J.W. (1967) *Tschechen und Deutsche 1918–1938*. Munich: Nymphenburger Verlagshandlung.
Candeloro, G. (1978) *Storia dell' Italia moderna. Volume ottavo: La prima guerra mondiale. Il dopoguerra. L' avvento del fascismo*. Milan: Feltrinelli.
Capoccia, G. (2001a) 'Defending democracy: strategies of reaction to political extremism in inter-war Europe', *European Journal of Political Research*, 39, 4: 431–460.
Capoccia, G. (2001b) 'Repression, incorporation, lustration, education: how democracies react to their enemies. Towards a theoretical framework for the comparative analysis of defense of democracy', Paper presented to the 29th ECPR Joint Sessions of Workshops, Grenoble, 6–11 April.
Capoccia, G. (2002a) 'Anti-system parties: A conceptual reassessment', *Journal of Theoretical Politics*, 14, 1: 9–35.
Capoccia, G. (2002b) 'Legislative responses against extremism. The "Protection of Democracy" in the first Czechoslovak Republic 1920–1938', forthcoming in *East European Politics and Societies*, 16, 3: 691–738.
Capoccia, G. (2004) *Defending Democracy: Responses to Extremism in Inter-war Europe*. Baltimore: Johns Hopkins University Press.
Dorpalen, A. (1964) *Hindenburg and the Politics of the Weimar Republic*. Princeton: Princeton University Press.
Eatwell, R. (2000) 'The rebirth of the "extreme right" in Western Europe'. *Parliamentary Affairs*, 53, 3: 407–425.
Étienne, J.-M. (1968) *Le mouvement rexiste jusqu'en 1940*. Paris: Armand Colin.
Farneti, P. (1978) 'Social conflict, parliamentary fragmentation, institutional shift, and the rise of Fascism: Italy', in Linz, J.J. and Stepan, A. (eds) *The Breakdown of Democratic Regimes: Europe*. Baltimore: Johns Hopkins University Press, pp. 3–33.
Fearon, J. (1991) 'Counterfactuals and hypothesis testing in political science'. *World Politics* 43: 169–195.
Fink, J.E. (2001) 'Electoral regimes and the proscription of anti-democratic parties', in Rapoport, D. and Weinberg, L. (eds) *The Democratic Experience and Political Violence*. London: Frank Cass, pp. 51–77.
Fox, G.H. and Nolte, G. (1995) 'Intolerant democracies', *Harvard International Law Review* 36: 1–70.
Gérard, E. (1985) *De katholieke partij in crisis: Partijpolitiek leven in Belgie (1918–1940)*. Leuven: Kritak.
Gusy, C. (1991) *Weimar – die wehrlose Republik? Verfassungsschutzrecht und Verfassungsschutz in der Weimarer Republik*. Tübingen: Mohr.
Hauner, M. (1986) 'Military budgets and the armament industry', in Kaser, M.C.

and Radice, E.A. (eds) *The Economic History of Eastern Europe 1919–1975*. Oxford: Clarendon Press, pp. 49–116.
Hodgson, J.H. (1967) *Communism in Finland. A History and Interpretation*. Princeton: Princeton University Press.
Höjer, C.-H. (1946) *Le régime parlementaire belge de 1918 à 1940*. Brussels; Uppsala: CRISP/Statsveteskapliga föreningen.
Ignazi, P. (1992) 'The silent counter-revolution: hypotheses on the emergence of extreme right-wing parties in Europe', *European Journal of Political Research*, 22, 1: 3–34.
Ignazi, P. (1994) *L'estrema destra in Europa*, Bologna: Il Mulino.
Jasper, G. (1963) *Der Schutz der Republik. Studien zur staatlichen Sicherung der Demokratie in der Weimarer Republik*. Tübingen: Mohr.
Lepsius, M.R. (1978) 'From fragmented party democracy to government by emergency decree and National Socialist takeover', in Linz, J.J. and Stepan, A. (eds) *The Breakdown of Democratic Regimes: Europe*. Baltimore: Johns Hopkins University Press, pp. 34–79.
Linz, J.J. (1978) 'Crisis, breakdown and reequilibration', in Linz, J.J. and Stepan, A. (eds) *The Breakdown of Democratic Regimes*. Baltimore: Johns Hopkins University Press, pp. 1–124.
Lippincott B.E. (1965) *Democracy's Dilemma: The Totalitarian Party in a Free Society*. New York: Roland.
Loewenstein, K. (1937a) 'Militant democracy and fundamental rights, I', *American Political Science Review* 31: 417–432.
Loewenstein, K. (1937b) 'Militant democracy and fundamental rights, II', *American Political Science Review* 31: 638–658.
Mabille, X. (1986) *Histoire politique de la Belgique. Facteurs et acteurs de changement*. Brussels: CRISP.
Mäkelä, J. (1987) 'The radical left and the communist party in Finnish politics', in Mylly, J. and Berry, M. (eds) *Political Parties in Finland – Essays in History and Politics*. Turku: University of Turku, pp. 153–186.
Mamatey, V.S. (1973) 'The development of Czechoslovak democracy, 1920–1938', in Mamatey, V.S. and Luza, R. (eds) *A History of the Czechoslovak Republic*. Princeton: Princeton University Press, pp. 99–166.
Rintala, M. (1962) *Three Generations. The Extreme Right Wing in Finnish Politics*. Bloomington: Indiana University Press.
Sander, F. (1935) *Die politische Gesetzgebung der Tschechoslowakischen Republik in den Jahren 1932–1934*. Reichenberg: Stiepel.
Sander, F. (1937) *Das Staatsverteidigungsgesetz und die Verfassungsurkunde der tschechoslovakischen Republik. Eine rechtsdogmatische Untersuchung*. Brünn: Rohrer.
Sartori, G. (1976) *Parties and Party Systems*. Cambridge: Cambridge University Press.
Sartori, G. (1982). *Teoria dei partiti e caso italiano*. Milan: SugarCo.
Schmitter, P. and Brouwer, I. (1999) *Conceptualizing, Researching and Evaluating Democracy Promotion and Protection*. Florence: EUI Working Paper Department of Social and Political Science 7/99.
Tetlock, P.E. and Belkin, A. (eds) (1996) *Counterfactual Thought Experiments in World Politics. Logical, Methodological and Psychological Perspectives*. Princeton: Princeton University Press.

Tomuschat, C. (1992) 'Democratic pluralism: the right to political opposition', in Rosas, A. and Helgesen, J. (eds) *The Strength of Diversity: Human Rights and Pluralist Democracy.* Dordrecht: Nijhoff, pp. 27–48.

Upton, A.F. (1973) 'The Communist Party of Finland', in Upton, A.F. (ed.) *The Communist Parties of Scandinavia and Finland.* London: Weidenfeld and Nicholson.

Van Donselaar, J. (1995) *De staat paraat? De bestrijding van extreem-rechts in West-Europa.* Amsterdam: Babylon-De Geus.

5 The defending democracy and the extreme right
A comparative analysis

Ami Pedahzur

Introduction

One of the paradoxes debated in democratic thought for many years focuses on the question: to what extent is it conceivable for a democratic polity to grant all its citizens – including those intent on undermining it – full liberty of action, thus, in effect, expediting efforts to bring about the possible demise of this very democracy. This quandary, otherwise labeled the paradox of tolerance' by Karl Popper (1962), embodies a further, inverse paradox which can be called the 'paradox of the defending democracy.'

This raises another question: to what degree does a democratic polity have the mandate to suppress or overpower extremist elements emanating from within its borders – elements that often seek to challenge its stability and core values? A heavy-handed response may lead to the erosion of those very same principles upon which the democracy is structured. A predicament may even arise where boundaries are rendered indistinct between the methods used by the struggling democracy, and the extremist threats aspiring to undermine it. An operative perspective deriving from this paradox focuses on the effectiveness of counteraction policy, and especially on whether a severe response initiated by the democracy – which evidently carries a high ethical price – does in fact eradicate extremism and violence and consequently uphold the polity's stability.

These convoluted dilemmas and their derivatives have occupied philosophers and scholars for many years. The core of the argument addressing the tension between the defense of the democracy and the guaranteed protection of its basic liberties was for a long time restricted to the philosophical playing field or the 'theoretical-normative level' (Ignazi 1999, p. 39). However, with time, and particularly in the second half of the twentieth century, this discourse was supplemented with another level of analysis – the political-institutional level. Close scrutiny of the argument involving this term indicates two principal lines of research. The first, i.e. the legal-judicial, focuses on the judiciary statutes and verdicts handed down against extremist parties and violent organizations (Loewenstein 1937a, b,

1938b; Capoccia 2001a). The second line of research, the military-operative, places its emphasis on military-intelligence–policing strategies and tactics in the battle against subversion, political violence and terror in democratic systems.

Although discussions couched in the theoretical-normative level were generally distinct from those on a political-constitutional scale, some theorists were successful in bridging these two levels of analysis (e.g. Cappocia 2001a,b; Cohen-Almagor 1997; Chalk 1995; Crelinsten and Schmid 1992). Works by these scholars were helpful in presenting a more inclusive theory regarding the democratic response to extremism, subversion and political violence. However, at the same time, their research still suffered from the absence of a comprehensive model that could account for additional levels of analysis and, in particular, the social level of analysis.

The first part of this chapter aims to present an academic discussion and analysis of democracy's response to extreme right-wing challenges. In addition to trying to cope with the ethical aspects, we will attempt to suspend somewhat the theoretical-normative aspect, and rather place at center stage the political-institutional frame as well as the social frame of analysis. These two latter frameworks carry the potential to take us a step further toward understanding whether the 'golden path' does in fact exist. Is there a course enabling democratic systems of government effectively to protect themselves without crossing the legal and ethical boundaries on which they are founded? The second part of the chapter will be devoted to an analysis of the responses of three democracies (Germany, Israel and the United States) by applying the analytical framework set out below.

In search of a definition

In the attempt to address democratic dilemmas encountered in the response to extremism and violence, scholars, and particularly those affiliated with judicial schools of thought, as well as judges and policy-makers, have searched for a terminology that would accurately describe democratic polities caught up in the struggle against powerful extremist elements. The first term of note is the 'militant democracy', prescribed by Loewenstein (1937a,b, 1938a,b) to indicate certain polities that held rule in the period between the two world wars. This designation carried normative implications and was intended to define the legal measures for use by European democracies in order to deal with the growth of fascism (see also Capoccia 2001a,b). Another term meriting attention is *wehrhafte Demokratie*, associated with the democratic constitution adopted by Germany in the wake of World War II. In English, this indicates a 'defensive,' 'protective' or 'watchful' democracy. The statutory-judicial interpretation of this construct in Germany was: '*wehr-hafte Demokratie* is one that does not open its doors to acts of subversion under the cover of legitimate parliamentary activity' (Cohen-Almagor 1994, p. 184).

This brief definition leaves the student of political science, who wishes to put it to empirical use, somewhat at a loss. Do subversive elements, which in fact pose a threat to democracy, solely take on the guise of parliamentary organizations, to wit political parties? Furthermore, what is the genuine intention behind the idea of keeping the doors of democracy shut in the face of these subversive groups? Does the *wehrhafte Demokratie* rule out these organizations from taking part in elections? Or, even more, does it outlaw them and cast their members into jail? These questions are, in general, left unanswered, despite the efforts of Carlo Schmid, chairman of the head committee in charge of consolidating the German constitution following World War II, to invest the construct with more meaning: 'It is not part of the concept of democracy that it creates the preconditions of its own destruction [...] we should also have the courage to be intolerant towards those who wish to use a democratic system in order to kill it off' (cited in Elmar 1987, p. 85). These words are indicative of the conventional approach assumed by democratic forms of government, according to which democracy has the absolute justification to protect itself from insurgents whoever they may be. Still, the key question remains – using what kind of methods? Are all ways and means legitimate in the democratic state's struggle for its existence?

In the effort to resolve this question, we elected to appropriate a second term: 'defending democracy.' This notion is also derived from the judicial school of thought and is associated with the State of Israel and its decision, in the mid-1960s, to prevent the Arab Socialist List from taking part in parliamentary elections. A 'defending democracy,' according to the Israeli court of law, is when 'the state possesses an implied power, similar to self-defense, to fight against subversive attempts designed to destroy it' (Cohen-Almagor 1994, p. 184). *Prima facie*, it appears that this definition is a significantly softer rendition than the German *wehrhafte Demokratie*. Yet, a review of the statements issued by Israeli Judge Zusman, who made broad use of the concept of defending democracy, shows that the difference between the two concepts is minimal. According to Justice Zusman: 'Just as a man does not have to agree to be killed, so a state too does not have to agree to be destroyed and erased from the map' (cited in Cohen-Almagor 1994, p. 183). Regardless of the fact that his conclusions are not very useful in bringing sharper relief to the definition, Zusman's assertion does provide an answer of sorts to the question of what measures the democracy is entitled to use in defending itself. Zusman clearly states that in a 'war like any war,' the democratic polity has the right to exercise its power, even in the absence of empowering legislation, if this power is applied in self-defense.

Surprisingly, the appropriation from the judiciary of the concept of defending democracy and its application to the sociological realm by two of the leading Israeli political sociologists, Dan Horowitz and Moshe Lissak, has neither assisted in developing the various dimensions of the concept nor relieved us of its ambiguity. They define defending democracy as 'a democracy which excludes from the democratic game those groups whose aims or actions may endanger the state, its political regime or its basic national consensus' (Horowitz and Lissak 1990, p. 197). This formulation indicates that these two scholars chose to pursue the same path laid down by legalists, while expanding it on two accounts. First, as Horowitz and Lissak see it, a democracy has the right to exclude all dangerous groups from the political system; that is, they do not limit democracy's jurisdiction of defensive action only to political parties. Second, groups that may be excluded from the democratic process are not only those allegedly endangering the state or the polity's stability, but also those that threaten its basic national consensus.

Most scholars concur that democratic governments can exclude from the political arena those organizations, and especially political parties, whose ideology or actions may endanger the actual democracy, and in certain cases also the system of principles forming the democracy's basis of legitimacy. However, an attempt to apply the construct of the defending democracy in its present form to the analytic use of inquiring into democracies' responses to extremism, subversion and violence will apparently not yield the anticipated result. Accordingly, the term must be elucidated, the elements comprising it must be underscored, and the distinctions among them illuminated. For this purpose, we submit a conceptual framework based on both the political-institutional level and the social level, spelling out the guiding principles and tools used by the various democratic countries in their struggle against perceived adversaries.

A framework for analysis

Before introducing the framework employed in our analysis, it is important to set out a methodological reservation in regard to the use of the term 'defending democracy' (Capoccia 2001a). The coupling of the word 'defending' with the word 'democracy' may in fact be misleading, because it produces an idiom the reader may think is a type of democracy along the lines of liberal democracy or consensus democracy, and this is not the case. Defending democracy and its various derivatives does not indicate a form of governmental system, but rather the course chosen by a democracy in its efforts to protect itself. Thus, we accept Giovanni Capoccia's definition according to which defending democracy is: 'the elaboration and enactment of short-term political strategies, whether inclusive or repressive in nature, which are explicitly aimed at reacting against those political forces that exploit the rights and guarantees of democracy in order to undermine its fundamental bases' (Capoccia 2001a, p. 432). However, contrary to this definition, we believe that long term strategies should not be excluded.

This still allows for the possibility that the nature of democracy may in fact dictate the nature of its response to provocation; often, certain courses of counteraction are identified with certain types of democracies. However, for the sake of clarity and to avoid confusion, modes of response should not be part of the definition of the political system. Therefore, we shall assume that all democratic systems endeavoring to protect themselves in the face of radical and violent elements, do indeed fulfill the requirements of the general framework of defending democracy. Having said this, it should be stressed that this term alone does not suffice to understand the various types and degrees of response. Hence, we propose that the notion of the defending democracy represents a multi-dimensional space that includes belligerent (militant) as well as less belligerent (immunized) approaches. These two exemplary approaches signify ideal types, which are not necessarily concepts that exist in the real world: rather, they represent a space in which the responses of the majority of democratic polities can be found.

The basis for the operative definitions of the militant and the immunized routes of counteraction principally draws on the various theoretical references to barriers or controls used by the democracy against antagonists. However, it also derives from an inductive review of the practices of Western countries against elements constituting a threat to their regime. Therefore, we will try to offer four principal categories of controls that will later serve as the basis for the definition of the various orientations.

Legal and judicial controls

Legal and judicial controls include, *inter alia*, constitutions or statutes stipulating under what conditions partisan political activity can be restricted, as well as laws establishing which tools are legitimate in instances of anti-governmental protest, such as incitement or subversive action. Included in this category are also those legal barriers regulating the relations among the different groups in society and, in particular, controls intended to restrict racist or other expressions which may offend various social groups. The notable aspect of these barriers is that they are most often predicated on constitutional or legal frameworks and are subject to continuous judicial review. Barriers of this type carry the potential for suppressing challenges posed by anti-governmental extremist factions, but at the same time they also have the power to check and restrain governmental response to these same extremist elements, thus preventing the undermining of the democracy's ethical foundations (Capoccia 2001a).

Administrative and intelligence controls

Contrary to legal and judicial barriers, which are distinguished by a complete adherence to the framework of the rule of law (Hofnung 1991, pp. 11–20), there are more flexible measures, often extending beyond the limits of state laws. In fact, occasionally they disregard the basic liberties inherent in the democratic idea, such as civil liberty, freedom of expression and of assembly. Despite the sharp contradiction between these orientations and the liberal democratic paradigm, there is abundant testimony of their use, particularly when the polity senses its stability is in significant jeopardy (Crelinsten and Schmid 1992). Under extreme circumstances, these measures may include the use of military forces against seditious elements, although more typically the security services or secret police are assigned this responsibility.

Unlike police forces, whose actions are bound by strict codes, the secret service in democratic countries enjoys a broader field of operation. In many cases it also has access to 'grey' means of control at variance with the tools available to the police (More 1994). In Germany, for example, there is extensive public criticism of surveillance systems used by the Federal Bureau for the Protection of the Constitution (BfVS) against parties listed as constitutionally-hostile. Although these steps, in most cases, receive constitutional endorsement and judicial review, criticism has been aimed at the fact that employing undercover police against citizens may cause grave harm to the same liberties purportedly upheld by the democracy.

Additional evidence of controls of this nature can be found in those cases where the state devises a broader infrastructure with the intent of paving the way for a more forceful policy of response to seditious events. This infrastructure may include: declaring a state of emergency, adopting emergency legislation, and the use of administrative regulations and modifications of the legal process. Occasionally, it entails the institution of special courts of law whose specific role is to preside over concerns related to subversive violence and, principally, terrorists (Hofnung 1994).

Educational controls

This area is of imperative significance because, by exercising educational controls, the state is able to contend with the challenges of extremism long before they materialize into political alternatives. To be specific, with the aid of the education system and particularly, but not exclusively, civic studies, the future citizens of the state can be introduced to the key democratic notions. Moreover, in many democracies, civics education consists of a diversified curriculum based on the instruction of basic democratic rights, such as: freedom of speech, assembly, worship, privacy and the right to hold property and take political action.

In addition, most students are exposed to the formal aspect of governmental process, i.e. the constitutional and statutory processes that form the basic structure of the liberal state. The social aspect is also taught, comprising the complexity of groups in society, the rights of these groups, the prominent cleavages dividing society and the major political concerns of the day (Levinson 1999). In this fashion, students become acquainted with the guiding principles of the polity in which they live, the outlines of its institutional essentials, the problems confronting it, and the general norms of the country.

Social controls

'Civil society' is another social domain historically absent from the discourse on defending democracy. Yet, in recent years it has acquired a high profile in the discussion of factors contributing to the normal functioning of democratic polities. Although there have been some recent reservations regarding the dangers of 'uncivil society' especially in new democratic systems (e.g. Kopecký and Mudde 2002), we confine our discussion to 'pro-democratic' civil society, i.e. groups and organizations that are explicitly committed to the protection of democracy. In our view, they hold a central role in the protection of democracy (e.g. Szocs 1998).

The regulating mechanism formed by civil society is manifested in the actions of social organizations that are non-government affiliated, yet are still concerned about the expansion of extremism in society and about flagrant acts of provocation against the democratic foundations of the governing state. Civil society organizations can operate in either political or community frameworks by employing educational and informational campaigns, or they may publicly respond to acts of extremism. In certain cases, they may mobilize efforts to influence governmental authorities. In these aspects, we find an additional contribution to the strength of democratic government. Civil society enjoys both worlds: it is able to voice objection to provocateurs but it may also form a system of accountability aimed at restraining over-aggressive government responses by mobilizing public opinion and/or turning to the law in the name of upholding democracy.

In between the militant and the immunized routes

In order to classify these numerous controls and measures, and to help elucidate the ideal types of the routes of response, they are categorized according to two criteria: scope and intensity. *Scope* indicates the democracy's range of response; does the state limit its response to extremist organizations alone or does it extend policy to the social level as well? *Intensity* denotes the type of mechanisms utilized by the state. That is, does the particular democracy choose to respond to extremist challenges by using more moderate means of countermeasure, such as education, allowing more room for civil society activity and imposing minimal statutory restrictions on antagonistic elements or, on the contrary, does it employ more drastic steps, which may entail stretching the idea of the rule of law? Setting out the controls and methods employed by democracies trying to protect themselves brings into prominence the two polarities, i.e.

the militant and the immunized routes, which can be pursued in the struggle against subversive elements (see Table 5.1).

In between the two models, there is a broad continuum along which it is possible to pinpoint most democratic countries and estimate the extent of their 'militancy' or 'immunization.' Furthermore, this continuum enables a diachronic analysis of isolated cases and the estimation of single countries' movement along the time axis from one type of response to another. The militant route denotes a political system whose goals are very narrow and principally restricted to defending the state from manifestations of political extremism, incitement and violence. A state that adopts the immunized route, on the other hand, seeks to shore up its

Table 5.1 Defending democracy: the militant and the immunized route

	Defending democracy	
	Militant route	*Immunized route*
Aim	Destroying the threat of extremism	Strengthening democracy
General characteristics	Limited scope, high intensity, most of the initiative is by the state	Wider scope, low intensity, the initiative is divided between the state and the society
Legal and judiciary controls	Maximal use of the administrative means for the purpose of repressing subversive and extremist elements	Maximal use of the legal framework which corresponds with democratic and constitutional foundations and is under continuous judicial review
Administrative and intelligence controls	Wide use of regulations and continuous expansion of the legal framework. Extensive use of special police forces and security services	Minimal use of controls which do not correspond with democratic values or expand the strict boundaries of the rule of law principle. Law enforcement is mainly in the hands of the police
Educational controls	Civic education is not perceived by the state as a tool for defending the democratic regime and thus is often reduced to the procedural aspects of the governmental process	Strong emphasis on state-initiated civic education in its broader context
Social controls	Low levels of civil society activities, often due to limitations imposed by the state on such activities	High levels of civil society activities

governmental system against subversive acts of defiance, and if and when these provocations are in fact realized, it deploys defensive means that form a more comprehensive and liberal treatment of these elements.

In order to help draw comparisons among the guiding principles of each model, a medical metaphor is proposed. The militant route adopts methods of treatment targeting the symptoms of the 'illness of extremism.' These symptoms are principally political parties, radical movements and manifestations of incitement, sedition, and political violence. In order to 'get rid of the Fascist cancer,' as the adherents of the militant route aspire, particularly strong medication must be prescribed, with the result that the patient (i.e. the polity itself) will most likely suffer from severe side and after-effects. This medicinal plan includes a list of unconventional measures that circumvent standard legal and judicial processes.

The immunized route, on the other hand, assumes a more holistic view by treating both the symptoms and the illness etiology. This orientation focuses primarily on preventive medicine, with the goal of maintaining a steady stream of antibodies against the spreading of disease. This is achieved mostly by using the inculcation of democratic values and tolerance, and by providing the opportunity for civil society to take an active role in the political theatre. Nevertheless, the holistic approach does not neglect the treatment of the symptoms of the illness in the event that extremism and violence still break out. However, in this case, since we are speaking of a more immunized body, the medical measures applied are more conventional, that is, they are within legal limits and do not threaten subsequently to weaken the body.

With respect to its policy toward radical parties, the immunized route underscores the legal-judicial aspect. In other words, the state employs constitutional and statutory measures that benefit from a broad consensus and the essential principles of the rule of law in its deliberations regarding a party's disqualification or the prevention of its registration. As for extra-parliamentary movements, the immunized route renounces the approach based on the extensive use of administrative procedures, i.e. the enforcement of regulations and injunctions outlawing these movements, their definition as terrorist organizations, or restriction of the freedom of movement of their members regardless of the conventions of state criminal law. Democracies that choose the immunized route will act against subversive movements using the same practices mandated by criminal law, while also maintaining a meticulous and invariable scrutiny of the judicial authority.

In concluding, we shall argue that although in the short run, the militant course may be more effective toward various manifestations of extremism and violence, the immunized route is more effective in the long-term. This analysis is primarily based in the immunized model's strong connection to society and on the perception that in order to fight extremism successfully, its roots must first be detected. Moreover, two flaws inherent in the militant route could impair its effectiveness in the long run.

The first shortcoming is related to the aforementioned paradox, i.e. the more a democracy adopts the militant mode, the more it undermines its own principles – a fact that may eventually lead it to becoming an authoritarian regime under the name of democracy. In the case of the second drawback, the practical-tactical perspective should replace the ethical aspect. Examination of the 'militant route' from this perspective demonstrates that its effectiveness is indeed questionable. A case in point is Germany (Backes and Mudde 2000), where labeling a particular political movement as illegal may lead to a self-fulfilling prophesy. That is to say, a movement that has so far operated in public view is now forced 'to go underground' and radicalize its operations in order to maintain its goals. On the other hand, a movement that has been legally banned can occasionally assume various other guises by changing its name or the composition of its key activists and, in the long run, make things more difficult for the democracy.

A comparative analysis

In this part of the chapter, an attempt will be made to apply the aforementioned analytical framework to a comparative analysis of Germany, Israel, and the United States. These three have all confronted challenges of extremism and violence in the last few decades.[1] However, it should be noted that there are some basic differences between these polities. The most important for our discussion is the constitutional structure of each of these countries. Contrary to the US and Germany, Israel has never adopted a constitution. The state has, therefore, much more space to maneuver in its struggle with extremist and anti-democratic challenges. Moreover, a comparative examination of the American and German constitutions reveals substantial differences with regard to the idea of defending the democratic regime.

While the American constitution stresses the freedoms of the individual, the German, whilst recognizing the importance of such liberties, emphasizes the defence of a stable democratic regime and thus allows the authorities more space in their attempts to defend the state. German anxiety about the possibility of history repeating itself has been so high that, according to clause 79 (3) in the constitution (the perpetuity clause), clauses 1 (civil rights) and 20 (the democratic nature of the country) may never be amended (Finer *et al.* 1996). Furthermore, the German constitution refers to domestic emergency situations and grants the authorities permission to deal with them in a more rigid manner than other constitutions allow (Finer *et al.* 1996, p. 33; Groenewold 1992, p. 144).

We turn first to a comparative institutional analysis, that is to say the state's use of legal and judiciary controls on the one hand, and intelligence and administrative controls on the other hand. Subsequently, the discussion will continue on the social level, i.e. attempts to root democratic values in the society by means of education and the role of civil society in responding to challenges of extremism.

Legal and judiciary controls

We will first compare the paths chosen by the different states in the response to extremist parties. However, before discussing the barriers imposed by democracies on extreme parties, an extra latent structural barrier – the electoral system – should be mentioned. This barrier is not intended to block extreme parties from gaining representation. However, different electoral systems or the level of the representation threshold may become crucial variables in explaining the success or failure of parties (Sartori 1997). Therefore, it should be noted that while considering the electoral and party systems variables, the US with its strong two-party system, and Germany with its 5-per cent representation threshold, enjoy good structural protection from extreme elements in parliament. Israel with its low representation threshold (1.5 per cent) enjoys only minimal protection.

Despite the almost insurmountable blocks facing small parties in the US, a National Socialist Party (NSPA) was established and even came to the forefront of public debate in April 1977, during its efforts to march in Skokie, Illinois. The Skokie affair has major importance in this discussion since it signaled the stance of the US Judiciary towards the restrictions that should be imposed upon extremist parties. Following a long judicial discussion, in January 1978, the Illinois Supreme Court, in a seven-to-one decision, ruled in favor of the Nazi march. This held that:

> Speech can be restricted only when it interferes in a physical way with other legitimate activities; when it is thrust upon a captive audience, or when it directly incited immediate harmful conduct. Otherwise, no matter what the content of the speech, the intention of the speaker, and the impact of the speech on non captive listeners, the speech is protected under the First Amendment to the US Constitution.
> (Cohen-Almagor 1994, pp. 132–133).

In this ruling, the court reinforced the US constitutional commitment to the broadest liberal approach. This ruling was extremely important in light of the far less liberal approach of the American authorities in the 1940s and 1950s, especially towards the Communist Party.

The US liberal approach towards the NSPA might be explained by two variables: a socio-historical one, the American tradition of sanctifying the freedom of the individual, and a practical one, the fact that due to the structural barriers, the party did not stand any real chance of becoming an influential political actor. Yet, other extreme right organizations found their way into the legislature and policy-making procedures, mainly through the Republican Party (Minkenberg 1993). Despite the limited success of David Duke and other extreme right-wing leaders, the American authorities never faced a large-scale emergence of such forces and hence did not adopt any special measures to counter the phenomenon.

Although structural and social conditions in Israel and Germany themselves are hardly similar, the two countries differ dramatically from the US in two major senses. First, both countries have variations of a multi-party system and, second, both have adopted legislation aimed at preventing the representation of extreme parties in their parliaments.

Clause 21 of the German Basic Law sets very strict rules with regard to political parties that are entitled to take part in elections to the legislature. For example, the law demands that the internal organization of parties should conform to democratic principles. Moreover, parties that, by reason of their aims or the behavior of their adherents, seek to impair or abolish the free democratic basic order or to endanger the existence of the Federal Republic of Germany risk being declared unconstitutional by the Federal Constitutional Court (Finer *et al.* 1996, pp. 137–138). It should be noted here that the German state makes an official distinction between 'radicalism' and 'extremism' (either from the left or the right). Radical groups are *verfassungsfeindlich*, i.e. in opposition to the principles of the constitution, while extremists are *verfassungswidrig*, i.e. unconstitutional. Or, in the words of the *Verfassungsschutz*, radicals aim 'at one-sided solutions that go "down to the root" of certain problems, without (yet) aiming at the full or partial elimination of the free democratic order.' The latter is specific for extremists, which are also the only ones that can be outlawed by the State – non-party organizations by the Minister of Interior, political parties by the Constitutional Court.

Israel's section 7A of the Basic Law puts similar barriers in front of extremist parties. According to this section, parties may be disqualified on the grounds of denying the Jewish nature of the State of Israel, incitement to racism, the manifestation of anti-democratic sentiments (Finn 2001, p. 61). In a 2002 amendment, support for an enemy country or a terrorist organization was added (*Haaretz* 16 May 2002).

Although the German, and especially the Israeli, laws give the state the authority to ban parties, both countries have chosen to use this authority only on rare occasions in the recent decades. In post-war Germany only two parties were banned because of clause 21 – the German Communist Party and the extreme right Socialist Reich Party (SRP), both during the 1950s. The constitutional court ruled that the SRP was an unconstitutional party, which did not exhibit commitment to civil rights, the rule of law, pluralism and equal opportunities for all political actors. Consequently, the court ruled that such a party has no place in the political arena and ordered its dismantling and the confiscation of all its assets (Einhorn 1993). Similarly, in Israel since 1965, when the (Arab) Socialist Party was banned (though without any specific legal authoritarization), only two parties have been banned – the racist Kach party, led by Rabbi Meir Kahane, and its splinter Kahane is Alive, both on the grounds of being anti-democratic and racist.

Despite these party bans, both Germany and Israel demonstrate a high commitment to liberal values. Extreme right-wing parties have continued to emerge in both countries, yet the authorities and the parties committed themselves to several ground rules. In Germany, while the state did declare them extremists, which gives it the authority to infiltrate the parties, it did not initiate a banning process. From their part, the parties were very careful with their language on issues such as liberal democracy and foreigners (Minkenberg 1993). However, a major change in policy occurred in the summer of 2000, when the German state decided to initiate a process to ban the German National Democratic Party because of its alleged plan for a racist revolution. By October 2001, the Federal Constitutional Court decided to commence hearings on the issue of a possible NPD ban. The ruling stated that the petitions from the constitutional bodies were valid and contained sufficient justification for such far-reaching legal proceedings.

The banning process of a political party in Germany resembles that of Israel, yet it is much lengthier and involves the executive, parliamentary and judicial authorities, thus ensuring that the constitutional rights of the party are not undermined. However, although the formal procedure of a party ban in Israel is indeed shorter, the fact that the Supreme Court has specified very detailed guidelines for the disqualification process assures its commitment to liberal values. Moreover, Israel's attitude towards extremist parties is, in general, more pragmatic than the German one – a point which is reflected in the decision made by the state not to monitor parties that are represented in legislative bodies.

It may be concluded that the policy of the US towards extreme parties is almost irrelevant due to the structural barriers imposed. Even in cases where such parties were active, the authorities' attitude towards them tended to be very liberal and thus fitted the immunized route. In Germany and Israel, the need to defend the regime from subversive elements was more pressing and, in both countries, extremist parties were banned in accordance with constitutional and legal arrangements. Over the years, the ban weapon was used only rarely. Therefore, Israeli as well as German policies may be characterized as approaching the immunized route.

In the US and Germany, as in Israel, the struggle against extra-parliamentary movements within democratic boundaries was more difficult than coping with political parties. This was due to the simple fact that social movements do not aspire to gain parliamentary access and thus are not bound by the rules of the electoral game. Moreover, social movements, which enjoy a loose organizational structure, do not have to register and are free to act within the social sphere, and transfer input into the political arena. In the US, the activity of such movements is a central element in the political culture and is widely protected by the First Amendment of the Constitution. Thus, although such associations, in their 'uncivil' form, may present grave challenges to authorities, their important role in the American democracy makes it almost impossible to restrict their actions.

These political and cultural settings encouraged the American authorities to adhere to a liberal approach in their response to political acts of violence (Chalk 1996). Smith's description of diverse reactions against several extremist movements during the 1980s confirms this assumption. These acts proved to be successful in terms of countering terrorism (Smith 1994), and at the same time did not cross democratic boundaries. Even the anti-terrorism legislation that was passed following the Oklahoma City bombing does not seem to exceed limitations of the idea of the rule of law, especially following the assessment of its constitutionality by the Supreme Court (Andryszewski 1997). Moreover, even the reform adopted in late 1999, which was aimed at giving the FBI wider powers in responding to terrorism, did not bring a radical change in the agency's actions. According to FBI Deputy Director Robert M. Bryant, the new policy will not change the FBI's long tradition of respecting civil rights (*Washington Post*, 11 November 1999). However, following the events on September 11, 2001, the picture has changed dramatically.

Intelligence and administrative controls

Like Israel, Germany demonstrates a very different example of counter extremism policies than that of the US. The rigid policy adopted by the federal government in the 1960s engendered much criticism. Although, according to Finn, this reaction model was restrained by the constitution and thus committed to civil rights, Loewenstein argued that this policy was 'probably among the most repressive anti-terrorist legislation existing in a liberal democracy' (Finn 1991, p. 206). Such criticism emerged as a result of the emergency regulations of 1968, which gave the federal government extended authority to fight terrorism. These regulations also gave extra powers to the Federal Criminal Police Office as well as the BfVS. The left-wing terrorist attacks, which Germany had endured between 1974 and 1978, encouraged the adoption of even more rigid legislation against acts of subversive and terrorist nature. These new regulations included Penal Code 88a, according to which a crime against the constitution could result in three years' imprisonment. This law was subject to severe criticism and was invalidated in 1981. Further examples of the non-liberal character of this policy can be found in amendments 129 and 129a to the penal code, the purpose of which was to impose higher limitations on the formation of terrorist organizations. Moreover, the German government adopted the *Radikalenerlaß* (Radicals Decree or Decree against Extremism) policy, according to which: 'only those persons who can show that they are prepared at all times to uphold the free democratic basic order and actively to defend this basic order, both on and off duty, may be appointed to public service' (Finn 1991, p. 207). Consequently, this regulation prevented many Germans from being employed in the public sector and many others faced unpleasant interrogations (Finn 1991). These policies, though legally better defined than the Israeli ones, reflect a tendency to expand legal frameworks and make them highly flexible. Consequently, very often such frameworks undermine their democratic nature and tend to acquire an administrative nature (Pedahzur and Ranstorp 2001).

Over the years, Germany's model of reaction underwent several liberal reforms, a process similar to Israeli attempts to depart from its own repressive model. Examples from the 1980s and 1990s reveal that although Germany still had in its possession various means to cope with the challenges of politically motivated violence, it tended not to make extensive use of them. For example, during the 1990s only 15 radical organizations were declared illegal, while the number of extreme-right movements and organizations in 1999 stood at 134.[2] In recent years, German policy towards right-wing violent organizations has become more vigorous, yet according to representatives of the police as well as the BfVS, it is still bound by legal democratic boundaries.[3] Indeed, contrary to Israeli security forces and especially the General Security Service (GSS), which operate under a state of emergency and are allowed to act much more freely, the modus operandi of the German BfVS, as well as special police forces, corresponds much better with democratic values. These forces are subject to parliamentary, judicial and public criticism and therefore usually cope with problems of extremism and violence by employing softer tactics.

Unlike the Israeli GSS, the BfVS, which is in charge of gathering intelligence on extremist movements, is prevented from acting against them. Therefore, in addition to gathering information, the organization issues reports on extreme right-wing activities. These reports are not distributed solely to decision-makers but to the general public as well. The purpose of publishing such intelligence information is to raise public awareness about the risks that emerge from the far right and about the expanding nature of its movements. Furthermore, the special police forces that were established for the purpose of countering the neo-Nazi scene are trained to use non-violent measures in dealing with violent crowds. Actually, one of the most important tasks of these forces is an educational one, i.e. trying, by persuasive means, to prevent radical youths from committing violence.

Israel's struggle against extremism and violence, as mentioned earlier, follows a far more rigid model. This is mainly a result of the Arab–Israeli conflict. However, Jewish radicals have to face some features of this policy as well. The most interesting fact about the Israeli approach towards the right-wing militants is the lack of consistency. This non-coherent policy may be described as a pendulum policy. Most of the time, the chosen strategies can be described as rather remote from the rule of law principle. This is mainly due to the central role of the GSS and the application of different regulations against the militants, which are derived from the state of emergency and are not part of the penal code. In several instances, and especially with regard to the Kahane gang, the state of Israel did not hesitate to adopt a pure militant model. In the early 1980s, Rabbi Kahane himself was sentenced to four months administrative detention in prison, without facing accusations or standing trial. Over the years, Kahane and his followers were constant targets of the security services and were subject to many administrative measures.

In 1994, following the Massacre in the Tomb of Patriarchs that was carried out by a former follower of Kahane, Dr Baruch Goldstein, both Kach and Kahane is Alive were outlawed and declared terrorist organizations. This step was taken in accordance with the Prevention of Terrorism Ordinance (No. 33 of 1948), according to which being a member in a terrorist organization, or even delivering a speech or propaganda on behalf of such an organization, could bring severe imprisonment penalties (Cohen-Almagor 1997, pp. 85–86). This was one of the most repressive steps ever taken towards a Jewish political movement in the history of the state of Israel.

It is interesting to mention that the same authorities took a totally different route towards another Jewish terrorist organization in the same period. In early 1994, a violent religious gang, led by charismatic Rabbi Uzi Meshulam, established itself in the Rabbi's house in the city of Yahud. Although this group was referred to by the chief of police at the time, Asaf Hefetz, as the most dangerous terrorist organization Israel had ever known, the authorities decided to treat it according to the most strict boundaries of the rule of law. Hence, both the Rabbi and his followers were taken into custody following a police operation, all faced criminal charges and were sentenced to long periods in jail in accordance with the penal code. The paradoxical result was that while the Meshulam group ceased to exist, the followers of Kahane are still active, mainly in spreading his racist ideology and provoking violence against Arabs. It seems as if outlawing had almost no effect on the movement.

To conclude, both Germany and Israel have tended to put security considerations to the forefront of their counter-violence activities and, as a result, were subject to criticism concerning the offense of liberal rights. While, in recent years, both countries have been aiming to limit their response to extremism to narrow and democratically acceptable policies, both still have a long way to go. The US, on the other hand, traditionally tended to stick to the narrow interpretation of the criminal justice model and was thus much more closely related to the liberal perception. The September 11 events, however, caused a priority change in the country. Countering terrorism has become a major priority and, as a result, the Homeland Security Office was established under the President's Executive Order 13228.[4]

It seems, at this point, that despite the increasing criticism with regard to legislative initiatives such as the Patriot Act, the use of military tribunals and the extended authority given the law enforcement agencies following the attacks, the US still enjoys stronger democratic foundations than Israel or Germany. However, in light of the lack of sufficient perspective which may allow us to assess better the US counterterrorism policies following September 11, and the degree to which they correspond with constitutional boundaries, we prefer not to reach a conclusive statement at this point.

At the same time, it is important to note that even today there are strong signs that acts initiated by the State authorities, which seem to cross democratic acceptability, are subject to much social criticism, forcing the State to reconsider its policies. For example, on 9 May 2002, following loud protest by civil rights organizations, the US Justice Department's Office of the Inspector General announced that it would be conducting an inquiry into the treatment of detainees arrested and held in custody during the investigation into the September 11 attacks.[5] Hence, devastating events can push even democratic regimes to adopt policies that often do not correspond with democratic principles. However, the presence of strong democratic foundations, which are manifested in the activities of pro-democratic civil society, as well as the public, may direct the State to more acceptable models of response. The following sections of this chapter will be devoted to the role of democratic foundations in the framework of the defending democracy.

Educational controls

Most democracies acknowledge the need to socialize their citizens to the rules of the democratic game. However, for many years, civic education in the US, Germany and Israel was rather similar, i.e. the emphasis was put on structures and functions of governmental institutions. Yet, in the last few decades the education systems in many democracies, including the US and Germany, have expanded the role of civic studies and shifted the emphasis from structures and procedures to democratic and liberal values. This was a result of the increase of political apathy, low electoral turnouts and declining levels of social and political participation that have characterized many polities in recent decades. At the same time, increasing manifestations of racist, sectarian, authoritarian and anti-humanitarian values alarmed many countries in Western Europe and North America, thus sparking a renewed interest in civic education (Frazer 1999).

Both in the US and Germany, which are characterized by federal structures, authority for education rests at the state level, resulting in some variation in the curricular requirements from one locale to another. Nevertheless, the majority of German students must take civic education or social studies courses that teach them about political concepts, institutions, and processes. In the USA more than 75 per cent of students take courses in civic education or government before they graduate from high school. Moreover, all high school students in the US have at least one year of US history that includes extensive political education. In both countries, students take courses that are designed to teach about the political arena and to prepare them for their role as citizens of a democracy. As for the contents of civic classes, Hahn's conclusions were that, in upper classes, especially in Germany, students are usually exposed to more complex issues, which include the West and the Third World, theories of democracy, political parties, political participation and economic problems (Hahn 1999, pp. 235–237).

Moreover, the ministries of education in many German states, especially in the former states of East Germany (GDR), are opening the gates of the education system to civil society organizations, which work to promote tolerance and democratic values.[6] The rapid development of civic education programs in the former GDR is in line with Frazer's contention that the new regimes in Eastern Europe adopt new educational programs to enable the citizens of those countries, who were socialized to communist values, to become acquainted with democratic ones (Frazer, 1999).

Contrary to the East European countries, or the US and Germany, Israel has not adopted a clear policy regarding civic education programs. This might be a result of the dual nature of the state, on the one hand Jewish and on the other a democracy. For many years the Israeli education system was oriented toward a Zionist nationalist direction, a fact that caused the marginalization of democratic values. Even following the expansion of extremism, and its manifestations in the 1980s, it seemed almost impossible for policy makers in the country to include liberal values that could contradict the nationalistic ones in the curricula. As a result, civic education in Israel remains marginal and lacks essential democratic ideas (Pedahzur 2001). Thus, upon graduation, most of the Israeli high school students are alienated from basic democratic values (Perliger 2001), a fact which could indicate that, contrary to the US and even Germany in terms of social infrastructure, Israel is still very far from the immunized model.

Civil society

As for the role of civil society in assisting a state's move towards the immunized model, as mentioned earlier, many of the civil society organizations promote tolerance and thus assist in the immunization process of the society. These activities make it far harder for extremist political leaders and activists to mobilize wide support from the population. Moreover, an active civil society may also assist in limiting the state's response – a point demonstrated in the US example following the September 11 events.[7]

Both in the German and US experiences of recent years, examples may be found of dynamic civil activity regarding challenges of an extremist nature. Following the success of the German People's Union (DVU) in the Sachsen-Anhalt elections in April, 1998, the German post office workers union asked the federal government to find ways to prevent the use of the German postal system in delivering racist mail. This step was taken before the national elections of September 1998 and reflected fear of the possibility that the party would enter the national parliament. Prior to the 1998 elections, many members of parliament (MPs) were addressed by the Organization of Christian Churches in Germany, which asked politicians not to use xenophobic rhetoric during the election campaign. Moreover, both the employers and the employees unions in Berlin asked their members not to vote for extreme right parties. They also asked them to act openly to stem the rising violence against foreigners.[8] Moreover, the *Lichterketten* demonstrations, where thousands of Germans formed human chains holding candles against racism, were examples of pro-democratic activity not only among institutionalized civil society organizations, but also at the grassroots level.

The American tradition of a strong civil society also found its expression in the struggle against racism and extremism. Such activity may be detected in all forms and shapes of civil society, beginning with grassroots activity inside the local community and ending with the continuous activities of strong interest groups. For example, when in New Town, Pennsylvania, violent extreme-right activists broke a window because a Hanukkah Menorah stood behind it, the local community organized itself and Menorahs were placed in almost every house in the neighborhood. A similar example might be found in the neo-Nazi graffiti attack in the District of Columbia. When the newspapers wrote that the city did not have enough resources to clean up the desecration, the local communities decided to take on this task and erased these drawings themselves (Porat *et al.* 1998).

Yet, according to longstanding American tradition, the most active members in American civil society are the more institutionalized organizations, especially interest groups (see also Chapters 2 and 8). Among the most prominent groups acting against racism, xenophobia and hate crimes are the Anti-Defamation League (ADL), the American Jewish Committee, the Southern Poverty Law Center, as well as many interest groups that represent other minorities. In such cases, the groups themselves bring society closer to the state by initiating joint activities. In 1998, the ADL cooperated with the state of New Jersey in proposing rewards for those who exposed racist graffiti perpetrators. In 1999, the same organization, jointly with the NYC police department, published a handbook for local communities. The purpose of the book was to help the members of the community to react to racist violence (ADL 1999). These organizations do not restrict themselves to local activities, but aim at the legislative level as well. The 'hate crimes' laws adopted by many states in the US are a direct consequence of the ADL's efforts to find a way to fight racist and xenophobic crimes within the constitutional boundaries, and a concentrated effort of the organization to establish lobbies to support such legislation (ADL 1999).

In Israel, civil society organizations, and especially pro-democratic ones, are still a new phenomenon (Ben-Eliezer 1999; Yishai 1998a,b). For many years the state dominated the social sphere and thus prevented the emergence of a powerful civil society. However, in recent years the picture has changed and there is a new opportunity structure for such organizations. Indeed, in the last decade, different types of pro-democratic organizations can be traced in the country. Many of these organizations – such as the Adam School, the Institute for Democratic Education and the Foundations Institute – focus on the promotion of liberal values mainly through democracy education, while others, and especially the Association for Civil Rights, are confronting the state's non-liberal policies and are trying to limit its response to democratic boundaries.

In conclusion, a comparison between the cases of the US, Germany and Israel reveals that civil society in the US is highly institutionalized and fulfills all its functions in assisting the defence of democracy. In Germany, and especially in the former GDR states, civil society has played a larger part over the years and is also becoming an essential element in the struggle to protect democracy. In Israel, on the other hand, civil society has the potential to attain such a role, yet there still is a long way to go before this will actually be achieved.

Conclusions

What, therefore, are the conceptual and empirical conclusions to be drawn from this study? And which questions are still left unanswered?

Earlier, we discussed the terms 'militant democracy' and 'defending democracy' used by both scholars and policymakers. These ambiguous terms ultimately rely on one basic assumption, i.e. democracy has the right to defend itself from its adversaries. In light of the events of the twentieth century, the most important enemy appears to be anti-democratic political parties. Yet, a closer look at the challenges facing democratic systems of governance today reveals a more intricate picture: whilst certain political parties pose a danger to the stability of these systems, there are also major threats from radical or revolutionary extra-parliamentary movements and terrorist organizations. Furthermore, the formal nature of the definitions of militant democracy and defending democracy, stresses the state institutions' judicial means in their struggle with anti-democratic challenges. This limits the discourse to the paradoxes generated by the need for democratic polities to defend themselves and which, in their very efforts to do so, are liable to undermine the ethical foundations on which they are structured.

In an attempt to address the complexity of challenges facing the self-defending democratic polity, we expanded the notion of defending democracy beyond conventional definitions, mainly by supplementing the formal-institutional perspective with a social one. The rationale was that simply investigating the measures employed by the state while dealing with defiant elements seemed inadequate when these elements were already highly visible. Defending democracy should thus be perceived as a more comprehensive term, which also involves actions effected in the political and social spheres, designed to reinforce the democratic bases of society and to reduce the mobilizing potential of extremist parties and movements. Furthermore, including the social perspective in this analysis also enables more penetrating scrutiny of the defending democracy paradox and suggests possible ways for its resolution. One of our fundamental assumptions is that as society enjoys a more stable democratic underlying social structure, the intensity of the extremist threat aimed at the state is reduced, and the inclination of state authorities to cross democratically-acceptable boundaries in their struggle against provocative elements is also weakened.

To facilitate the use of the concept of the defending democracy for analytical purposes, we proposed two ideal types: the militant and the immunizing routes. These concepts are structured on both institutional and social components, forming a continuum. Presenting these types imparts the notion of the defending democracy with a dynamic aspect. It enables examination of the change of how a certain country's confrontation with extremist phenomena changes over time, and in fact provides the means for comparison across several countries.

The use of the analytical framework yielded some interesting findings in the comparative analysis. Positioning the three countries on the continuum between the militant and the immunized models indicated that in any aspect of the analysis, and even following the September 11 events, the US is still the closest to the immunized ideal. Although the US is not unpolluted by manifestations of extremism and violence, a close look at its political culture reveals a relatively high commitment to democratic principles. Moreover, civil society, which is an essential element of American political life, has a major role in responding to extremist threats and actually helps in controlling the levels of extremism within society as well as challenges to the state. Analysis of the institutional response to extreme parties reveals high levels of restraint and commitment to the idea of the rule of law. Even in the case of terrorism, especially before 2001, the State response was confined to strict constitutional boundaries. It can thus be concluded that the danger that American democracy will become a victim of emerging extremist forces, or of its own actions, is relatively low. However, there is a need to look into the US example again, once a clearer perspective is attained about the September 11 attacks.

Generally, Germany can be described as located in between the militant and the immunized models. However, we should make a distinction between the Western states, where democracy has been entrenched since the end of World War II, and states that were part of the GDR and are still going through processes of democratization. Many German citizens lived under non-democratic regimes during the twentieth century. Consequently, the federal government, the state administrations, and many of the emerging civil society organizations are committed to the goal of establishing a democratic political culture in the country. Thus, issues such as tolerance and democracy have become an integral part of the education process. As for the state response to extreme parties and violent racist manifestations, a comparison between the policies that were employed by the state in the period 1950–80 with those of the 1990s reveals a slow but continuous process of liberalization. Despite the emergence of right-wing violence in many states of the former GDR, as well as in some states of former West Germany, the responsible intelligence authorities usually have refrained from crossing German constitutional boundaries and do not use repressive means against the perpetrators. Even the move to ban the NPD cannot be regarded as crossing the boundaries of democratic acceptability. In order to ban the party, the state will have to go through a long legal process and to show solid proof that this party is indeed unconstitutional, a rather difficult task.

The Israeli case is much more complicated. A first look at the response to extreme parties and violent organizations indicates that the state has come a long way in the last 50 years and is moving to the immunized model. This change can be accounted for by the increased awareness of the judiciary and part of the political elite of the importance of democratic values. This awareness was reinforced by the court's decision to allow Baruch Marzel, the former leader of Kach, to take part in the 2003 elections as a member of the new Herut party. However, a close look at the social sphere reveals that Israeli society still lacks a solid liberal infrastructure and that the state is largely responsible for this. The complicated nature of Israel as a Jewish and as a democratic state created two sets of education policies, one Jewish-nationalistic and the other more democratic. An analysis of the attempts to increase the role of democratic values in the education system reveals that most policy makers were against such a move. This fact kept civic education, as well as other courses that could help students acquire democratic values, in a very marginal position. Moreover, for many years Israel's image as a centralist state prevented civil society from performing its role in helping to make democracy work. The recent signs of an emergence of a civic society may indicate that the social sphere in Israel is becoming more involved in protecting the democratic regime, yet these are only (first) initial intimations. Thus, one has to conclude that though it did depart from the militant model, Israeli democracy is still far from immunized and, as a result, is much more vulnerable both to manifestations of extremism and the response to them.

Notes

1 There are some basic differences between the extreme-right threats in the three countries. These differences are taken into account in the comparative analysis.
2 http://www.tau.ac.il/Anti-Semitism/asw99–2000/germany.htm
3 Personal interview with Officer Zimmerman, Mega Task Force, Franfurt-Oder, 23.10.2000; Personal interview with Dr Annegret Ortling and Mr Jorg Milbradt, BfV, Ministerium des Innern, Land Brandenburg. 24.10.2000.
4 http://www.fbi.gov/congress/congress02/caruso032102.htm
5 http://www.amnesty-usa.org/usacrisis/
6 From an interview with Mr. Karsten Friedel, coordinator, Tolerantes Benadenburg. 23.10.2000.
7 For description of some of the civil society organizations active in this arena and their activities, see http://jurist.law.pitt.edu/terrorism/terrorism3b.htm# Groups
8 http://www.tau.ac.il/Anti-Semitism/asw98–9/germany.htm

Bibliography

ADL (1997) *Hate Crimes Laws*. New York: Anti-Defamation League.
ADL (1999) *Security For Community Institutions. A Handbook*. New York: Anti-Defamation League.
Andryszewski, T. (1997) *The Militia Movement in America*, Brookfield: Milbrook.
Backes, U. and Mudde, C. (2000) 'Germany: extremism without successful parties', *Parliamentary Affairs* 53, 3: 457–468.
Ben-Eliezer, U. (1999) 'Is civil society emerging in Israel? Politics and identity in the new associations', *Israeli Sociology* 2, 1: 51–98.
Cappocia, G. (2001a) 'Defending democracy: strategies of reaction to political extremism in inter-war Europe', *European Journal of Political Research* 39, 4: 431–460.
Cappocia, G. (2001b) 'Repression, incorporation, lustration, education: how democracies react to their enemies. Towards a theoretical framework for the comparative analysis of defense of democracy', Paper presented at the ECPR Joint Sessions of Workshops, Grenoble, 6–11 April.
Chalk, P. (1995) 'The liberal democratic response to terrorism', *Terrorism and Political Violence* 7, 4: 10–44.
Chalk, P. (1996) *West European Terrorism and Counter-Terrorism: The Evolving Dynamic*, Basingstoke: Macmillan.
Cohen-Almagor, R. (1994) *The Boundaries of Liberty and Tolerance in the Struggle against Kahanism in Israel*, Gainesville: University Press of Florida.
Cohen-Almagor, R. (1997) 'Combating right-wing political extremism in Israel: Critical Appraisal', *Terrorism and Political Violence*, 9, 4: 82–105.
Crelinsten, R.D. and Schmid A.P. (1992) 'Western responses to terrorism: A twenty-five year balance sheet', *Terrorism and Political Violence* 4, 4: 307–340.
Einhorn, T. (1993) *Statutory Proscription of Political Parties that have Racist Platforms: Article 7A of the Basic Law: Ha-Knesset*, Jerusalem: The Israeli Association for Parliamentary Issues.
Elmar, H.M. (1987) *The Democratic Tradition: Four German Constitutions*, Leamington: Berg.
Finer, S.E., Bogdanor, V. and Rudden, B. (1996) *Comparing Constitutions*, Oxford: Clarendon.

Finn, J.E. (2001) 'Electoral regimes and the proscription of anti-democratic parties', in Rapaport, D.C. and Weinberg, L. (eds) *The Democratic Experience and Political Violence*, London: Frank Cass, pp. 51–77.

Finn, J.E. (1991) *Constitutions in Crisis: Political Violence and the Rule of Law*, New York: Oxford University Press.

Frazer, E. (1999) 'Introduction: the idea of political education', *Oxford Review of Education* 25, 1–2: 5–22.

Groenewold, K. (1992) 'The German Republic's response and civil liberties', *Terrorism and Political Violence* 4, 4: 136–150.

Hahn, C.L. (1999) 'Citizenship education: an empirical study of policy, practices and outcome', *Oxford Review of Education* 25, 1–2: 235–237.

Hofnung, M. (1991) *Israel – State Security vs. Rule of Law, 1948–1991*, Jerusalem: Nevo (Hebrew).

Hofnung, M. (1994) 'State of emergency and ethnic conflict in liberal democracies: Great Britain and Israel', *Terrorism and Political Violence*, 6, 3: 340–365.

Horowitz, D. and Lissak, M. (1990) *Trouble in Utopia: The Overburdened Polity in Israel*, Tel-Aviv: Am-Oved.

Ignazi, P. (1999) 'Reaction to thoughts by Giovanni Capoccia on Doctoral Research in Progress', *ECPR News*, 10, 3: 39.

Kopecký, P. and Mudde, C. (eds.) (2002) *Uncivil Society? Contentious Politics in Post-Communist Europe*, London: Routledge.

Levinson, M. (1999) 'Liberalism, pluralism and political education: paradox or paradigm?', *Oxford Review of Education* 25, 1–2: 39–58.

Loewenstein, K. (1937a) 'Militant democracy and fundamental rights, I', *American Political Science Review* 31, 3: 417–432.

Loewenstein, K. (1937b) 'Militant democracy and fundamental rights, II', *American Political Science Review* 31, 4: 638–658.

Loewenstein, K. (1938a) 'Legislative control of political extremism in European democracies I', *Columbia Law Review* 38: 591–622.

Loewenstein, K. (1938b) 'Legislative control of political extremism in European democracies II', *Columbia Law Review* 38: 725–774.

Minkenberg, M. (1993) 'The new right in comparative perspective: the USA and Germany', *Cornell Western Societies Papers* 32: 40–46.

More, G. (1994) 'Undercover surveillance of the Republikaner Party: protecting a militant democracy or discrediting a political rival', *German Politics* 3, 2: 284–292.

Pedahzur, A. (2001) 'The paradox of civic education in non-liberal democracies: the case of Israel', *Journal of Education Policy* 16, 5: 413–430.

Pedahzur, A. and Ranstorp, M. (2001) 'A tertiary model for countering terrorism in liberal democracies: the case of Israel', *Terrorism and Political Violence* 13, 2: 1–26.

Perliger, A. (2001) 'Political attitudes and behaviors as a result of civic education, Haifa: Department of Political Science, unpublished MA dissertation.

Popper, K. (1962) *The Open Society and its Enemies*, London: Routledge and Kegan Paul. Vols. I, II.

Porat, D., Vago, R. and Shtauber R. (eds.) (1998) *Anti-Semitism and Radical Movements in the World: Data, Characteristics and Estimations*, Tel Aviv: Ramot–Tel-Aviv University (Hebrew).

Rubinstein, A. (1991) *The Constitutional Law/Legislation of the State of Israel*, Jerusalem: Shoken (Hebrew).

Sartori, G. (1997) *Comparative Constitutional Engineering: An Inquiry into Structures, Incentives and Outcomes*, New York: New York University Press.

Smith, B.L. (1994) *Terrorism in America: Pipe Bombs and Pipe Dreams*, Albany: State University of New York Press.

Szocs, L. (1998) 'A tale of the unexpected: the extreme right vis-à-vis democracy in post-communist Hungary', *Ethnic and Racial Studies* 21, 6: 1096–1115.

Tocqueville, A. (1979) *De La Democratie en Amerique*, Jerusalem: Bialik Institute.

Yishai, Y. (1998a) *Civilian Society in Israel towards the Year 2000 – Between State and Society*. Jerusalem: Paul Baerward School of Social Work.

Yishai, Y. (1998b) 'Civil society in transition: interest politics in Israel', *Annals of the American Association for Political and Social Sciences* 555: 147–162.

6 Institutional inclusion and exclusion of extreme right parties[1]

Laurent Kestel and Laurent Godmer

Introduction

Since the 1980s, many parliamentary elections in different European countries have clearly demonstrated that the extreme right is making an electoral revival. The most dramatic break with the post-1945 European tradition concerns the fact that, in some cases, extreme-right parties have become coalition partners with conservative parties in national government.

The first country to have integrated the extreme right at the national level was Italy in 1994, followed by Austria (2000), Denmark (2001), and populist right parties entered governing coalitions in both Portugal and the Netherlands during 2002. However, whilst the extreme right remains powerful in other countries (especially France and Belgium), it has never become part of any governing coalition (although the National Front (FN) has briefly shared power with the mainstream right in some localities in the past).

The existing literature on extreme-right parties either ignores or fails to account adequately for this pattern of integration or non-integration. The central point of this chapter, therefore, is to show that institutional integration – defined as the participation at any level in governing alliances – of the extreme right within the national political market is a function of its degree of inclusion in regional parliaments, particularly through more or less transparent coalitional practices. The notion of a peripheral coalitional market allows us to emphasize the coherence of the German model of exclusive oligopoly, as well as the Austrian model of maximum institutional inclusion of the extreme right. Finally, the French case serves as an experimental field for the analytical scheme which is developed in relation to these two dichotomised models. We will particularly focus our observations on the way different democratic systems and sub-systems (especially in France) have reacted to the extremist electoral breakthrough without 'de-democratizing' themselves either by a total exclusion of such fringe parties, or by their integration into regional and national governments.

A theory of coalitional political markets

The fact that there is a differentiated integration of the extreme right parties within the diverse national political markets (i.e. central as well as peripheral markets) allows us to understand better the institutionalization mechanisms of these parties.

First, two 'substantialistic' biases have to be avoided. One concerns seeing political parties as a unified, homogeneous 'whole', manipulating the same 'symbolic goods' (Bourdieu 2000) (which is implied by the common essentialist conception of ideology), with the same practices in the different political markets. Second, one should not forget the existence of different political fields, i.e. the national political field and peripheral political fields. Whilst there has undoubtedly been a homogenization of these two categories of markets over the years (Gaxie and Lehingue 1984), this does not mean that one can neglect the differentiated distribution of political practices (such as demonstrations) and political products (programmes, discourse) on these markets. 'The political system does not present itself as a compact, homogeneous block [...] ruled by a monolithic order, rather it is a structured and stratified ensemble, formed with heterogeneous elements, sometimes pulled towards the centre, but sometimes pushed towards the periphery.' (Chevallier 1985, pp. 107–108)

Analysing the integration attempts of extreme-right parties within these different markets forces us to raise the issue of the differentiated cost of entry in these markets. Our own observation is that research in political sociology and political science studies tend excessively to focus on central political markets. We aim to show that the integration of the extreme right – or its exclusion – derives from its position within the peripheral coalitional markets.

Since extreme right parties are almost never in a position to conquer major power positions, their institutional integration requires a more or less open coalition with other political groups, mostly conservative ones (even though groups with other political complexions may be involved). Indeed, the historian Robert Paxton has observed that 'extreme right activism, in the twentieth century, never succeeded without the help, or at least the complicity, of the conservative elites' (Paxton 1997, pp. 21–22). The entry into the Austrian national government by leaders of the Austrian Freedom Party (FPÖ) in 2000 vividly illustrates the importance of conservative collaboration. However, the emergence of extreme right parliamentary groups in regional assemblies poses questions for all the actors in the political system – not just conservatives.

This is the reason why we use the notion of a coalitional political market, empirically defined as a space of possibilities that can provide either symbolic goods (such as institutional recognition) or positional ones (i.e. access to diverse degrees of power). This coalitional market – mostly regional and national coalitions in our research – is primarily structured around two axes: maximization of benefits in terms of access to 'power and representation positions', and 'political positions' (Godmer and Kestel 2001). These are produced by opinion makers who define the possibilities of extreme right representatives entering coalitional markets – a 'symbolic' aspect that is not really covered by the coalition-building theorists who emphasize ideological linkages without considering the internal borders drawn by the opinion makers within political markets (Bourdieu 1982).

With the help of this conceptual tool, which will be further refined in the light of discussion of empirical examples, it is possible to study the Austrian case, which is the ideal type of a high level of integration of an extreme-right party into an open peripheral coalitional market, and the German case, which is the counter-model of the 'containment' of the extreme right. These two case studies will allow us to use the two paradigms so as to analyse precisely the French model which we qualify as an 'evolving' one as it is essentially a model of progressive exclusion of the major extreme-right party from peripheral coalitional markets.

The German model: exclusionary oligopoly

In the Federal Republic of Germany, there was no possible entry to the regional coalition market for successive extreme-right parties after the first post-war Bundestag elections in 1949. Whilst there was some porosity on the fringes of the Liberals (FDP) and the Christian Democrats (CDU/CSU), which allowed some lower-ranking ex-members of the NSDAP to start a new regional, even national, political career, extreme-right parties were completely excluded from all levels of government. The regulation of coalitional markets was directly linked to the construction of a new democracy that sought actively to protect the Basic Law and democratic parties (e.g. *Parteiengesetz* in 1967). The most famous example of constitutional-regulatory control is the proscription of the clearly Nazi Socialist Reich Party (SRP) in 1952 by the Federal Constitutional Court, which led to the dismantling of the SRP parliamentary groups in the Bundestag and in the Lower-Saxon Land parliament.

One can characterize the German coalitional market as an oligopoly and as an exclusive (or closed autarchic) space. A high level of entry costs means broad consensus. This has led to the exclusion of all the major extreme right regional electoral groups from all regional governments since the Second World War. Even a 'conservative' region like Baden-Württemberg was obliged, according to this logic, to set up a grand coalition between the CDU and the Social Democrats (SPD) to keep out the rise of the Republicans (REP) in the early 1990s. This example remains one of the best illustrations of a regulation that does not permit any exceptions and which symbolizes a high level of nationally-defined discipline. The democratic parties of the 'oligopoly' (CDU, FDP, SPD and, since the 1980s, the

Greens) effectively shun all coalition possibilities with the extreme right (Schmidt 1997). This can be called, after the United States' foreign policy during the cold war, a 'containment' policy (which is incidentally very different from a destructive strategy).

The Austrian model: maximum integration

The Austrian way of dealing with the extreme right parties in regional parliaments is the exact opposite of the German model. The ubiquitous figure of Jörg Haider, *Landeshauptmann* (regional governor) of Carinthia (1989–91 and 1999–2004) and former federal president of the FPÖ (1986–2000) embodies this fundamental difference compared with the German system. The Austrian political system is the perfect example of a coalitional market that is regionally and nationally unified according to an oligopoly logic that is absolutely inclusive, in the sense that there is no differentiation between extremist and democratic political parties. The major extreme right parties, the post-1945 Union of Independents (VdU) and its successor the FPÖ, have been permanently represented in national and regional parliaments since 1948 and have been widely accepted as coalition partners (Höbelt 1999, Gerlich and Müller 1983). Indeed, Austrian regional coalition governments have defied the classical laws of coalition building, such as the 'minimum winning coalition' and 'ideological proximity' for six decades since 1945.

For three decades, this participation in regional governments was relatively hidden because the FPÖ's weak position did not allow it to have many ministers. Even support for the national coalition governments of Socialist (SPÖ) chancellors Kreisky and Sinowatz between 1971 and 1986 (especially from 1983 to 1986) aroused little comment. The high level of acceptability of extreme-right parties and leaders (who included former Nazis) was largely due to a more 'tolerant' view of the former collaborators of the Third Reich. This was, in part, the result of the peculiar geopolitical situation of the small Austrian Republic on the border of the communist block, which favoured internal political 'pacification'. Moreover, the 1938 *Anschluß* was typically portrayed as German annexation, which allowed official discourses to position the country on the side of the 'victims' of the Second World War. The official radicalization (1987–2000) of the FPÖ under the direction of Jörg Haider led to an 'Ausgrenzung' policy at national level, i.e. a 'strategy of the incumbent and of the two smaller opposition parties oriented towards the exclusion of Jörg Haider from' the federal government (Puntscher-Riekmann 1999, pp. 78–79). Nevertheless, even when Haider himself was obliged to resign from his position as *Landeshauptmann* in 1991, he still retained the regional vice-president position (1991–2) (Kräh 1996, p. 282). And whilst he did not become part of the national ÖVP-FPÖ coalitions in 2000, several leading members of his party entered the Cabinet.

Of great interest is the process of homogenization that occurred in

Austria and Germany. Indeed, the rules governing the regional coalitional markets historically tended to be similar to those affecting the national market. The huge difference is that in Germany, the homogenization – set up in the 1950s and never questioned – was to exclude definitively the extreme right from coalitions, thereby generating an invisible wall between *representation*, which is largely accepted for the successive extreme-right parties, and *government*, which is strictly reserved for an oligopoly of democratic 'anti-extremist' political parties (i.e. refusing any kind of alliance and rapprochement with extreme groups or parties). On the other hand, in Austria, the FPÖ has been present in almost all the regional governments since the 1970s. The result of this particularly open consociational, cooperation-based system is that the FPÖ has governed not just with the conservative ÖVP, but even with the socialist SPÖ (for instance in the famous Haider-led Carinthian government)

Although the FPÖ faces ideological hostility in some areas (such as in the Vienna region), in general the hurdle it needs to cross to enter government is not ideological. In practice, the issue is more related to levels of support: first, a party needs to cross the electoral threshold (normally 4 per cent of the regional vote), and second it needs to pass an internal threshold that technically justifies a presence in a regional government (generally only a little more than 10 per cent). Needless to say, such a logic prevails in an even more organized way at local level (in many regions, it is even compulsory to integrate important parties in local government). In fact, it can be assumed that 'Haiderization' is just the progressive recognition of deep-rooted regional rules.

France: between co-operation and distinction

Our main objective is to understand how the FN leaders, especially Jean-Marie Le Pen who has come to symbolize the party, have envisaged their relation with the political system. These relations are viewed through the dialectic of distinction and cooperation. In this perspective, 'cooperation' may be defined as participation in the political game, i.e.:

- Minimal acceptance of the democratic rules of the game (especially contesting different elections)
- Action in the current political sphere: namely, positioning on key issues, events, and the quest for media coverage.

'Distinction' may be conceived as:

- A political resource (objectively oriented) which results from differentiation from rival products.
- The main resource of a political entrepreneur excluded from the coalitional market (i.e. from elected positions) who tries to distinguish

himself/herself is mostly a *discursive* one. A charismatic leader such as Jean-Marie Le Pen uses (and abuses) a common-sense rhetoric, typically portraying himself as a true man of 'the people', though sometimes using explicit homophobic, sexist and racist metaphors, etc (Taguieff 1984; Wahnich *et al.* 1997).

However, relations between the FN and the political system must also take into account the interactions with the other actors in the political field. That is the reason why we insist on the fact that this is a highly *constrained* relation: the FN leaders can never totally control interactions with other actors (for instance, the FN has been classified as an extreme-right party by opponents, which has had important consequences, including encouraging radical elements within the party to adopt a higher profile, containment by the other parties, etc). The analysis of relations between the FN and the political system thus raises Carl Schmitt's classic friend–enemy distinction (Schmitt 1962). More precisely, the heart of the matter lies in the process of *designation* and *definition* (Bourdieu 1982) of the FN within the political system as a whole. The struggle for a legitimate definition of this party is a discursive one (Edelman 1991). It produces discourses with the goal of modifying common representations of the National Front. However, it is also a practical struggle, i.e. the product of interactions, of a political context, and of the practices of actors involved in the political game.

What follows is a brief section that outlines the sudden emergence of the FN as a political force. The next section shows how the FN was progressively excluded from any kind of participation in the political game. The third and final section takes into account the fact that the diverse electoral laws produced a double party system (Parodi 1997), allowing some parties which were not part of alliance systems (namely the Greens and the FN) to obtain elective mandates to reward their political staff.

The entry of the FN into the political arena

Founded on 5 October 1972, the FN was an attempt to federate the different components of the extreme right into a single organization. It was a *sociation* (Weber 1965, p. 78) of the neo-fascist New Order (ON), former 'Poujadists', and nostalgics for *Algérie française* gathered around Jean-Marie Le Pen (Camus 1996). But this first *sociation* failed after the FN's dismal showing in the 1973 legislative elections, which resulted in most ON leaders leaving the FN to found the Party of New Forces (PFN). This seemed to leave the extreme-right even more organizationally diverse than before, with numerous monarchist, populist, 'solidarist', and neo-fascist movements (Camus and Monzat 1992, Algazy 1984). All this changed when the FN suddenly experienced an increase in electoral support in some localities during 1982–3 (especially the election of Jean-Pierre Stirbois, Secretary-General of the party as deputy-Mayor of Dreux, partly helped by support from local mainstream right).

The FN had produced for several years a discourse based on anti-immigration positions, a supply-side oriented economic programme, and violent anti-communism. Therefore, it can be said that the symbolic goods specifically attributed to the extreme right (ethnic nationalism in particular) have been in the hands of the FN leader since the beginning of the 1980s. The permanence of that status was facilitated by the 'counter-societal' aspects of the FN (Askolovitch 1999, p. 147), publicly known through its two major annual meetings in Paris, on 1 May (to celebrate Joan of Arc) and in September the 'Blue-White-Red' (BBR) fair. After its 1983 electoral breakthrough, no other political grouping managed successfully to contest FN's monopoly of representation of that political sector. As a consequence, the FN was to face a high number of splits, but has always kept its dominant position as *the* party of the extreme right.

From quasi-alliance to exclusion: the FN facing progressively regulated coalitional markets

Despite its ability to structure positions around its specific symbolic goods, the FN has been progressively excluded from the *central coalitional market*. On the eve of the 1980s, the FN had acquired a monopolistic situation as far as 'extreme right' topical symbolic goods were concerned. This space was all the more important as it gave rise to particular attitudes of the 'parliamentary' parties and major mobilizations (such as anti-racist demonstrations and the creation of SOS-Racism), the raison d'être of which was, in fact, the proscription of the FN. The electoral rise of the president of the FN was not essentially the result of his own ability to become the leader of the extreme right nor by his personal charisma, which is a typical 'screen concept' (Bourdieu 1982, p. 152). Such a success was, on the contrary, the outcome of a fight over the monopoly of representation of a political sector. The emergence of the FN obliged the main actors of national political life to take part in a struggle – one of the stakes of which was to *define* the FN. The practical consequences of such a definition was the inclusion or the exclusion of the FN from political coalitional markets.

To a certain extent, the future of the FN was decided in Dreux in 1983, when the local Gaullist Rally for the Republic (RPR) merged its municipal list with the one led by Stirbois (Pons 1983). After the victory of the RPR-FN coalition, in numerous social fields (the media, universities, and the political field) agents defined their position with regard to the electoral development of Le Pen's party.[2] Many authors have emphasized the existence of media-electoral windows of opportunities to explain the success of the Front (Birenbaum 1992; Perrineau 1998a; Marcus 1995). The televised performances of Le Pen, local electoral breakthroughs (Molfessis 1989;

Perrineau 1998a; Mayer 1999) and the structuring of the 'symbolic goods' market by imposing immigration and insecurity in the political debate were apparently among the main key success factors of the FN. They were obviously reinforced by the failure of the Socialist Party (PS)-Communist Party (PCF)-led coalition government to tackle unemployment and other problems, and their backtracking on much of their 1981 left-wing programme.

Agenda-setting of the FN's symbolic goods by mainstream parties (mostly the conservative right) transformed the 'symbolic goods market' for the FN. Le Pen's success was indeed largely based on the porosity between the programmes of the right and the FN parties, especially as regards immigration and insecurity issues. For instance, in mid-December 1984 at the RPR Grenoble convention, party leaders agreed on the principle of 'returning unemployed immigrant workers' (Letigre 1988, p. 114). The RPR-Union for French Democracy (UDF) 1986 programme 'used the popular stereotypes: foreigners abusing benefits from the Social Security [...], are favoured in social housing attribution and are more often delinquent than the French. The spirit of the project insisted on the right and duty of the French to protect their cultural identity, sole condition for the country's survival' (Gastaud 2000, p. 211).

The political consequence was the proposed legal reform of the Code on Nationality (which implied a 'voluntary' dimension instead of automatic naturalization), first promoted by Jean-Claude Gaudin, President of the Provence region (with a right-FN regional 'government') and of the UDF national parliamentary group (Gastaud 2000). Although numerous protests blocked the project in 1987, it was passed in 1993 (and modified by the left government in 1997). Another side effect of the FN's symbolic upheaval was the reactivation of the anti-racist laws. The Gayssot Law of 1990 mostly reinforced the 'Pleven Law' of 1972. However, implementation limited the impact of this legal instrument, since very few people were condemned: in 1993, for example, there were only two cases, whereas there were 2324 trials in the United Kingdom for racial discrimination (Wieviorka 1998, p. 89). In short, it is obvious that during the last two decades of the twentieth century, particularly over the issue of nationality, the FN played a major role. Le Pen analysed this situation in 1987: 'I am in a way the centre of the political life, everyone situating himself in relation to me and to my declarations on all major current issues' (quoted by Birenbaum 1992, p. 115). Widespread reactions to his surprisingly good national score of 14.3 per cent in the first ballot of the 1988 presidential election confirmed that status.

In the early 1980s, the FN had been hampered in local elections because its organizational weaknesses did not allow it to present lists in the biggest cities. It could obtain isolated good results though, for instance in Paris's 20th arrondissement where Le Pen gathered more than 11 per cent of the vote in 1983. More importantly, the 16.7 per cent won by Stirbois's list in

Dreux and its successful alliance tended to legitimize the FN as a player in the political field. Further election gains added fuel to the fire. This inevitably led to debates within the mainstream right parties about relations with the FN (*La Lettre de la nation*, 16 February 1985).

Within the UDF, there was a division between the centrists and the liberals, with Pierre Méhaignerie considering Le Pen as an 'adversary' and Jean-Claude Gaudin (Republican Party, PR) as a competitor – the latter view could involve cooperation in the right circumstances – usually where the FN was relatively strong (*Libération*, 22 February 1985). The case of Dreux shows that there was also a division within the RPR: its president, Jacques Chirac (1976–94), refused any type of alliance with the extreme right (Ysmal 1984), but some others were willing to consider local understandings. This was especially true of Charles Pasqua, co-founder of the RPR in 1976, who commented that 'local elections concern our local instances and not the central committee of the RPR [...] If they consider this must be done to get rid of the communists, they do it' (*Le Monde*, 2 November 1983). Similarly, Jacques Toubon, Secretary-General of the party, asserted, in an even clearer way: 'The federations will be free to do want they want. The RPR does not have any hostility towards the National Front' (*La Lettre de la Nation*, February 1985).

Only leaders of the National Centre of Independents and Peasants (CNIP) showed relatively clear support for an understanding with the FN. Two CNIP leaders, Pierre Sergent and Bernard Antony, even became FN leaders after 1984. CNIP President, Philippe Malaud (1980–7), and Michel Junot promoted a real alliance on the national level with the FN, and the CNIP Mayor of Nice, Jacques Médecin, supported the FN in a local context (*Libération*, 27 February 1984). Malaud opposed the tendency of 'numerous UDF as well as RPR leaders to refuse any negotiation and alliance with the FN' (*Quotidien de Paris*, 29 June 1984). However, the CNIP in general was a relatively small party, and its leadership too weak to impose a uniform line.

The proportional representation system chosen for the legislative elections of March 1986 allowed the creation of an FN parliamentary group. With 9.8 per cent of the national vote, in coalition with the CNIP and the Committees of Republican Action (CAR) led by the ex-RPR Bruno Mégret, the FN obtained 35 MPs. But the right parties had an absolute majority and the question of support from the FN was not raised. Under the direction of Le Pen, the National Rally (RN) group (FN-CNIP-CAR) did not vote for Prime Minister Chirac after his first speech in the National Assembly.[3] Subsequently, Yvon Briant (future President of the CNIP) and Bruno Chauvierre (ex-RPR) left the FN-led group as they opposed the anti-Chirac strategy, which most of the group supported (Birenbaum 1992). During the two years in which the FN had a significant parliamentary presence (1986–8) many FN Deputies were tempted to switch sides. Interestingly, the only female deputy of the RN group, Yann Piat, revealed that she was 'contacted, invited for lunch [with the leaders of the right]. The proposition was simple: quit the FN and join the CNIP group, with the assurance of receiving the UDF-RPR investiture for the next legislative elections' (Piat 1991, p. 165).[4] However, there were also notable links between the various parliamentary groups. An example of rapprochement was the 'pro-life' study group that facilitated contacts between Frontists and RPR-UDF colleagues. That group produced a proposition issued by Michel de Rostolan (RN), Christine Boutin (Catholic UDF) and Hector Rolland (RPR), co-signed by more than 100 MPs, which sought to stop the reimbursement of non-therapeutic abortions by Social Security (Maisonneuve 1991).

However, after the return to the majority voting system and the re-election of a left government, the leaders of the parliamentary right operated a containment policy aimed at containing the National Front and at keeping it as far as possible from political bargaining and from the 1980s' alliances. The former UDF Prime Minister, Raymond Barre (1976–81), even proposed to forbid mergers of municipal lists in order to avoid 'another Dreux'. Meanwhile, the RPR and UDF leaders explicitly condemned the alliances with the FN (Perrineau 1998b). In 1990, the concept of a 'republican front' was canvassed to build an alliance of all the 'democratic' parties. However, it was only partially applied and rapidly abandoned.

Le Pen continued specifically to court publicity and to remain the public persona of the FN – sometimes via provocative speeches. In 1987 he qualified the Nazi gas chambers as a 'detail' of the Second World War. He also insulted a centrist Minister using clearly Holocaust-'revisionist' rhetoric (Birenbaum 1992). Using this logic of radicalization, he created an additional source of distinction from other leaders in the political field. This partly explains why Le Pen concentrated more and more of his attacks on Chirac during the 1990s (quipping famously in 1995: 'Chirac, he's Jospin but worse'). Moreover, he systematically opposed consensus on key political issues (for example, he was against the participation in the Gulf wars and against the Maastricht Treaty). The aim was a re-radicalization through different processes: re-integration of nationalist-revolutionary activists such as Pierre Pauty (ex-PNF), Liliane Boury (ex-neo-fascist), Jean-Jacques Susini (sentenced to death for OAS terrorism in Algeria); radicalization of anti-establishment discourse; 'ethnicization'; a less supply-side oriented economic perspective ('Neither left, nor right' was the slogan after the 1995 Presidential election). This was Le Pen's answer to the containment policies of the parliamentary right.

This evolution of the moderate right and the FN has to be analysed in terms of interdependence if one wants to avoid naive assessments. The coalitional market is structured by struggles over the possible legitimization of an electoral agreement. The re-establishment of the '*Koalitionsfähigkeit*' (i.e. acceptability in a coalition) of the FN was nearly reached after the 1997 defeat of the right. The FN had in fact helped many Socialist MPs to be elected by maintaining 133 candidates for the second round. On the other hand, several RPR or UDF incumbents clearly wooed the FN. For example, Christian Martin (UDF) supported 'national preference' (a reform proposed by the FN which aims to give the French people preference over the foreigners (especially non-EU citizens) as far as social welfare and social housing are concerned) and Jacques Limouzy (RPR) declared that the anti-racist laws had to be abrogated (*Le Monde*, 6 June 1997). As a consequence, several leaders and opinion-makers thought of including the FN in an alliance. Philippe de Villiers, president of the Eurosceptical Movement for France (MPF) was in favour of an alliance, stating that 'if the right keeps on considering the FN as its primary adversary, when it is the left in power, it will never return to power'. A former RPR minister, Robert Pandraud asserted that 'the Socialist Party was never criticized for his alliance with the Communist Party' (*Le Monde*, 4 June 1997), whereas the Republican Party leader Claude Goasguen thought that 'the moment has arrived to get out of the impasse of the "diabolical" treatment of the FN' (*Le Monde*, 20–21 June 1997).

This disorder was also the result of internal divisions within the FN, as many leaders favoured alliances and wanted to limit the distinction policy. After the right's defeat, the Delegate General Mégret, who was to become the President of the Republican National Movement (MNR) after the split in 1998–9, called for 'all those who are deceived by the political class, and mostly by the RPR and the UDF, to join us and to take initiatives that allow them to turn in our direction'. He added that 'if restructuring of the parties of the old majority were to the basis of homogeneous convictions, there would be no organisation on the right that would have any reason not to work with us, to sign agreements, even government agreements [...] on the basis of a priority given to the imperative of national sovereignty in relation to globalisation, in its migratory manifestations as well as in its economic manifestations' (*Le Monde*, 11 June 1997). Of even greater interest was the quick answer by Le Pen: 'One does not ally with forces in decomposition, one waits to pick up the debris. [...] If [RPR-UDF] voters do not find in their parties what they expected from them, very naturally we will welcome them within our movement' (*Présent*, 17 June 1997).

These words underline that each party of the parliamentary right was divided by fighting over alliances with the FN that seemed theoretically possible. These debates were also undoubtedly transfigured by the struggle for internal positions, and among local organizations as well (Kestel 1999). It is even more visible in the case of the FN. Internal conflicts between the supporters of Le Pen and Mégret crystallized on the issue of alliance.

The study of political parties according to a strictly 'centralist' (i.e. national) point of view reinforces the common illusion of a homogeneity of practices and of activists' strategies. Rather, pre-eminence of the national political field should not obscure the existence – particularly in France – of a double party system (Parodi 1997) partly due to the multiplicity of electoral systems. The regional PR system (Godmer 1998) allows smaller parties, which are not part of an alliance system (e.g. the Greens in 1986–8 and the FN), to reward their political personnel, a pay-off which was not possible at local government level.[5] In 1986, the FN obtained 137 regional councillors. This allowed the implantation of a large part of its political personnel across the whole territory (Kestel 1998). Ever since, the FN regional councillors have taken part in different political games. In spite of 'the homogenisation of political markets' (Gaxie and Lehingue 1984), we will see that the control exercised by the parties on all of the peripheral markets is not univocal.

The 'Regional Front'. A monopolistic extreme-right political enterprise in the regional governmental oligopoly

Although the FN obtained its first MEPs in 1984 and Deputies in 1986, above all it took advantage of the post-1986 new regional party system, which was of great importance to rewarding its elite and ensuring its organizational survival.

During the first regional elections in metropolitan France, there did not really exist a willingness to develop a containment policy against the FN in the regional assemblies (Godmer and Kestel 2001). Thus, the new FN regional parliamentary groups managed to become key actors in the election of RPR-UDF regional Presidents in six regions (Higher Normandy, Franche-Comté, Aquitaine, Picardie, Languedoc-Roussillon, Midi-Pyrénées). Moreover, they obtained one Vice-Presidency in three regions (Higher Normandy, Picardie, Languedoc-Roussillon) and two[6] – along with an explicit regional government alliance (Downs 1998) – in Provence-Alpes-Côte d'Azur (PACA). The process was twofold: there was direct personal reward and also institutional recognition – i.e. a symbolic acceptance of the integration of the extreme right into the regional political market. The degree of FN integration was largely proportional to institutional weight. In the assemblies where the number of regional councillors was only one or two (or even none in Limousin), there was absolutely no integration. There was a *low* degree of integration where the FN regional parliamentarians had a considerable group but could not change the regional majority. And there was a *high* degree of integration where they were largely able to do so.

However, the 1992 regional elections showed progressive exclusion and differentiated integration of the FN. Due to a landslide for the right and to possible alliances with numerous ecologist councillors, the right parties were freer than in 1986. It was also only after the March 1992 elections that RPR-UDF leaders tried to exclude totally the FN from regional coalitional markets, although it had doubled their representation (*Français d'abord*, No. 348, 2001). This process of exclusion had been under way at national level since 1986 and at peripheral level since 1988. But the RPR-UDF landslide and centralized regulation (facilitated by new possibilities of central control, for example due to new rules governing political finances) may have accelerated it. As a result, there was no explicit right-FN alliance for the elections of regional Presidents in 1992.

However, the exclusion from the coalitional markets was not total since, in many cases, integration meant the installation of a permanent deliberative commission whose members are designated by a PR system, thus giving positions (for example, being a member of the permanent commissions, the 'government' of the regions) to elected leaders of important FN groups. 'It becomes possible to soften the alliances, to envisage "good manners exchanges", to defer certain decisions; and this is made easier because precise definition of the "group" is made by internal rules' (Patriat 1993, p. 308). With again the sole exception of Limousin – the only structurally 'left' region, led by a PS-PCF coalition – which *de facto* excluded the newly-arrived FN councillors by restricting the number of commission members, the other regional executives tended on the contrary to conceive the rule in a rather extensive way, allowing a 'soft integration' of the FN councillors, characterized by low visibility. However, when compared with 1986, the degree of integration is low in all regions, in Provence in particular. Another temporary and historically unique exception is the 1992–3 United France (FU, i.e. the future MDR)-PS-Radicals-FN majority that elected and supported the President of the centrist Movement of Reformers (MDR), Jean-Pierre Soisson in Burgundy.

Containment by RPR-UDF leaders was clearly and definitively implemented during the election of the regional Presidents in March and April 1998. With 15 per cent of the national votes and 275 councillors, FN leaders tried to enter the coalitional markets by proposing a six-issue 'minimum programme' to the mainstream right. These six points were as follows: a reduction in taxes, security in high schools, transparency of public markets, development of regional cultural policy, PR-elected groups in commissions, and the strengthening of professional education. There were official and clear interventions by the Secretary General and by the President of the RPR, then by the President of the UDF (himself a candidate in PACA against the President of the FN) and President of the main component of the UDF coalition, with threats of exclusion from the respective parties for those who accepted alliances with the FN. The President of the Republic, Jacques Chirac (RPR), and the Prime Minister, Lionel Jospin (PS), made official declarations to force Presidents elected with help from the FN to withdraw. As a consequence, the Presidents of Aquitaine, Franche-Comté, Centre, Midi-Pyrénées, and Higher Normandy resigned, refusing a compromise with the FN.

The Presidents of Picardie, Rhone-Alps, Languedoc-Roussillon refused to apply the national decisions and remained in place. They were excluded from the UDF. In Rhone-Alps a new election in 1999 allowed the leadership of the new UDF to organize better control over its representatives and to take over the regional government by obliging the 'Plural left' (PS-PCF-Radicals-Greens) to enter a temporary alliance. Thereby, it underlined the party HQ distinction between extremist and democratic (or 'republican') forces. The three remaining right-FN coalitions for the 1999–2004 period thus constitute the last 'free zones', in which there is autonomy of the regional coalitional market. In the other regions, the exclusion of the FN has been effective. For example, the right helped the left to gain the presidency of Provence so as to counter the candidacy of Le Pen himself to this position (Le Pen lost his regional mandate in 2000 after his condemnation for physical violence against a socialist Mayor).

At the national level, the isolation of the FN has been complete since the loss of its last Deputy in 1998 (after 12 years of continuous presence in the National Assembly). Moreover, it has not managed to maintain a parliamentary group in the European Parliament (it barely reached the electoral threshold, polling only 5.7 per cent and winning just five MEPs in the 1999–2004 parliament). Nevertheless, the breakaway of the MNR in 1999 (which also contested the European elections that year, even less successfully than the FN) did not really diminish the monopolization of the extreme-right symbolic goods and electoral results by the FN. The failure of the MNR was underlined in the 2002 presidential election, when Mégret won only 2.3 per cent of the votes whereas Le Pen qualified for the second ballot run off with Chirac. Nevertheless, this took place in a reconfiguration process which is only to be completed in the post-Le Pen era.

Conclusions

The notion of a 'peripheral coalitional market' offers the advantage of no longer envisaging the political field from a uniquely national angle. It also allows us to see how differentiated the political practices of the diverse political entrepreneurs are, despite the very essentialist vision of political parties which tends to prevail. A major debate concerns the place of 'ideology' (i.e. of explicit normative criteria, aimed at excluding political parties that refuse the minimal rules of representative democracy) in the regulation process of those markets. In fact, the ideological criterion plays a comparatively limited role in relation to the admission of the extremist party into this field.

The containment logic is based on a distinction between access to 'representation' – which is, in general, accepted for extreme-right parties that achieve sufficient electoral success to elect supporters – and access to coalitional markets (i.e. participation in governance processes). This analytical scheme was designed to understand the different possible systemic responses to the rise of the extreme parties. In addition, it takes into account the post-war institutional evolution of the West European countries that followed the German example by developing a dual political market with regional representative assemblies – notably in Spain, Italy, Belgium, France and the United Kingdom (though devolution has in some cases been asymmetrical).

The German and Austrian cases represent poles with which one can benchmark other states as we have done with France. Belgium, for example, seems to follow the German 'containment' example by excluding a very important party, namely the Vlaams Blok (VB) from coalitional government at the national, regional (Flanders) and metropolitan (Antwerp in 2000 – where it became the largest party) levels. A very different situation prevails in the Second Italian Republic, which has been characterized by two significant extreme right parties – the Northern League (LN) and the National Alliance (AN). It is interesting to note that its political markets tend to follow the 'Austrian' paradigm, in the sense that their participation in regional governments (especially after the 1995 and 2000 regional elections) is the rule because they are part of the Forza Italia (FI)-led national coalition (which returned to national government in 2001). It can thus be seen that a dual Europe has emerged, divided between inclusionary and exclusionary power systems in relation to the rise of the extreme right.

Notes

1 We thank Bruno Perreau, Tangui Coulouarn (both from Paris-I University) and Matthew Langsley for their helpful comments.
2 A symbolic fight that occurred also within the academic sector, as historians, sociologists and political scientists tried to form an opinion (Taguieff 1984; Milza 1992).
3 When a new government presents itself for the first time to the National Assembly, it almost automatically asks for an official vote of confidence, which defines the majority.
4 She was the only FN MP to remain in Parliament in 1988 (after the return to the majority system), being re-elected in the Var department. However, she left the FN in the same year to join the PR, under which label she was re-elected in 1993 before being murdered by the local criminal underworld in 1994.
5 On the local level, there were allegedly about 1,000 FN opposition councillors, but these positions are not rewarding (no salary, no office, etc) since the FN was excluded from almost all municipal majorities. Thus, it did not obtain a single Mayor in 1977 and 1983. Apart from very small villages, it obtained only one city office in 1989 (Saint-Gilles), four in 1995–7 (the major city of Toulon, Marignane, Orange and Vitrolles), but lost all of them – except Orange in the 2001 local elections.
6 Among them we find the interesting case of Jacques Bompard, leader of the FN in the Vaucluse department, who was also elected MP there in 1986 and Mayor of Orange in 1995. After his re-election in 2001, he remained the only FN Mayor of a city for the 2001–7 period.

Bibliography

Algazy, J. (1984) *La tentation néo-fasciste 1944–1965*. Paris: Fayard.
Askolovitch, C. (1999) *Voyage au bout de la France. Le Front national tel qu'il est*. Paris: Grasset.
Birenbaum, G. (1992) *Le Front national en politique*. Paris: Balland.
Bourdieu, P. (1982) *Ce que parler veut dire*. Paris: Fayard.
Bourdieu, P. (2000) *Propos sur le champ politique*. Lyon: PUL.
Camus, J.-Y. (1996) 'Origine et formation du Front national, 1972–1981'. In Mayer, N. and Perrineau, P. (eds) *Le Front national à découvert*, 2nd edn. Paris: PFNSP.
Camus, J.-Y. and Monzat, R. (1992) *Les droites nationales et radicales en France*. Lyon: PUL.
Chevallier, J. (1985) *Éléments d'analyse politique*. Paris: Presses Universitaires de France.
Downs, W.M. (1998) *Coalition Government, Subnational style. Multiparty Politics in Europe's Regional Parliaments*. Columbus: Ohio State University Press.
Edelman, M. (1991) *Pièces et règles du jeu politique* (French translation of *Constructing the Political Spectacle*). Paris: Le Seuil.
Gaxie, D. and Lehingue, P. (1984) *Enjeux municipaux*. Paris: Presses Universitaires de France.
Gastaud, Y. (2000) *L'immigration et l'opinion politique en France sous la Ve République*. Paris: Le Seuil.
Gerlich, P. and Müller, W.C. (eds) (1983) *Zwischen Koalition und Konkurrenz. Österreichs Parteien seit 1945*. Vienna: Wilhelm Braumüller/UP.
Godmer, L. (1998) *La démocratie éclatée. Les modes de désignation des membres des assemblées régionales dans les principaux États d'Europe occidentale*. Master's thesis. Paris-I Sorbonne University: Department of Political Science.
Godmer, L. and Kestel, L. (2001) 'Extremism and democratic coalitions. The institutional integration of extreme right parties in the regional parliaments of Germany, Austria and France'. Paper presented at the 29th Joint Sessions of Workshops of the European Consortium for Political Research (ECPR), Institute for Political Studies, Grenoble, 9 April.
Höbelt, L. (1999) *Von der vierten Partei zur dritten Kraft. Die Geschichte der VdU*. Graz/Stuttgart: Lepold Stocker.
Kestel, L. (1998) *Les candidats du Front national aux élections législatives de 1986 à 1997*. B.A. thesis. Paris-I Sorbonne University: Department of History.
Kestel, L. (1999) *Structuration, homogénéisation des groupements, di-sociation. La fédération Front national de Paris, (1972–1999)*. MA thesis. Paris-I Sorbonne University: Department of Political Science.
Kräh, G. (1996) *Die Freiheitlichen unter Jörg Haider: rechtsextreme Gefahr oder Hoffnungsträger für Österreich*. Frankfurt on Main: Lang.
Letigre, H. (1988) *La réaction du RPR à la percée du Front national*. Paris: La Pensée universelle.
Maisonneuve, C. (1991) 'Le Front National à l'Assemblée Nationale: histoire d'un groupe parlementaire, 1986–1988'. MA thesis. Paris, Institute for Political Studies.
Marcus, J. (1995) *The National Front and French Politics: The Resistible Rise of Jean-Marie Le Pen*. Basingstoke: Macmillan.
Mayer, N. (1999) *Ces Français qui votent FN*. Paris: Flammarion.

Milza, P. (1992) 'Le Front national: droite extrême ou national-populisme?'. In Sirinelli, J.F. (ed.) *Histoire des droites en France*. Paris: Gallimard.

Molfessis, N. (1989) *Images de l'homme politique et mises en scène télévisuelles. L'exemple de Jean-Marie Le Pen à 'L'Heure de vérité' et à 'Questions à domicile'*. Master's thesis. Paris: Institute for Political studies (IEP).

Parodi, J.-L. (1997) 'Proportionnalisation périodique, cohabitation, atomisation partisane: un triple défi pour le régime semi-présidentiel'. *Revue française de science politique*, 47, 3–4: 292–312.

Patriat, C. (1993) 'Pouvoirs régionaux en chantier. Le réglage régional des majorités nationales?'. In Perrineau, P. (ed.) *Le vote éclaté. Les élections régionales et cantonales de mars 1992*. Paris: Presses de la FNSP.

Perrineau, P. (1998a) 'Les étapes de l'implantation du Front national'. In Delwit, P., De Waele, J.-M. and Rea, A. (eds) *L'extrême droite en France et en Belgique. Interventions*. Brussels: Complexe.

Perrineau, P. (1998b) *Le symptôme Le Pen. Radiographie des électeurs du Front national*. Paris: Fayard.

Paxton, R.O. (1997) *Le Temps des chemises vertes* (French translation of *French Peasant Fascism: Henry Dorgere's Greenshirts and the Crises of French Agriculture, 1929–1939*. Paris: Le Seuil.

Piat, Y. (1991). *Seule, en haut, à droite*. Paris: Fixot.

Pons, B. (1983) 'L'essentiel est de faire confiance à Jean Hiaux'. *La lettre de la nation*, September.

Puntscher-Riekmann, S. (1999) 'The politics of Ausgrenzung, the Nazi Past and the European dimension of the new radical right in Austria.' In Bischo, G., Pelinka, A. and Karlhofer, F. (eds) *The Vranitzy Era in Austria*. New-Brunswick/London: Transaction.

Schmidt, M. (1997) *Die Parlamentsarbeit rechtextremer Parteien und möglichen Gegenstrategien. Eine Untersuchung am Beispiel des 'Deutschen Volksunion' im Schleswig-Holsteinischen Landtag*. Munster: Agenda.

Schmitt, C. (1962) *La Notion de politique* (1962) (French translation). Paris: Flammarion.

Taguieff, P.-A. (1984) 'La rhétorique du national-populisme'. Mots 9, pp. 113–139.

Wahnich, S. et al. (1997) *Le Pen, les mots. Analyse d'un discours d'extrême droite*. Paris: La Découverte.

Weber, M. (1965) *Économie et société* (I) (French translation of *Wirtschaft und Gesellschaft*). Paris: Plon.

Wieviorka, M. (1998) *Le racisme, une introduction*. Paris: La Découverte.

Ysmal, C. (1984) 'Le RPR et l'UDF face au Front national: concurrence et connivence'. *Revue politique et parlementaire*, 86, 913, November–December, pp. 6–20.

7 The diversified approach
Swedish responses to the extreme right

Anders Widfeldt

Introduction

In recent years, much attention has been paid to the growth of extreme right electoral activity in Scandinavia. In Norway and Denmark, populist right parties have provided support for minority governments after national elections in 2001. In Norway, the increased acceptance of the Progress Party can to some extent be explained by the party's apparent move towards the centre ground. Most notably, the party has toned down its anti-immigration rhetoric. The Danish People's Party, on the other hand, has shown no signs of de-radicalization, and appears to have gained its increased legitimacy via other parties and the electorate accepting its political agenda. Immigration was a key issue in the 2001 campaign, and after the election the new centre-right government introduced several measures to tighten immigration and asylum policy (Qvortrup 2002a,b). In both Denmark and Norway, therefore, two parties previously treated as pariahs by the other parties, gained unprecedented positions of legitimacy and influence.

In Finland, however, no populist right party has been able to fill the gap left by the Rural Party, which went bankrupt in 1995 – although its successor, the True Finns Party, won one seat in 1999 and three seats in the 2003 parliamentary elections (cf. Pekonen 1999). In Sweden, the New Democracy party, which erupted onto the political scene from nowhere in 1991, turned out to be a short-lived phenomenon. No party has so far managed to fill the void. The more radical Sweden Democrats received 1.4 per cent in the 2002 election. This was well below the level required for parliamentary representation, although the party significantly increased its presence on local councils.

The rise of the extreme right in Scandinavia also encompasses neo-Nazi activity and racist violence, which have attracted considerable concern in the Scandinavian region. Members of racist organizations have been found guilty of racially motivated killings. There is a thriving Nazi subculture, with a highly successful 'white power' music industry. This extreme right wave is not equally spread throughout the Nordic region either, but it is an issue and a political force that cannot be ignored. Neo-Nazi and militant racist organizations are particularly strong in Sweden. They also exist in Denmark and Norway, but have so far not gained a foothold in Finland (Pekonen 1999; Bjørgo 1997).

Thus, although it might be an exaggeration to state that the extreme right is continuously increasing in support and activity in Scandinavia, it has become an important phenomenon in the region. Populist right parties are important players in the Norwegian and Danish party systems and, while currently insignificant, should not be ruled out for the future in Finland and Sweden. Racist violence occurs to varying extents in the whole Scandinavian region, and the absence of neo-Nazi groups so far in Finland may well prove not to be permanent. Thus, the Nordic political systems, hitherto characterized by consensus and a low level of social and political conflict, are facing a completely new challenge.

In this chapter, the main focus will be on responses to the extreme right challenge in the largest of the Scandinavian states, Sweden. Of course, what is loosely labelled the 'extreme right' is a broad and diversified phenomenon. Indeed, as Mudde (2000) has argued, the 'extreme right' is in many ways a misleading choice of words, and is mostly used for the want of a better shorthand term. Here, the term 'extreme right' will be used in a broad sense, and include New Democracy, a right-wing party that comes across as relatively mild in an international comparison, as well as the much more extreme neo-Nazi and militant racist groups. It will, however, be argued that New Democracy represented something new, different and unwelcome for the remaining political parties when it broke through in 1991.

Responses to political extremism

The extreme right challenge can be divided into two subcategories, the *parliamentary challenge* and the *extra-parliamentary challenge*. The former has been provided by New Democracy. The latter comes from racist and neo-Nazi groups. There are, of course, important differences between these two challenges. On the one hand, there was a political party that mocked the Establishment, but which was completely legalistic and democratic. On the other hand, there are groups and organizations that sometimes use violence, which often operate outside the legal framework, and are anti-democratic. Despite these obvious differences, they both represent challenges in their own right.

New Democracy politicized new issues, most notably immigration. To a significant extent, its raison d'être was to challenge the established political order. Swedish politics has a long-standing reputation as being consensual, where policy-making takes place according to a 'slow, deliberating mode' (Särlvik 1983, p. 146), with extensive participation from interest organizations. New Democracy explicitly set out to challenge this. The party wanted to run the country according to business principles, with a quicker and more efficient decision-making process. The party programme of 1991 stated that 'the rule of politicians and the bureaucracy must be significantly reduced' and demanded that corporatist arrangements be broken up (Ny Demokrati, p. iv).

Demands such as these were not new or unique in themselves, but together with the party's provocative political style, they represented a challenge against the established political order. Schedler (1996, p. 293) argues that an anti-Establishment party orders the world into an anti-political triangle consisting of (a) the political class as malicious rogues; (b) the people as innocent victims; and (c) the anti-establishment party itself as redeeming heroes. This aptly summarises New Democracy's rhetoric. In addition, it had charismatic leadership and claimed to represent the 'common man' against the Establishment, which are key characteristics of a populist party (see Taggart 2000). Thus, despite not being anti-democratic, and despite several of its policies being shared by other parties, New Democracy provided a challenge against the established parties and the political system.

The response to the *parliamentary challenge* will be studied by focusing on the other parliamentary parties and their treatment of New Democracy during the 1991–4 parliamentary term. A problem here is that New Democracy was not only a new and different newcomer, which deliberately set out to challenge the established parties. It was also a new competitor for votes. Thus, it is of interest to try to establish whether the established parties treated New Democracy as an untouchable pariah that would hopefully soon disappear, or whether the party was treated as a 'normal' competitor for votes (cf. Downs 2001).

The *extra-parliamentary* challenge is of a different nature. We are now dealing with groups and organizations that often revert to violence. Some of them are openly racist and anti-democratic. Thus, unlike New Democracy, these groups provide a clear-cut challenge to democracy. This means that the analysis of the response to the extra-parliamentary challenge will have to be adjusted accordingly. Since neo-Nazi and racist groups do not operate within the democratic and legal framework, this means that administrative and judicial institutions as well as parties can be expected to respond. In addition, the response to the extra parliamentary challenge will not only be studied at the national level, but also at the local government level, as it is local levels that have to deal with the concrete manifestations of this challenge.

There are many possible ways of responding to a challenge from politically extreme groups or parties. To give some structure to the subsequent discussion, two distinctions will be made. The first is between *accommodation* (co-optation) and *marginalization* (restriction). The second is the distinction between *specific* responses (targeted at the extremist organizations as such) and *general* responses (targeted at the public). These distinctions can be put together into a typology depicted in Figure 7.1.

General accommodation (1) is designed to acquiesce public opinion, by accommodating, or co-opting, some of the demands of the extreme right. It could, for example, take the shape of introducing stricter asylum laws in an attempt to stem the growth of anti-immigration sentiment.

An example of *specific accommodation* (2) could be to involve an extremist party in government, in order to expose its lack of realism, and to force the party to take political responsibility. It could be argued that this was the strategy used by the Austrian ÖVP, when they decided to form a government coalition with the FPÖ in 2000. It is also possible for a government to cooperate in parliament with the extremist party, without including it in a formal coalition. An example of this was when the Danish liberal-conservative minority government took office with support from the Danish People's Party after the 2001 election. However, it should be noted that the inclusion of an alleged extreme right party in government could have other motives. For example, it might be the case that other parties quite simply do not regard the 'extreme right' party in question as extreme, or as unacceptable. If this is the case, then it can hardly be a case of accommodation; rather a case of acceptance.

General marginalization (3) has the purpose of restricting the expression of racism, xenophobic and other extreme views among the public. For example, it can encompass laws against racist remarks or political symbols. Such measures can be employed to make it more difficult openly to express support for the extreme right, but can also be a symbolic act – to show that anti-democracy and racism have no place in a democratic society.

Specific marginalization (4), finally, can include bans or restrictions against extremist groups or parties. The most obvious example is an outright ban of a party or organization (Finn 2000). Less radical examples can involve the seizure of party newspapers, bans against political uniforms or restricting the right for extreme groups and parties to hold public meetings. It can also involve parties forming coalitions to ensure that the extremist party is excluded from power. Such anti-extremist coalitions can often include parties that would not consider cooperating with each other in different circumstances. An example is the *cordon sanitaire* against the

	General	Specific
Accommodation	1	2
Marginalization	3	4

Figure 7.1 A typology of responses to political extremism.

Vlaams Blok in the Flemish part of Belgium (Mudde 2000). The agreement included a commitment not to engage with the Vlaams Blok in any way, at any level (national, regional or local), or in any context. This strategy is an example of the power of the established parties, but it is not foolproof, as shown by the continued success of Vlaams Blok in recent years.

It should be noted that, in the real world, these four types of response are not mutually exclusive. For example, a ban on the display of Nazi symbols could be targeted at extreme right groups or at the general public and could thus be an example of specific as well as general marginalization. Similarly, to take an extreme party into a government coalition could include elements of both general and specific accommodation. Thus, a certain action taken by a government, political party, etc, may contain elements of more than one of the responses in the typology in Figure 7.1. Still, while the four types of response may empirically appear as mixtures, it is useful to keep them analytically separate. The main question of this chapter is the extent to which the four types of response are included in the overall response in Sweden, and whether there is any difference between the responses to the parliamentary and the extra-parliamentary challenges.

An important issue here is where the response actually comes from. In this chapter, the party political response will be discussed as well as the response from state institutions, such as the public administration and the judiciary. In practice, of course, the distinction between parties and the state is not clear cut. According to the well-known cartel party theory, political parties are in the process of colluding with the state, at the same time as they are becoming detached from the civil society (Katz and Mair 1995). The political independence of civil service is also sometimes questioned, given the tendency of some parties to politicize the bureaucracy. Along the same lines, it could be claimed that a state does not in itself take decisions, and cannot therefore marginalize, or accommodate. Rather, it is the parties, and their representatives in parliament and government, that take such decisions.

Against this it can be argued that state institutions cannot be expected always to act in complete accordance with the wishes of the parties. The civil service has some degree of independence when it implements laws and regulations, an independence it may choose to make use of when facing an extremist challenge. This is particularly important when it comes to the challenge from neo-Nazi and militant racist groups, whose opposition is not only directed at the established political forces, but the entire state. It is, however, also relevant to the challenge from populist right parties, who frequently criticize the bureaucracy and the legal system. Therefore, although the state and political parties to a degree share the same interests, it is possible that in some situations they may act independently of each other.

Of course, when a democracy responds to an extremist challenge, it runs the risk of carrying its own contradiction. In order to deal with extremists, democracy will often feel the need to take measures that can be criticized for being undemocratic. Neo-Nazi and militant racist groups are often, directly or indirectly, subjected to restrictions in freedom of expression (e.g. laws against Holocaust denial or racist statements) or freedom of assembly (bans on public meetings). In some countries, certain extremist groups or parties have been banned altogether (e.g. in the Netherlands; see Mudde 2000).

These examples illustrate a democratic dilemma. If taken too far, measures taken to protect democracy can in themselves be a threat to democracy. This dilemma is less pronounced when it comes to responding to populist right parties than neo-nazi and militant racist groups. Still, systematic attempts to exclude a party from the degree of influence its electoral strength would otherwise entitle it to, can be regarded as problematical from a democratic perspective. Along these lines it can be argued that the *cordon sanitaire* in Belgium has denied the Vlaams Blok the political influence it has earned via the ballot box. At the same time, it is worth remembering that the motives for marginalizing a political party may not exclusively be based on concern for democracy, even if lip service to this effect is paid; the measures taken may just as well be used as a weapon in the competition between parties.

Thus, the relationship between democracy and extremism is not always that clear cut. Under pressure, democracy can become a threat against itself. At the same time, an insufficient response against an extremist challenge would also be a threat against democracy. This dilemma cannot be resolved here. Nevertheless, it is of interest to study how a country like Sweden, with a reputation as open and consensual, responds to a challenge from the extreme right.

The following account will focus on the 1990s. The section on the response to New Democracy will, for obvious reasons, be limited to the period when this party was a force to be reckoned with, i.e. until 1994, but some attention will also be paid to the subsequent period, when a possible democratic response could be regarded as a precaution against the emergence of new challenges from the populist right. The section on responses to violent racism and neo-Nazism will cover a longer period, into the 2000s.

The parliamentary challenge: New Democracy

The events that led to the formation of New Democracy have been documented elsewhere (e.g. Widfeldt 2000; Taggart 1996; Arter 1992). Already in late 1990, before the party had been formally founded, opinion polls suggested that it had enough popular support to pass the 4 per cent threshold for parliamentary representation. The immediate reaction among the democratic establishment was one of disbelief. All parties, right, left and centre, reacted with horror at the prospect of a sister party to the Norwegian and Danish Progress parties entering the Riksdag.

As was argued above, it was not primarily the policies that made New Democracy so controversial. Rather, it was the political style that caused such resentment. There was a lack of respect for democratic institutions and procedures, something which was illustrated when co-leader Bert Karlsson, who among other things is a pop music producer, compared his entry into parliament with his involvement in several Eurovision song contests. The party's representatives often used drastic language and were quick to ridicule established parties and politicians. In addition, New Democracy's criticism of the Swedish immigration and asylum policies differentiated it from other parties, and was met with widespread criticism.

The initial response from the established parties could be summarized as very cautious. Very few parties and party leaders tried to take on New Democracy during the 1991 campaign. Instead, there was a general tendency to avoid direct debate and confrontation. The main exception was the leader of the Liberal Party, Mr Bengt Westerberg. Throughout the 1991 campaign, he repeatedly criticized New Democracy and its parliamentary candidates for xenophobia and for simplistic policy proposals. On election night, he demonstratively left the TV studio when the joint leaders of New Democracy, Ian Wachtmeister and Bert Karlsson, entered, after the party had received 6.7 per cent of the vote, comfortably clearing the representational threshold. Westerberg was praised from many quarters for being honest and brave in his uncompromising attitude. It certainly was not an opportunist strategy, given the opinion climate at the time. For all the praise and respect, Westerberg's party suffered a serious election defeat, with what at the time was the second worst result in its history. Thus, it could be argued that, with Westerberg and the Liberals as the main exception, the initial response from the established party system was not to engage with New Democracy (Downs 2001). The hope seemed to be that a lack of attention would prevent the party from generating too much interest (cf. Elmbrant 1993). However, New Democracy did enter parliament, and the other parties now had to respond to this challenge. The four responses in the typology in Figure 7.1 will, therefore, be discussed one by one. The tactic of *general accommodation* would imply that the established parties could try to minimize support for New Democracy by adapting its views on immigration. New Democracy openly and strongly criticized the alleged generous refugee and immigration policies. The anti-immigration rhetoric was, although not extreme in comparison to that of some extreme right parties in continental Europe, by far the most outspoken ever expressed by a Swedish parliamentary party. New Democracy argued that political refugees should be given loans instead of allowances, that immigrants should be expelled in cases of serious or repeated crime, and that immigrant children should not be entitled to education in their 'home language'. The party also argued that the definition of a political refugee should be made stricter (*Riksdag* motion 1991/92:SF630). In a private member's motion to the *Riksdag*, New Democracy MP John Bouvin linked the increasing unemployment to immigration, and proposed that immigration should be reduced to a minimum for 'one or more years' (*Riksdag* motion 1991/92: SF622).

New Democracy's proposals to change the Swedish refugee and immigration policies received no direct support from the established parties. Indeed, the party was heavily criticized, and sometimes even accused of racism. However, it seemed as if New Democracy had struck a chord with the Swedish public. New Democracy's time in parliament coincided with a period of high pressure on Sweden's capacity to accept refugees, mainly due to the war in the former Yugoslavia. In 1992, 84,000 persons applied for political asylum in Sweden, the highest figure so far recorded in a single year. It also coincided with a peak in anti-immigration attitudes among the Swedish public (Demker 2000). The party made successful summer tours with public meetings around the country in 1992 and 1993, where criticism against the existing refugee and immigration policies was a key feature. In July 1992, Ian Wachtmeister asked an audience in Göteborg: 'What should we do about the Somalians? Bring them here?', which was received with widespread amusement (direct observation by the author). New Democracy did well in opinion polls, with figures of over 10 per cent in mid 1992. Despite a decline in support in 1993, the party looked well capable of holding on to its parliamentary status, until Wachtmeister announced in February 1994 that he was resigning from the party leadership. From then on its support collapsed.

The high number of asylum seekers in the early 1990s came despite the fact that the Swedish asylum policy had been tightened in late 1989, when the Social Democratic government decided on a stricter definition of refugees, which basically was in accordance with the UN Convention on Refugees. Asylum seekers would no longer be accepted on humanitarian or 'refugee-like' grounds. The decision was taken by the government. It was debated, but not voted on, in parliament (*Riksdag* minutes 1989/90: 46 (14/12), 9 §; see also Pred 2000, p. 49f). In June 1993, the non-socialist government decided to grant asylum to all pending applications from Bosnia-Herzegovina, unless there were strong reasons against it. At the same time, however, visa restrictions were imposed on Bosnian citizens, which significantly reduced the number of new applications from Bosnia-Herzegovina. Despite this, an all time high number of 79,000 asylum claims were granted in 1994, although the numbers went down significantly from 1995 onwards (http://www.immi.se/asyl/198097.htm).

After the 1994 election, a one-party Social Democratic government took office. The minister responsible for immigration between 1994 and 1996, Mr Leif Blomberg, was criticized for being a hardliner. In December 1996, parliament approved a government proposal, which included the removal of certain grounds for asylum, including refusal to serve in military forces. The concept of '*de facto* refugees' was also abolished. This was criticized as a tightening of the Swedish asylum policy, especially by the Left, Green and Liberal parties (*Riksdag* private members motions 1996/97: SF13, 1996/97: SF18 and 1996/97: SF19). MPs from these parties even argued that the government was introducing policies that resembled those previously proposed by New Democracy (*Riksdag* minutes, 1996/97: 39, 5/12; see also *Riksdag* private members motion 1997/98: SF14). Support for such allegations can be found in the changes in asylum policy which took place in 1996, including a tightening of the definition of a political refugee, which had been among New Democracy's proposals. On the other hand, some of New Democracy's demands, such as the abolition of 'home language' teaching and the automatic expulsion of immigrants that have committed repeated crimes, have not been introduced.

Thus, whether the policy changes in the second half of the 1990s actually amounted to general accommodation is a matter of judgement. On the one hand, it is undeniable that the peak in New Democracy support in 1991–2 coincided with a peak in anti-immigration sentiments among the public, as shown by comparing the party's ratings in SIFO polls (Oscarsson 1998, p. 328) and variations in the public attitude on asylum policy (Demker 2000). Thus, it might be possible to argue that the decision to impose visa restrictions on Bosnian citizens in 1993, and the changes in asylum policy in 1996, were designed to accommodate public discontent with the influx of refugees, and take away the potential for support for New Democracy. By 1996, New Democracy was a completely spent force, but it could be argued that these policies were implemented to prevent renewed support for the party, or the growth of other parties with a similar agenda. It is also possible to find statements from government representatives that support such a conclusion, such as that the previous, more generous, refugee policies lacked 'popular anchoring' (Pred 2000, p. 52).

However, this is mostly circumstantial evidence. It is hardly possible to prove that concern with support for New Democracy was behind the changes in asylum policy. Nor can it be conclusively proven that the policies were primarily designed to accommodate anti-immigration attitudes among the public. The official line of both the non-socialist government between 1991 and 1994, and the Social Democratic government after 1994, was that Sweden had already accepted a large number of political refugees, and that the country could not handle a continued intake of the same scale.

Specific accommodation would have meant involving New Democracy in a government coalition, or a formalized cooperation pact. Certainly, the situation after the 1991 election meant that it was impossible to ignore the party. Out of the total of 349 *Riksdag* seats, the socialist bloc consisting of the Social Democrats and the Left Party had 154 seats. The non-socialist bloc, consisting of the Moderates, the Liberals, Christian Democrats and the Centre Party, had 170 seats. Thus, the latter four parties, which formed a coalition government after the election, were five seats short of a majority. New Democracy held a pivotal position with their 25 seats. Although the parliamentary situation was complicated, there is nothing to suggest that any of the coalition partners seriously contemplated including New Democracy in the government. When the government was installed on 3 October, New Democracy abstained in the vote of investiture (*Riksdagens årsbok* 1991/92, p. 14f). This was generally regarded as passive support for the government, since the Swedish constitution states that a government is tolerated by parliament as long as there is not a majority of the elected MPs voting against it.[1]

Despite this passive support, the situation for the government was not enviable. To get its bills through parliament, it had to rely on support from New Democracy, or on cross-bloc agreements with the Social Democrats. This dilemma was most urgent during the unsuccessful attempts to defend the Swedish currency against speculation in the autumn of 1992. The *Krona* had been tied to the ECU since 1988, but in 1992 it became increasingly apparent that it was significantly overvalued. In order to defend the *Krona* against speculation, the Central Bank raised the marginal interest rate, briefly to 500 per cent. At the same time, the government tried to work out austerity packages, in order to regain the confidence of the money market in the Swedish economy. Owing to the complicated parliamentary situation, support from New Democracy or the Social Democrats was necessary to carry such packages through the *Riksdag*.

Throughout the crisis, it seemed apparent that major cross-bloc deals with the Social Democrats was always the government's preferred option. Indeed, broad consensus was considered a value in itself in the quest to rebuild the reputation of the Swedish economy. However, Jan Teorell's study of the events during the turbulent period between September and November suggests that the Moderate leader and Prime Minister Carl Bildt may have been open to discussions with New Democracy during the first phases of the crisis. Wachtmeister openly expressed interest in participating in the negotiations, and Bildt said on TV that Wachtmeister had behaved in a 'responsible and impressive manner', while others did not have the same 'crisis awareness', a statement that infuriated the Social Democrats (Teorell 1998, p. 57; Elmbrant 1993, pp. 303ff).

Whether these words revealed genuine openness towards New Democracy, or were intended as a provocation to get the Social Democratic leadership moving, is not clear. According to Teorell, Bildt did suggest to the government that talks with New Democracy could be an 'alternative strategy', if the negotiations with the Social Democrats were to collapse (Teorell 1998, p. 56). Such ideas were, however, firmly resisted by Westerberg and any thoughts of involving New Democracy were soon abandoned (Teorell 1998; Elmbrant 1993). Wachtmeister (1992, p. 142) claims that it was the Liberals and Social Democrats that were the main obstacles to including New Democracy in the negotiations. During the subsequent phases of the crisis, New Democracy was clearly out of the picture, and Wachtmeister belonged to the minority who started to question the prevailing consensus that the *Krona* must be defended at all costs (Teorell 1998, p. 67).

Thus, although Prime Minister Bildt may at some stage have toyed with the idea of including New Democracy in the package deals to defend the Swedish currency, the government went for cross-bloc deals with the Social Democrats. Two such deals, which together included unprecedented welfare cuts and significant tax increases, were reached in late September 1992. On 19 November, however, the government finally had to give up the defence of the overvalued *Krona*, which was allowed to float. Its value promptly sank like a stone (Teorell 1998).

After the defence of the *Krona* had failed, there was no room left for further cross-bloc agreements. With their eyes set on the 1994 election, the Social Democrats went in for a fully-fledged opposition policy, and the government had to rely on New Democracy. This reliance turned out to be highly unreliable, however. The main strategy of the government parties was to negotiate with New Democracy in the parliamentary committees, rather than trying to reach wider agreements with the party leadership. The success of this strategy varied, largely depending on which New Democracy MPs they were dealing with. New Democracy's three years in parliament were riddled with internal conflicts, defections and poor party discipline, which made systematic cooperation difficult, especially towards the end of the 1991–4 period. There were cases where New Democracy took one side in a parliamentary committee, only to change its mind in the chamber.

This happened with the government proposal to introduce *vårdnadsbidrag*, an allowance for parents with children. The New Democracy representative had opposed the proposal in the parliamentary committee on social affairs. In the chamber, other New Democracy representatives proposed that the bill should be resubmitted to the parliamentary committee. When the bill was finally brought to the chamber, the New Democracy group was split, but a sufficient number of the party's MPs voted with the government for the bill to be passed (*Riksdag utskottsbetänkanden* SoU 1993/94: 25; SoU 1993/94: 34; *Riksdag* minutes 1993/94: 106, 18/5, 2 §; 1993/94: 108, 20/5, 4 §).

In addition, there were cases when the party sided with the opposition to abolish laws, whose introduction New Democracy had supported shortly before. An example of the latter was when the *Riksdag* voted to abolish a reform of the health care system, the so-called 'house doctor reform', in 1994. The reform had been introduced, with support from New Democracy, a year earlier.

Thus, there is no evidence of specific accommodation. No other party tried to make far-reaching deals with New Democracy. The fact that the party held the parliamentary balance meant that it was impossible to completely avoid contacts and agreements. But such agreements were made on an ad-hoc basis. There were no systematic attempts to force New Democracy into taking political responsibility. Indeed, Ian Wachtmeister himself often complained about the cold treatment received by himself and his party, for example in his book from 1992, *Krokodilerna* (the crocodiles). The title refers to mainstream politicians who, according to Wachtmeister, have big mouths but no ears.

General marginalization was never a likely strategy against New Democracy. It could have involved restrictions against expressing support for the party, carrying its symbols, etc. There is no evidence of such measures taken against New Democracy. General marginalization will be returned to in the next section in connection with the discussion on the response to neo-Nazism.

The refusal to involve the party in coalitions or cooperation pacts could perhaps be regarded as evidence of *specific marginalization*. There is, however, much that speaks against such a conclusion. It is true that some parties, especially the arch rival Liberals, did not wish to touch New Democracy with a barge pole, but there was no *cordon sanitaire* against the party. Cooperation was confined to ad-hoc agreements in the parliamentary committees; but for the most part the government worked on the assumption that it could rely on New Democracy's votes – a reliance that, as we have seen, was not always rewarded. The one occasion where deals with the Social Democrats were preferred rather than seeking New Democracy support was during the currency crisis in 1992, but this was a unique situation, portrayed by leading politicians as something of a national emergency. After the currency crisis, the Social Democrats did not seem to have any qualms about siding with New Democracy, if they could damage the government that way. There is definitely no evidence of plans of more severe marginalization. No attempts were made by the other parties to restrict New Democracy's chances of re-election by amending the electoral laws; nor the rules for receiving the state subsidies, that Swedish parties with parliamentary representation, or at least 2.5 per cent of the votes in a parliamentary election, are entitled to.

To sum up the discussion in this section, there is little evidence of specific or general marginalization, nor of specific accommodation in the response to New Democracy. It might be possible to trace elements of general accommodation, but this would be somewhat tenuous. Rather, the response during the 1991–4 parliamentary period had similarities with the response during the 1991 election campaign; in other words trying to avoid engaging with the party. Downs' (2001: p. 26) words, 'Ignore it and it will go away', may be something of an exaggeration, as the majority situation made it impossible to completely ignore New Democracy. But the other parliamentary parties tried to keep New Democracy at arm's length, and kept any cooperation to an ad-hoc basis.

There are several reasons why New Democracy was treated like this. First, although it was not extreme in its policies by international comparison, it represented something new and different in the Swedish party system. More important, however, the rhetoric and style of New Democracy alienated it from the other parties. A party, which constantly ridicules and makes fun of its political competitors can hardly expect much cooperation. Third, New Democracy soon earned a reputation as unreliable and lacking in seriousness. Thus, it was its behaviour at least as much as the policies that gave New Democracy its outsider status. It should also be noted that this was a position the party did not mind. New Democracy relied on its image as an outsider, and was not interested in appearing as too closely connected to the establishment (see Wachtmeister 1992).

The extra-parliamentary challenge: neo-Nazism and militant racism

Nazism does not have a particularly strong tradition in Sweden. A number of extreme right groups and parties did exist during the inter-war period. At times, they were quite noisy, but their political impact should not be overstated. Electorally, they were minuscule. Potential fifth-column groups existed during the war, but it seems as if the German regime never had much trust in the potential Swedish 'Quislings'. Although Sweden escaped occupation, Nazism was as discredited among Swedes as anywhere in Europe at the end of the war. The Nazi and fascist groups that survived were completely insignificant. Paul Wilkinson (1983) pointed out a number of racist incidents in Sweden in the early 1980s, but also noted that the Swedish government had gone further than many other countries in efforts to combat prejudice and conflict.

However, the second half of the 1980s saw a significant increase in the activities of extreme right groups. By the early 1990s, members of neo-Nazi groups had been convicted of murder, arson and bomb attacks (Larsson and Lodenius 1991). Extreme right activity continued to increase in the 1990s, with highly publicized incidents, such as racist attacks in Trollhättan in 1993 and the murder of the syndicalist trade unionist Björn Söderberg in the autumn of 1999.

In late 2000, the European Monitoring Centre on Racism and Xenophobia (EUMC) estimated that Sweden had the second highest level of racial and extreme right violence in the EU, behind Germany. In the 1999 Annual Report, the EUMC stated that in that year there were 2363 reported crimes with racial or xenophobic motives. These incidents included cases of illegal threats, assaults and molestation, and signified a continuous increase since 1997. Nearly 1000 crimes were committed by neo-Nazi organizations, including four reported cases of murder, and four attempted murders (EUMC 1999, pp. 28ff).

While estimations and international comparisons are extremely difficult to make, owing to the multitude of problems connected with the reporting and classification of racist and extreme right crime, the report reinforced the impression that Sweden is struggling to come to terms with its transition into a multiethnic society. Available evidence suggests that modern extreme right groups in Sweden have caused more harm and loss of life than their predecessors in the 1930s and 1940s.[2]

Thus, the seriousness of the extra-parliamentary extreme right challenge is clear. It could be argued that the response has had elements of *general accommodation*, in the sense that the tightening of the asylum laws discussed in the previous section were not only designed to prevent support for New Democracy from growing, but also to stifle support for more extreme organizations. Again, however, it is difficult to substantiate any such conclusion.

Specific accommodation can at once be ruled out as a possible response. The neo-Nazi and racist groups in question have not been represented in parliament, and could therefore not be subject to coalitions or systematic cooperation even in the highly unlikely event of the established parties entertaining such thoughts. Nor would it appear likely that there would be much interest in such cooperation among the Nazi and racist groups.

Instead, the debate in Sweden about the extra-parliamentary extreme right challenge has been focused on *marginalization*. Laws dealing with racism and extremism have existed for many years. A law against political uniforms was first introduced in 1933 (SOU 2000:88; Berg 1995; see however further below). Since 1948, there has been a law against the persecution of population groups (*'hets mot folkgrupp'*).[3] The law was changed in 1970, 1982 and 1988, and refers to verbal threats, and expressions of contempt, in a disseminated statement, against population groups or groups of persons, with reference to race, skin colour, national or ethnic origin, or faith (SOU 2000:88). This provision is also included in the constitutional Freedom of the Press Act of 1949, which regulates printed matter,[4] and the Fundamental Law on Freedom of Expression of 1991, which regulates broadcasts, film and video.[5] In addition, the constitutional Instrument of Government of 1974 states that 'Freedom of association may be restricted only in respect of organizations whose activities are of a military or quasi-military nature, or which involve the persecution of a population group of a particular race, skin colour or ethnic origin'.[6] So far, however, such legislation has not been used.

During the latter half of the 1990s, the increased activity of neo-Nazi groups meant that the existing legislation was subjected to unprecedented tests. In separate court verdicts in 1996 and 1997, it was ruled that the law against political uniforms could not be applied, as it 'manifestly' (i.e. obviously) conflicts with the Instrument of Government's protection of freedom of expression. The court cases in question involved individuals who had publicly worn armbands with Swastikas. The law against political uniforms still exists, but is to all intents and purposes impractical (SOU 2000:88). In another verdict, however, the Swedish Supreme Court ruled in 1996 that public display of emblems or symbols, or the wearing of clothes, connected with extreme right ideologies or racial hatred, is to be regarded as a case of persecution of population groups ('*hets mot folkgrupp*'; see above). Other court verdicts have established that the Roman/Nazi salute and 'Sieg Heil' shouts should be treated in the same way.

These changes have given the police increased powers to deal with neo-Nazi gatherings. Several arrests, some of which have led to prison sentences, have been made for offences under the law against persecution of population groups (SOU 2000:88). Thus, some of the most important changes in the way in which Swedish authorities deal with militant extreme right groups have been initiated at the judicial level. These changes have not involved the amendment of laws, or the introduction of new laws. Instead, they are cases of adjustments of the application of existing laws. It could be argued that the changes in question amount to making existing marginalization more precise.

This is not to say that the rise of neo-Nazi groups has been ignored by the main political parties. The 1988 decision in parliament to amend the law against persecution of population groups was explicitly designed to constrain extreme right activity. The change meant that any dissemination of racist statements was made illegal; earlier only statements made in public had been illegal (*Riksdagens Årsbok* 1987/88; *Riksdag utskottsbetänkanden* 1987/88 KU36). In 1994, parliament decided that more severe penalties for crimes such as assault etc, should be considered if the motive of the crime was to infringe on a person, or group of persons, due to their ethnic origin or faith. Again, this was explicitly designed to constrain the activities of extreme right groups (Bjørgo 1997; *Riksdag utskottsbetänkanden* 1993/94 JuU13). However, proposals to ban extreme right groups have so far been rejected by the *Riksdag* majority. Such proposals been made in private members motions by the Christian Democratic, Green, and Left parties – and New Democracy.

The problems with neo-Nazi groups have, to a great extent, been experienced at local government level. In a report published in 1999, Anna-Maria Blomgren has studied the local response to the neo-Nazi activity in the 'Trestad' area, which includes the cities of Trollhättan, Vänersborg and Uddevalla in western Sweden. Of the three studied cities, Trollhättan has experienced the most serious problems. After some incidents in 1992, troubles flared up the following year. The incident that received the most attention was when a mosque was burnt down by Nazis. There were also incidents of serious violence directly aimed at individuals.

Blomgren argues that a racist underground culture has existed in Trollhättan since the early 1990s. During the decade, neo-Nazi groups such as White Aryan Resistance (VAM) and National Socialist Front (NSF) were represented in the city. There have also been links to the militant magazine *Storm*, and a number of 'White Power' rock bands have existed in Trollhättan. It should be noted that the extreme right has also made an impact on the party political level. The Sweden Democrats have been represented in the Trollhättan city council since 1998. The Sweden Democrats have no open links to Nazi groups, but it appears as if informal links have existed in Trollhättan (Blomgren 1999).

Blomgren's study shows that the initial reaction by local politicians in Trollhättan was to treat the incidents as youth problems, and to deny the possibility of links to the Nazi ideology. Even after the burning of the mosque, the problems were considered to be at worst expressions of xenophobia, and the youths involved were thought to be 'mere' hooligans not afflicted by Nazism. The response included symbolic gestures and manifestations, such as a 'night walk' against violence, where circa 300 people walked around the city. A book with information and arguments against prejudice was distributed to every household, and a local action plan against racist and xenophobic violence was planned but apparently not implemented (Blomgren 1999). After an initial flurry of activity, the issue dropped off the political agenda, and became the concern of the police, social authorities and local youth centres. Gradually, as awareness grew that the problems had clear links to Nazism, the response became more decisive. However, most of the relevant decisions were taken at the administrative rather than political level. These included bans on the wearing of Nazi and racist symbols in schools, youth centres and other council-owned properties (this was before it was established that Nazi symbols were illegal; see above).

Council officials also tried to restrict the possibilities for extreme right organizations to hold public meetings in council-owned properties. According to Swedish law, it is not possible to refuse someone to use council properties to hold public meetings merely on the grounds of a political ideology. It is, however, possible to make such a refusal if the organizer has given incorrect information about the purpose of the meeting, or if the meeting is considered to be a risk for disorder (Blomgren 1999). Other ways of dealing with the problem have included the involvement of police, youth centres and schools in projects to reduce tensions between ethnic groups, provide alternative activities for youths who may be in danger of being recruited to extreme right groups, and to create an ideological climate that restricts the growth potential for racist and extreme right ideologies. The success of such projects has varied, and much research remains to be done on the response to Nazi groups at the local level. A key finding in Blomgren's study is that the responses in the cities she studied suffered from a lack of communication between different levels, such as the police, local politicians, schools and youth centres. Once these communications had been improved, the response against the Nazi groups became more effective.

Rundqvist (1999), who has studied the response in the southern city of Karlskrona, a stronghold for the NSF, has come to a similar conclusion. Much of the response in Karlskrona has taken the shape of information campaigns and public displays of disapproval of the Nazi ideology. Local politicians have taken part in such campaigns and manifestations, and have also tried to communicate with members of NSF. On the administrative level, Nazis have been refused to hire council-owned properties, even though council officials admit that this may not be legal. These measures did not lead to the disappearance of NSF, as discussed further below.

Thus, the response to neo-Nazi and militant racist organizations has mainly included elements of *marginalization*. Several decisions on the national political level have been designed to restrict the activities of neo-Nazi and racist groups. The extension of the law against persecution of population groups, the inclusion of such a provision in the Fundamental Law on Freedom of Expression, and the decision to subject offences with a racist motive to more severe penalties can all be interpreted in this way. All these decisions were explicitly designed to provide difficulties for racist organizations; in other words *specific marginalization*. At the same time, it should be noted that they also made it more difficult for the general public to express support for such organizations, or their ideas. Hence, they could also be regarded as including elements of *general marginalization*.

At the same time, there is much to suggest that the most important recent changes in the policy against neo-Nazi organizations have not been caused by political decisions. Instead, it was a verdict by the Supreme Court that widened the applicability of the law against persecution of population groups to include Nazi symbols. It was, furthermore, lower court decisions that widened the applicability of the law even further, also to include Nazi salutes and shouts. It is also worth remembering that the most severe form of specific marginalization, an outright ban on neo-Nazi and/or racist organizations, has so far been rejected by the parliamentary majority.

The case studies of local responses by Blomgren and Rundqvist reinforce this impression. It appears as if the most concrete decisions have been taken at the administrative rather than at the political level. It was just argued that a significant part of the response on the national level came from the judiciary rather than parliament. Thus, it seems as if the national and local responses had it in common that elected politicians did not provide the most decisive response. However, this assertion should be qualified somewhat. Some local politicians, notably the Social Democrat Björn Fries in Karlskrona, have defied threats and intimidation to express publicly their disapproval of racism and Nazism. Such manifestations are largely symbolic, but their significance should not be underestimated.

It is also worth noting that manifestations against racism and neo-Nazism have come from the media and parts of civil society. On 30 November 1999, four leading Swedish newspapers – *Aftonbladet*, *Expressen*, *Dagens Nyheter* and *Svenska Dagbladet* – published photographs and names of 62 activists in neo-Nazi groups and criminal motorcycle gangs. The initiative was taken by Anders Gerdin, editor of the Social Democratic tabloid *Aftonbladet*, which is Sweden's biggest circulation newspaper. This one-day campaign, which has not been repeated, received praise, but also criticism. For example, the Press Ombudsman argued that several of the included persons were young and had not been convicted of serious crimes and were therefore singled out because of their political beliefs (*Aftonbladet*, 2 December 1999). Other critics argued that some leading neo-Nazis had not been included, that some of the included persons were no longer active, and that the huge headlines created an atmosphere of panic that played into the hands of the neo-Nazis (Lodenius 2000).

Civil society has responded to the extreme right challenge in various ways. In March 2003, the bank Nordea decided to close an account held by the NSF (*Aftonbladet*, 6 March 2003). Trade unions do not accept open neo-Nazis as members. The murder of Björn Söderberg, mentioned above, was apparently motivated by the expulsion of an exposed neo-Nazi from a trade union, and some of the 62 individuals included in the 'name and shame' newspaper campaign were later expelled from unions. Anti-racist organizations are active in some parts of Sweden. The best known is Anti-Fascist Action (AFA), which frequently attempts to disturb neo-Nazi gatherings, and also became known for its involvement in the protests at the EU summit in Göteborg in June 2001. Another example is EXIT, a voluntary organization that receives government funding. It was founded in 1998 by Kent Lindahl, a former neo-Nazi, and aims to provide moral support for those who wish to leave racist and extreme nationalist organizations (Lindahl 2000).

Conclusions: a diversified response

The evidence presented in this chapter suggests significant differences in the response to the parliamentary and extra-parliamentary extreme right challenge. Beginning with the parliamentary challenge, it can be argued that the response to New Democracy, at least to some extent, included attempts to accommodate popular discontent with immigration, which was a contributory factor behind the party's initial success. If the argument is accepted that the Swedish refugee policy since the mid 1990s has included the introduction of some of the demands of New Democracy, then there may be some truth in such an allegation. It is, for example, possible to argue that the tightening of asylum criteria in 1996 may have been motivated by concern for support for (other) anti-immigration parties.

Still, as has been pointed out, there is little concrete evidence that there were such considerations behind the government policy.

Instead, the response to New Democracy is better characterized as tolerance without acceptance. New Democracy was regarded with contempt by the political establishment. It was certainly not given the same acceptance as the Christian Democratic Party, which also entered parliament for the first time in 1991, and went straight into the non-socialist government coalition. The other parties did not treat New Democracy as an equal in the party system; someone you compete with for votes, but whose existence you accept. Rather, it was treated as a relatively harmless, but unwelcome, guest. The other parties certainly hoped that the intruder would disappear as soon as possible, but no direct measures were taken to make this happen.

To ignore the party completely would hardly have been possible, given the difficult majority situation in the *Riksdag*. The government needed New Democracy's support, or at least to make sure that New Democracy did not support the opposition proposals. This became especially important when the level of conflict between the government and opposition increased after the unsuccessful attempt to rescue the Swedish currency. Thus, New Democracy was not systematically neglected. Wachtmeister, Karlsson *et al.* may have been considered as 'pariahs' by their political opponents, but they were not repulsive enough to break up traditional left–right bloc politics. Indeed, the opposition Social Democrats seemed more concerned to make life difficult for the government than to form, or participate in, a *cordon sanitaire* against New Democracy. The response may well be different if the Sweden Democrats enter the Riksdag in the future. There are reports of local *cordons sanitaires*, involving parties from the left and right blocs, in councils where the Sweden Democrats hold a pivotal position after the 2002 election.

If the response to New Democracy is somewhat tricky to characterize, the response to neo-Nazi and racist organizations seems to be more straightforward. The evidence presented in this chapter suggests that it has been dominated by marginalization; primarily specific but also general. Most of the measures taken have been designed to make life more difficult for neo-Nazis and racists.

Thus, the overall response to the extreme right in Sweden has been diversified. The parliamentary and extra-parliamentary challenges have been met with different responses. This difference can be regarded as appropriate, considering the relative seriousness of the respective challenges. The effects of the respective responses have also varied. New Democracy has disappeared, although the direct reasons for this were internal and difficult to attribute to the response from other parties. Meanwhile, neo-Nazi and militant groups continue to exist, even though their strength and activity has fluctuated. Nazi groups often tend to appear in some places, then disappear, usually to reappear somewhere else. There is little doubt that the tightening of the laws discussed in the previous section have facilitated a stronger response from the authorities than would otherwise have been possible. Still, there is a widespread feeling that neo-Nazism and militant racism continue to be a threat, which will require continued attention from politicians and authorities.

Bjørgo (1997) argues that responses to racism and neo-Nazism will not work if they are too simplistic or unidimensional. For example, attempts to soothe popular xenophobia by restricting immigration may have a negative effect unless they are combined with other policies, such as a forceful reaction against racist violence. Conversely, attempts to marginalize racist groups or parties may not be sufficient, unless they are combined with better integration policies and/or measures against poverty or youth unemployment. Thus, there is no simple remedy against the extreme right challenge. Much will depend on the concrete situation. What works in one context may be counter-productive in another.

In conclusion, the issue of extreme-right activity will be subject to continued debate. In the winter of 2001, the government presented to parliament a national action plan against racism, xenophobia, homophobia and discrimination. The document includes a report on actions already taken against these problems, as well as a number of new initiatives. Another government initiative was the International Forum on Combating Intolerance, which was held in Stockholm in January 2001. This received widespread international attention, and the initiative was given much praise. A cynic may have regarded it as a PR exercise, but the Forum dealt with concerns that are central to democracy. Research reports were presented and local and national counter-strategies were discussed. However, neo-Nazi activity has not ceased. In September 2002, the National Socialist Front participated in the local election in Karlskrona. The NSF held public marches and meetings, and the last week before the election supporters from elsewhere in Sweden, as well as Denmark and Germany, travelled to help the NSF campaign. The mainstream parties issued pleas not to vote Nazi, and there were counter-demonstrations against the public marches and meetings held by the NSF. There were several skirmishes between NSF supporters and counter-activists, but on the whole the Karlskrona election passed without major incidents. Still, it was the most coordinated election attempt by a full-blown Nazi party in Sweden since the 1930s, and the election received much attention in the national media, despite coinciding with the national parliamentary election. It could, perhaps, be argued that the strategy of a fairly limited response by the mainstream parties was successful, since the NSF failed to gain representation on the Karlskrona local council (the NSF received 208 votes, or 0.5 per cent, which was just over 300 votes short of what would have been necessary to gain one seat). Still, some representatives of other parties expressed concern that an openly Nazi party could receive as much as 200 votes (it could also be mentioned that the Sweden Democrats got 3.3 per cent of the vote, and three council seats, in the same election) (*EXPO*, issue 3, 2002). As these examples show, racism and right-wing extremism continue to be high on the political agenda in Sweden.

Notes

1 New Democracy also abstained during a vote on a finance bill on 17 March 1993, where the government had declared that it would dissolve parliament if the bill was defeated. *Riksdagens årsbok* 1992/93: 11, pp. 41ff.
2 This is not to say that Swedish Nazi groups of the 1930s and 1940s were harmless. The most serious case was the arson attack in 1940 on the communist newspaper *Norrskensflamman*, in which three adults and two children were killed. The perpetrators had Nazi sympathies, but there were no direct links to any particular organization. (Johansson 1973, p. 274). Still, the number of lives lost due to extreme right attacks in the 1980s and 1990s almost certainly exceed the corresponding figures from the 1930s and 1940s.
3 Literally, the word *folkgrupp* means 'group of people'. It is translated as 'population group' in the official translation of the Freedom of the Press Act, in which the law against persecution of population groups is mentioned (see note 4 below).
4 Freedom of the Press Act, chapter 7, article 4, section 11. The wording has been changed on a number of occasions. The current wording is that 'persecution of a population group, whereby a person threatens or expresses contempt for a population group or other such group with allusion to its race, skin colour, national or ethnic origin, or religious faith' shall be regarded as an offence against the freedom of the press, if the statement is punishable under law.
5 Fundamental Law on Freedom of Expression, chapter 5 article 1.
6 Instrument of Government, Chapter 2, article 14; SOU 2000:88, pp. 186f.

Bibliography

Arter, D. (1992) 'Black faces in the blond crowd: populist racialism in Scandinavia', *Parliamentary Affairs* 45, 3: 357–372.
Berg, L. (1995) *Lagen om förbud mot politiska uniformer*. Göteborg: unpublished undergraduate thesis (*B-uppsats*), Department of Political Science.
Bjørgo, T. (1997) *Racist and Ring-Wing Violence in Scandinavia. Patterns, Perpetrators and Responses*. Oslo: Tano Aschehoug.
Blomgren, A.-M. (1999) *Vad gör samhället? Offentlig politik mot rasistiskt och främlingsfientligt våld i Vänersborg, Trollhättan och Uddevalla*. Stockholm: CEIFO.
Demker, M. (2000) 'Attityder till flyktingar: unga flickor och unga pojkar på var sin sida', in Holmberg, S. and Weibull, L. (eds.) *Det nya samhället*. Göteborg: The SOM Institute, pp. 59–68.
Downs, W.M. (2001) 'Pariahs in their midst: Belgian and Norwegian parties react to extremist threats', *West European Politics* 24, 3: 23–42.
Elmbrant, B. (1993) *Så föll den svenska modellen*. Stockholm: T. Fischer.
Finn, J. (2000) 'Electoral regimes and the proscription of anti-democratic parties', *Democracy and Violence* 3–4, 12: 51–77.
EUMC (1999) *Annual Report 1999*, available at: http://www.eumc.at/publications/ar99/AR99.htm.

http://www.immi.se/asyl/198097.htm. Website of the *Immigrant Institute*; Research and documentation center on migration.
Johansson, A. (1973) *Finlands sak. Svensk politik och opinion under vinterkriget 1939–1940*. Stockholm: Allmänna förlaget.
Katz, R.S. and Mair P. (1995) 'Changing models of party organization: the emergence of the Cartel Party', *Party Politics* 1, 1: 5–28.
Larsson, S. and Lodenius, A.-L. (1991) *Extremhögern*. Stockholm: Tiden.
Lindahl, K. (2000) *Exit – min väg bort från nazismen*. Stockholm: Norstedts.
Lodenius, A.-L. (2000) 'Tveksam mediakampanj mot nazistiskt hot', *Politik i norden*, 1.
Mudde, C. (2000) *The Ideology of the Extreme Right*. Manchester: Manchester University Press.
Ny Demokrati (1991) *Partiprogram 1991*.
Oscarsson, H. (1998) *Den svenska partirymden. Väljarnas uppfattningar av konfliktstrukturen i partisystemet 1956–1996*. Göteborg: Department of Political Science (Göteborg Studies in Politics 54).
Pekonen, K. (ed.) (1999) *The New Radical Right in Finland*. Jyväskylä: The Finnish Political Science Association.
Pred, A. (2000): *Even in Sweden. Racisms, Racialized Spaces, and the Popular Geographical Imagination*. Los Angeles: University of California Press.
Qvortrup, M. (2002a) 'The emperor's new clothes: the Danish General Election 20 November 2001', *West European Politics* 25, 2: 205–211.
Qvortrup, M. (2002b) 'The emperor's new clothes: the Danish General Election 20 November, 2001', *European Political Science* 2, 1: 17–22.
Riksdagens årsbok, 1987/1988; 1991/1992; 1992/1993. Stockholm: Sveriges riksdag.
Rundqvist, M. (1999) *Demokratins muskler. Kommunpolitikers och lokala myndighetspersoners åtgärder mot nationalsocialismen i Karlskrona*. Stockholm: CEIFO.
Schedler, A. (1996) 'Anti-political establishment parties', *Party Politics* 2, 3: 291–312.
Särlvik, B. (1983) 'Coalition politics and policy output in Scandinavia: Sweden, Denmark and Norway', in Bogdanor, V. (ed.) *Coalition Government in Western Europe*. London: Heineman, pp. 97–152.
SOU 2000:88: *Organiserad brottslighet, hets mot folkgrupp, hets mot homosexuella, m.m. – straffansvarets räckvidd. Betänkande från Kommittén om straffansvar för organiserad brottslighet m.m.* Stockholm: Fritzes (Statens Offentliga Utredningar).
Taggart, P.A. (1996) *The New Populism and the New Politics. New Protest Parties in Sweden in a Comparative Perspective*, Basingstoke and London: Macmillan.
Taggart, P.A. (2000) *Populism*. Buckingham: Open University Press.
Teorell, J. (1998) *Demokrati eller fåtalsvälde? Om beslutsfattande i partiorganisationer*. Uppsala: Acta Universitatis Upsaliensis.
Wachtmeister, I. (1992) *Krokodilerna*. Stockholm: AB IW Ventures.
Widfeldt, A. (2000) 'Scandinavia: mixed success for the populist right', *Parliamentary Affairs* 53, 3: 486–500.
Wilkinson, P. (1983) *The New Fascists*. London: Pan.

8 Right-wing extremism in the land of the free
Repression and toleration in the USA

George Michael

Introduction

By most accounts, right-wing extremism appeared to make a comeback in the United States during the 1990s. Although, this did not manifest itself in electoral success, due in large part to the nature of the American electoral system, the far right seemed to gain ground as a social movement. What is more, recent trends in technology, such as the Internet, have enabled the far right to reach out to a potentially larger audience than it has in the past. Finally, some high profile confrontations with law enforcement authorities and horrific acts of political violence – most notably the 1995 bombing of Murrah federal building in Oklahoma City – have seared the issue of right-wing terrorism into the public's mind.

By contrast to, for example, Germany and Israel (see Chapter 5), the United States has a strong civil liberties tradition and because of First Amendment protections, the government does not officially have the authority to disband extremist groups or proscribe extremist speech just because they may espouse unpopular ideas. While it is axiomatic to say that virtually all terrorists come from the ranks of extremists, most extremists are not terrorists. This puts authorities in a bit of a conundrum. From a comparative legal perspective, the US government appears to be more constrained in responding to political extremism. However, what is often ignored is that private non-governmental organizations (NGOs) have interjected themselves into this area of public policy and have done much to fill the void. Compared with other western nations, the federal government's response to right-wing terrorism and extremism is unique insofar as it engenders much greater participation from NGOs. Moreover, these NGOs have persuaded the government to take a strong position vis-à-vis the far right.

This chapter examines the US response to domestic right-wing terrorism and extremism. It is argued that, in essence, the response is a joint effort by both the government and private watchdog groups. The next section introduces the major NGOs, which figure prominently in this area of public policy. The section after examines how the US government has responded to the far right with particular emphasis on those episodes of collaboration with NGOs. Measures are then explored by which the NGOs have sought to counter the far right. The final section explains why the NGOs have been successful in this regard and speculates on what effect they have had in curbing right wing extremism.

NGOs and the far right

The number of NGOs, or so-called watchdog groups, which monitor the activities of the extreme right, has grown considerably over the past two decades. In fact, a recent University of Florida study estimates that there are now approximately 300 such groups nationwide (Padilla 1999). Like its far right opponents, the watchdog community is a variegated combination of groups – there seems to be a good deal of variation in the staff composition and orientations of the various NGOs.

First, there are the so-called Jewish defense organizations, which seek to safeguard the interests of Jews both in the United States and overseas. The chief organization in this category, and indeed for all NGOs in this area of policy, is the Anti-Defamation League (ADL). The ADL is well financed and maintains 33 regional offices in various American cities as well as foreign countries, including Austria, Canada, and Israel. This NGO sets the pace for the others as it has taken the lead in countering the far right through various measures including, *inter alia*, the promotion of legislation (e.g. anti-paramilitary training statutes and hate crime legislation), cooperation with law enforcement agencies, training programs, and the promotion of software that blocks access to extremist web sites. Through its nationwide intelligence apparatus, the ADL has been able to closely monitor developments in the far right.

The most recent Jewish defense organization to gain prominence is the Simon Wiesenthal Center (SWC), which has its headquarters in Los Angeles, California. For most of its history, the SWC has concentrated on educational efforts, but in recent years has expanded the scope of its domestic agenda to include monitoring right-wing extremist groups in the United States and abroad.

The Southern Poverty Law Center (SPLC) in Montgomery, Alabama is unique and in a category of its own. It is arguably, second only to the ADL, the most influential watchdog group. It has pioneered the use of civil suits to hold far-right groups responsible for the actions of their individual members. Some of these civil suits have resulted in very large judgments and in doing so, have bankrupted several far-right groups. Thus, the SPLC is among the most feared NGOs by the far right. The major Jewish defense groups together with the SPLC constitute, in my opinion, the first level of watchdog organizations. Those that follow are essentially second-level organizations.

The progressive-oriented NGOs constitute the third category of this taxonomy. Prominent among them is the Center for Democratic Renewal (CDR) of Atlanta, Georgia. The CDR has favored a grass roots approach as it seeks to form coalitions with like-minded progressive activists. Another prominent organization of the progressive-oriented NGOs is Political Research Associates (PRA) in Sommerville, Massachusetts. It is primarily a research center, which provides a clearinghouse of information for people who want either to study the American political right wing or organize against some of its public policy positions.[1] Much like the CDR, several members of its staff have progressive and left-wing political backgrounds.[2] One characteristic that differentiates the progressive watchdog groups from their better-established counterparts is their relationship to law enforcement agencies, as they are much less likely to get involved in intelligence sharing.

The regional watchdog groups compose a fourth category of NGOs. Chief among them is the Northwest Coalition Against Malicious Harassment (NWC), which currently has its headquarters in Seattle, Washington. The NWC was founded in 1986 as a community-based initiative to counter right-wing extremism in the Northwest emanating primarily from the Aryan Nations compound in Hayden Lake, Idaho. The NWC employs a variety of strategies to counter the far right, including providing assistance to communities to prevent acts of racist violence and harassment; educating communities about far right groups, and related issues, such as bias crime; and monitoring extremist activities in the region. Another NGO in this category is the Center for New Community, a regional watchdog group based in Chicago, Illinois with a faith-based approach, which enlists support primarily from liberal religious organizations, but also civic, education, labor, business, and government agencies as well. Its primary focus is on regional far right activity, such as Matt Hale's World Church of the Creator, which has its headquarters in East Peoria, Illinois, and Midwestern Christian Identity groups.

In recent years, right-wing extremists have taken to the Internet with great enthusiasm. Consequently, a fifth category – the Internet-based watchdogs – have created websites to counter their on-line propaganda. Some important examples in this category are the Nizkor Project, which focuses primarily on countering the claims of Holocaust revisionists; Hatewatch, which seeks to warn web surfers of the threat of on-line extremists; and the Militia Watchdog, which tracks the activities of those in the Christian Patriot/Militia movement.

The miscellaneous category has been included to complete this taxonomy. In recent years, loose networks of self-styled anarchists have confronted their far-right opponents in the streets and other public venues. Most notable in this regard is Anti-Racist Action (ARA). According to the organization's history, the first ARA chapter was formed in Minneapolis, Minnesota in 1986, when an anti-racist skinhead gang joined forces with a group of self-styled punks in a campaign to rid the twin cities of a racist skinhead gang.[3] Today, ARA claims to have chapters in over 130 cities and towns in the United States and Canada, and plans on opening new chapters in Mexico, Columbia, and Asia (Ferguson 2000, p. 1). Generally, ARA is an outlier in the watchdog community in that it does not enjoy the considerable credibility and good standing with the general public that other NGOs do. What's more, ARA chapters in general do not have the close working relationship with governmental authorities that many of the other watchdog groups enjoy. The ARA sees itself as willing to do the dirty work by confronting their opponents directly in the streets. However, this approach has also alienated other watchdog groups and governmental authorities alike. Perhaps what is most significant about the ARA is that it could conceivably ride on the coat-tails of a nascent anarchist movement, which has gained momentum in recent years in response to globalization, and could therefore serve as a gateway for younger people to get involved in watchdog and other anti-racist activities.

Now that the major NGOs have been identified it is time to take a closer look at how the US government has grappled with this issue. On numerous occasions NGOs have augmented the government's efforts.

US government's response to right-wing extremism and terrorism

Episodes of right-wing extremism and violence have sporadically punctuated American history almost from the founding of the republic. Consequently, this issue has frequently impelled the federal government to respond. Although several agencies and branches of the government – including Congress, the Supreme Court, and the Department of Defense – have dealt with this issue, this chapter focuses primarily on the Federal Bureau of Investigation (FBI) insofar as it has historically been the chief government agency responsible for investigating political extremism and domestic terrorism.

Historical background

The origins of the close working relationship between the federal government and NGOs in the effort to counter right-wing extremism can be traced back to the 1930s when the Unites States was in the throes of the Great Depression, which ushered in an era of renewed far-right activism. A variety of measures were used to counter right-wing extremism during this period. By 1936, President Franklin D. Roosevelt was concerned that potentially hostile fascist and communist governments might have an influence on domestic extremist groups. To meet this potential challenge, Roosevelt instructed Hoover to develop an intelligence apparatus to gather information on extremist groups (Davis 1992, p. 26). The bureau was authorized to gather domestic intelligence, in this case by presidential directive rather than by statute.

The ADL and the American Jewish Committee augmented the intelligence efforts of the government, as the two organizations worked closely together and provided information to government authorities including congressional committees, Army and Navy Intelligence, and the FBI (ADL 1965, p. 32; Schonbach 1958, pp. 436–437; Schachner 1948, pp. 123, 159–162). According to a claim by Arnold Forster, an important member of the ADL's fact-finding division during that period, most of the data on pro-Nazi propaganda that federal agencies possessed came from the ADL field investigators and other private organizations (Forster 1988, p. 55). The ADL often employed agents from outside investigative agencies who operated as independent contractors. Many were retired federal government investigators (Forster 1988, p. 56).

By the end of World War II the American far right was demoralized and imploding. However, events in the 1950s allowed it to rebound as a renascent Klan emerged in the aftermath of the *Brown v. Topeka Board of Education* Supreme Court decision in 1954. After 1956, the FBI conducted a campaign of surveillance against left-wing extremist groups. In 1964 though, the FBI decided to add the Klan and various 'white hate groups' to the list of targets under COINTELPRO.[4] According to the 1964 FBI memorandum that initiated this effort '[t]he purpose of this program is to expose, disrupt and otherwise neutralize the activities of the various Klans and hate organizations, their leadership and adherents' (FBI 1964). In total, 289 different programs of action were approved and used against various Klan and far-right organizations (Finch 1983, p. 158). Cumulatively, these COINTELPRO measures had a devastating effect on the morale of right-wing extremist groups. It created so much suspicion among members that they were extremely loath to initiate violence in any kind of organizational setting. By 1971, membership in the Klan had plummeted from its high of 14,000 members in 1964, to 4,300 members (Davis 1992, p. 93).

From the perspective of the government, these efforts were generally successful as the targeted extremist groups were effectively neutralized by the program. However, when details of COINTELPRO became available, it provoked both a legislative and public backlash against the government. The negative publicity surrounding the program pressured the Justice Department to make changes to the law enforcement and investigative policies of the FBI. Hence, the Levi Guidelines were adopted on April 5, 1976 in an attempt to de-politicize the FBI.[5] The guidelines marked a significant departure from traditional policy in that it moved federal law enforcement away from its preventive functions. Furthermore, these changes came on the heels of the Privacy Act of 1974, which attempted to stop the FBI from spying on people because of their political beliefs. The overall results of these changes were dramatic. The number of domestic intelligence cases initiated dropped from 1,454 in 1975 to only 95 in 1977 (Davis 1992, p. 176). Significantly, however, there was nothing in the guidelines that precluded the FBI from opening an investigation based on information received from private groups such as the SPLC and the ADL.

1980–93: from 'Operation Clean-Sweep' to Waco

By the early 1980s, terrorism had become a salient issue in the public mind. Several high profile acts of international terrorism against US personnel overseas compelled the government to take measures to protect American territory from such eventualities. To meet such potential challenges, Oliver Buck Revell, then the head of the FBI's Criminal Investigative Division, persuaded FBI Director William Webster in 1983 to authorize the creation of an elite anti-terrorist division in the FBI. Webster agreed, and Special Agent Danny O. Coulson was made the first commander of the Hostage Rescue Team (HRT) – an elite squad of 50 agents who could be deployed at a moment's notice to handle such emergencies (Revell 1998, pp. 254–255).[6]

The first major deployment of the new unit occurred in 1985 when it was called upon to arrest members of the Covenant, Sword, and the Arm of the Lord (CSA) at the group's compound in Arkansas. The operation was a stunning success as the violent-prone CSA, and fugitive members of the Order that had sought sanctuary there, surrendered without incident after two days of negotiations with HRT Commander Coulson (Coulson and Shannon 1999). Increasingly the activities of the radical right caught the attention of federal authorities and a concerted effort was made to stymie them.

From mid 1983 through the end of 1985, the underground revolutionary group, the Order, electrified the radical right and alarmed the government with a series of spectacular crimes that included bank robberies and armored car heists. To counter the threat of renascent right-wing terrorism, in 1985 the FBI, the IRS Security Division, the Justice Department, and the Bureau of Alcohol Tobacco and Firearms (ATF) joined forces in one of the largest joint efforts in law enforcement history, known as 'Operation Clean-Sweep', to investigate leaders of the movement (Seymour 1991, p. 5). It was, however, primarily a Department of the Treasury initiative and was allegedly the brainchild of an Assistant US Attorney, Steven Snyder (Coulson and Shannon 1999, p. 533).

Operation Clean-Sweep culminated in the Fort Smith sedition trial of 1988 in which a who's who of some of the most radical elements of the far right were prosecuted for conspiring to overthrow the United States government. James Ellison, the former leader of the CSA, turned state's evidence and was the government's star witness at the trial. Despite great effort on the part of federal prosecutors and the ADL, an Arkansas jury acquitted all of the defendants and the far right enjoyed a rare upset victory.[7]

This legal victory notwithstanding, at this stage the radical right was in disarray and the domestic terrorist threat from both the left and the right had largely evaporated by the mid-1980s. However, this lull in activity would prove to be short-lived. The 1990s would witness several high profile confrontations between political and religious extremists and law enforcement authorities.

The 1992 siege at Ruby Ridge was one of the first such incidents to gain widespread notoriety. The raid, which had begun as an ATF operation to arrest Randy Weaver on minor firearms violations, escalated into a firefight in which Weaver's son Sammy and an AFT Deputy Marshal were killed. Once a federal agent had been slain, the FBI assumed responsibility for the incident and the HRT was deployed. A series of bad policy decisions compounded the crisis, which tragically resulted in the fatal shooting of Weaver's wife, Vicki. Eventually, Weaver and co-defendant Kevin Harris surrendered to authorities but were ultimately acquitted of all of the most serious charges. Moreover, the jury fined the federal government for withholding evidence and for lying, and concluded that the federal government had acted with a 'callous disregard for the rights of the defendants and the interests of justice' (Kopel and Blackman 1997, p. 38). The government eventually settled a civil suit with Weaver and paid $3.1 million to him and his surviving children. In sum the incident had a devastating effect on the morale of the FBI as several agents with stellar service records effectively had their careers ruined.

Although the Ruby Ridge fiasco captured only a limited amount of public attention when it occurred, other incidents soon followed that would later magnify its significance. Just a few months later, the siege at Waco, i.e. the Branch Davidian compound in Mount Carmel, would lay bare the consequences of faulty planning in responding to dissident groups as well as the pitfalls that can occur when authorities rely on intelligence from NGOs without adequate corroboration (Kopel and Blackman 1997; Ammerman 1995, p. 289; Wright 1995, pp. 88–89).

This siege and subsequent conflagration at Waco galvanized the far right as the militia movement spread throughout many states. What's more, it provoked Timothy McVeigh to strike out against the government in revenge.

The Oklahoma City bombing and its aftermath

The April 19, 1995 bombing of the Murrah federal building in Oklahoma City, which killed 169 people, was, at the time, the most lethal act of terrorism committed on American soil. It did not take the authorities long to find the suspects. The mastermind of the bombing, Timothy McVeigh, was apprehended the same day of the attack and ultimately sentenced to death for the crime. His accomplice, Terry Nichols, was sentenced to life in prison. A third defendant, Michael Fortier, plea bargained with authorities, and received a sentence of 12 years in exchange for cooperating with the prosecution (Jones and Israel 1998, p. 96).

Prior to the bombing, the FBI did not pay much attention to the militia movement. Furthermore, one of its most extensive investigations failed to turn up a significant militia connection to the bombing. However, after this attack, the association between the two stuck in the public mind and the FBI began to monitor the militias and other far-right organizations much more closely. In the aftermath there were many calls to alter and expand counter-terrorism policy. This event, more than any other factor, was the impetus behind the expansion of counter-terrorism programs.

For starters, FBI Director Louis Free loosened the attorney general guidelines for investigating extremist groups (Redden 2000, p. 71). He also formed the Executive Working Group on Domestic Terrorism, which meets every two weeks to consider intelligence and plan strategy. Not even a year after its founding, FBI militia investigations had increased fourfold (Klaidman and Isikkoff 1996, p. 47). As a result of these policy changes, the number of politically oriented domestic surveillance operations increased substantially. Just prior to the Oklahoma City bombing, the FBI was working on roughly 100 terrorist investigations. This figure jumped to roughly 900 two years after the bombing (Kaplan and Tharp 1997–8, pp. 22–27).

After the fiascos of Ruby Ridge and Waco, the federal government began responding to right-wing extremists more gingerly, but still resolutely. The 1996 siege of the Montana Freemen at their 'Justus Township' estate in Jordan, Montana was a success story in this regard. Members of the Freemen were accused of committing a variety of acts of 'paper terrorism' in the Midwest region of the country such as issuing billions of dollars in phony checks and filing illegal property liens against their enemies. The FBI enlisted the support of high-profile figures in the Patriot movement to help negotiate an end to the standoff. It ended peacefully and the ensuing fallout in the Patriot community led to the diminution of a movement that the FBI had identified as a serious threat to domestic security. However, both the FBI and NGOs continued to monitor far-right groups and warn of their potential danger.

For example, just prior to the turn of the century in the fall of 1999, the FBI released a report, *Project Megiddo*, which alerted various chiefs of police around the country to the potential violence that groups holding millenarian beliefs could perpetrate. The report focused almost exclusively on the political right. Surprisingly, the subject of Islamic extremism was completely ignored. It was highly suspected by some observers that both the ADL and the SPLC had a hand in the preparation of the report.[8] For its part the FBI denied any such collusion.[9] Fueling this suspicion was the coincidence that the ADL issued a report *Y2K Paranoia: Extremists Confront the Millennium*, at the same conference – the International Association of Chiefs of Police in Charlotte, North Carolina – at which the FBI released its report. As it turned out, no significant far-right activity occurred at the turn of the new millennium.

Another example that illustrates the vigilance with which the government and NGOs have responded to the radical right is the case of Alex Curtis. Until recently, Curtis, a young man from San Diego, California, was the most vociferous advocate of the leaderless resistance approach to right-wing terrorism. Through audio programs on his *Nationalist Observer* website, he reviewed and critiqued recent episodes of right-wing violence. He would point out mistakes and offer suggestions on how they could be avoided. Not surprisingly, Curtis' violent rhetoric caught the attention of authorities and the watchdog organizations. In November 2000 the ADL issued a critical report on Curtis entitled *Alex Curtis: Lone Wolf of Hate Prowls the Internet*. About a week later he was arrested along with two other individuals for various alleged civil rights violations. The arrests were the culmination of an extensive two-year joint investigation by the FBI and the San Diego Police Department dubbed 'Operation Lone Wolf'. Failing to follow his own advice, Curtis allegedly acted with others to harass several prominent figures in the San Diego area.[10] Despite the amateurish characteristics of the alleged offenses, the authorities have taken Curtis and his accomplices seriously, as they remain in prison as of 2003.

The September 11 attacks on the World Trade Center and Pentagon brought home the issue of terrorism like no other previous attack in America's history. The government was strongly criticized in many quarters for its failure to anticipate and prepare for such a horrific eventuality. This perception notwithstanding, the Clinton administration had in fact given high priority to the issue of domestic terrorism. For example, President Clinton issued Presidential Decision Directive (PDD) 39 in 1995, which designated the FBI as the chief government agency responsible for investigating and preventing domestic terrorism. It was the first directive to make terrorism a national top priority and concluded the United States was threatened from within (Blitzer 1997).

Soon thereafter, new legislation was passed including the Anti-Terrorism and Effective Death Penalty Act of 1996, which contained the most thoroughgoing measures heretofore, aimed at combating terrorism. The various new laws and initiatives nearly doubled the amount of money spent on counter-terrorism to $11 billion a year (Redden 2000, p. 71). Much of the money went to the FBI, whose annual funding for its counter-terrorism program had grown from $78.5 million in 1993 to $301.2 million in 1999. Moreover, the number of agents funded for counter-terrorism investigations grew from 550 in 1993 to 1,383 in 1999 (Freeh 1999).

In the aftermath of the September 11 attack, the federal government, with support from the American public and US Congress, called for more vigilant measures to root out potential terrorists at home and abroad.[11] To meet the exigencies of the new terrorist threat, Congress passed the US PATRIOT Act, which was signed into law by President Bush on October

26, 2001. The thrust of the new law was to give authorities more options for surveillance with less judicial supervision (Herman n.d.). These new measures were welcomed by the ADL (ADL 2001a).

President Bush also approved the use of special military tribunals to streamline the trials of suspected foreign terrorists, as they allow for greater secrecy and faster trials than ordinary criminal courts. The ADL endorsed this new measure, as it issued a press release praising the new guidelines as 'a significant step forward in efforts to balance national security interests with traditional rights accorded criminal suspects in American courts' (ADL 2002a).

From the perspective of the far right and other unpopular dissident movements, these new measures are worrisome. Since the 9/11 attack, several far right activists – including David Duke, Matt Hale, Ernst Zündel, and several members of the National Alliance – have been arrested on charges which a fair reading would suggest were at least in part politically motivated. Thus, the far right's fears that the war on terror could turn inward against domestic extremists is not unfounded.

Now that the government's response has been examined, it is time to take a closer look at the various methods by which the NGOs have sought to counter their ideological opponents.

The watchdogs' response to the far right

The watchdog groups take a multifaceted approach to countering right-wing terrorism and extremism. One obvious concern to both the watchdogs and the government alike is paramilitary training by extremist groups. Even prior to the emergence of the contemporary militia movement, other segments of the far right have occasionally gained notoriety for this type of activity. These activities quickly caught the attention of watchdog groups and they wasted no time in looking for ways to curb this trend. The ADL took the lead in this effort by crafting legislation, which proscribed paramilitary training by unauthorized groups. The SPLC followed suit and also introduced its sponsored legislation. When the contemporary militia movement surfaced in 1994, more attention was brought to this issue. The watchdogs were ready to respond with a media campaign to heighten public awareness of the fledging movement and its potential for danger. The campaign has proven to be very successful as 24 states have enacted such statutes, 13 of which are based on the ADL's model (ADL 1998a). The thrust of the legislation is to make it illegal to operate paramilitary camps (ADL 1995).

Another measure aimed largely at the militia right is ADL-sponsored legislation proscribing so-called 'common law courts.' These pseudo-legal venues became popular with some militia groups during the mid-1990s. Typically these courts render judgments including property liens, criminal indictments, and other forms of 'paper terrorism' against their enemies and state authorities whom they believe have violated the Constitution and the public's trust.

To meet this challenge the ADL's Legal Affairs Department drafted a model statute in 1996 that criminalizes the practice of common law courts and introduced this measure into state legislatures (ADL 1997a, p. 2). What's more, the federal government has focused more attention on the issue, as evidenced by the FBI's *Terrorism in the United States 1997* report on domestic terrorism, which carried a story on the problem (FBI 1998, pp. 11–12). These combined efforts appear to have had a deterrent effect as the reported number of these courts has dwindled substantially over the past few years.[12] The current trend of hate crime legislation could have even greater potential in countering the far right in that it makes expressions of racial and ethnic hostility potentially very costly.

Hate crime laws are occasionally used to prosecute perpetrators of right-wing violence. Essentially a 'hate' or 'bias' crime is one that is directed against a victim because of some immutable attribute such as race, ethnicity or some affiliation (religion) or particular lifestyle (gay and lesbian, interracial marriage). Right-wing terrorists very often choose targets they perceive as 'outsiders' for no other reason than some ascriptive characteristic mentioned above. Moreover, because of the organizational fragmentation of the American far right, the distinction between terrorism and hate crimes is often blurred. Although very few right-wing groups regularly commit terrorism, some advocate violence and can presumably influence the 'lone wolves' that do.[13] Thus, hate crime laws can be used to counter right-wing violence. Most offenders arrested for hate crimes do not formally belong to organized far right groups and even those that do belong to such groups usually act independently without any directive from their organizations.[14] Be that as it may, watchdog groups have done much to link organized far right groups with the issue.

The ADL has been the most important advocate of hate crime legislation by far, and began lobbying for it in the 1970s. Its model statute, or a close facsimile, had been adopted in all but nine states by 1998 (ADL 1998b). Some local police departments have developed close working relationships with NGOs in this area.[15] Many politicians at the local, state, and national levels are now eager to champion such measures under the cause of combating bigotry and promoting greater inter-group tolerance.

Although the perpetrators of hate crimes are usually juveniles or young adults and without much wealth, the SPLC has on occasion used civil suits to hold far-right organizations responsible for the actions of their law-breaking members. This novel and controversial use of the civil suit has effectively put some right-wing organizations out of business. In essence, this approach seeks to hold leaders of far right organizations vicariously liable for the actions of their members, even in some instances where there is no evidence of any directive to commit an illegal act. The SPLC has effectively used this tactic on many occasions and has won judgment against several far right organizations, including Louis Beam's Knights of the Ku Klux Klan, Robert Shelton's United Klans of America, Tom Metzger's White Aryan Resistance, and most recently Richard Butler's Aryan Nations.

Some of the SPLC's detractors assert that the center is opportunistic in that it supposedly takes advantage of some of its clients for its own personal gain (e.g. Silverstein 2000; Wilcox 1999). The argument usually goes that although the plaintiffs might be awarded huge multi-million dollar judgments, they actually see very little of that money because these right-wing organizations are usually poorly financed. The SPLC counters that its aim is not so much to make money for its clients from damage awards, but rather to bankrupt the organizations and individuals responsible for crimes and effectively put them out of business (Dees and Bowden n.d.).

The ever-expanding Internet medium presents the opportunity for groups and individuals that would otherwise not have access to the marketplace of ideas a chance to have their views heard. The far right has enthusiastically taken advantage of the new medium and sees it as a powerful vehicle through which to spread its message. According to some estimates, by 1999, there were somewhere between 600 to 2,100 such websites worldwide.[16]

Not surprisingly, the use of the Internet by right-wing extremists has caused much consternation among the watchdog groups as several of them have taken measures to meet this new challenge. The Simon Wiesenthal Center produced a CD-ROM called *Digital Hate 2000* that lists extremist sites that it finds offensive (Arent 1999). Since 1985, the ADL has released several reports on the topic; for example, *Computerized Networks of Hate* (ADL 1985), *Web of Hate* (ADL 1996), *High-Tech Hate* (ADL 1997b) and *Poisoning the Web* (ADL 1999a). Moreover, on at least one occasion the ADL has testified before the Senate on the issue (ADL 1999b). In 1999, the ADL created *HateFilter* – a software program that blocks access to far right websites. Somewhat related to this issue, pressure is occasionally exerted on Internet Service Providers to prohibit offensive discourse on bulletin boards and dissuade various dot.com merchants to restrict the sale of items with extremist themes.

Training and educational programs are important instruments by which the NGOs can influence public policy towards extremism. For quite some time, the ADL has been active in this area. For example it periodically presents lectures on extremism at the FBI academy in Quantico, Virginia (ADL 1980). More recently, in April 2002, the ADL announced that is was distributing a CD-ROM entitled, *Extremism in America: A Guide*, to law enforcement officials across the country (ADL 2002b). Other watchdog groups have joined in this effort as well and offer similar programs of their own, which they conduct for both government agencies and private organizations.

The most effective effort in countering the far right has been in the area of intelligence sharing. Once again the ADL has taken the lead in this area. The SPLC has moved into this area as well and, as Morris Dees put it, the organization 'has long shared intelligence with law enforcement agencies' (Dees 1993, p. 19). The SPLC is thought to have one of the most comprehensive databases on right-wing extremism. Its researchers and investigators are reported to clip about 1,000 newspaper articles a week and read 150 far right magazines, which it receives through disguised addresses (Shapiro 1999). Furthermore, the SPLC reportedly monitors approximately 500 extremist websites daily to alert researchers to any changes (Arent 1999). Both the ADL and SPLC regularly issue newsletters and research reports to law enforcement agencies on the activities of far right groups.

FBI documents obtained under the Freedom of Information Act (FOIA) indicate that the ADL has made considerable efforts to cultivate a close working relationship with the FBI.[17] In 1985 the ADL won a remarkable coup when the FBI issued a memorandum instructing its field offices to 'contact each [ADL] Regional Office to establish a liaison and line of communication' (FBI 1985).

Some critics believe that the intelligence sharing between the FBI and the watchdog groups constitutes a circumvention of the Attorney General's Guidelines in that the former can prevail upon the latter's files when it sees fit to do so. Moreover, watchdog groups do not have to concern themselves with strict civil liberties restrictions to which the FBI must adhere when gathering information on its subjects of investigation. Finally, another area of concern is the circulation of personnel between law enforcement and the watchdog groups. For example, Neil Herman, a retired high-ranking FBI official who once led the agency's Joint Terrorist Task Force, became the head of the ADL's Fact-Finding Division upon his retirement from the bureau in 1999. Not long after assuming this position, he lobbied senior Justice Department officials to relax the constraints that inhibit the FBI from investigating extremist groups (Rosenlum 1999). He resigned from this position in 2000.

The various NGOs opposed to right-wing extremism – most notably the Jewish defense organizations – have responded to the 9/11 challenge as well. The ADL has been monitoring the response to this crisis from Arab, Muslim, and right wing extremists. Its Internet website features a section entitled *What They are Saying* in which the comments of extremists on the 9/11 are posted. The ADL has also sought to debunk various rumors circulating on the Internet that the Israeli government, specifically the Mossad, was complicit in the September 11 attack.[18] The Simon Wiesenthal Center has made efforts in this area as well (e.g. Brackman 2001).

The far right's reaction to the September 11 attacks was mixed. In some quarters, the far right expressed a palpable degree of *Schadenfreude* over the terrorist attack. Others were less sanguine about the current state of affairs and feared that the American government's war on terror could spillover into a witch hunt against domestic extremists. Many in the movement also expressed feelings of vindication insofar as many of the issues about which they feel strongly, featured prominently in the current crisis – as all of the 19 hijackers were immigrants this underscored the potential problems of America's liberal immigration policy. The most articulate critic in this respect was probably Jared Taylor of American Renaissance, who warned of the possibility of more terrorist attacks in his article 'Will America Learn its Lessons?' (Taylor 2001a).

The most frequent refrain however, was that the terrorist attack was visited upon America because of the government's unstinting support for Israel. Many in the far right derided President Bush's explanation that the terrorists had attacked America because of its freedom and democracy. For example, Jared Taylor (2001b: 4) sarcastically commented: 'Does President Bush really imagine Osama bin Laden saying to his men: "Those Americans are just too damn free" [...] The idea is absurd. Islamic militants have a grudge against us because of our attacks on Afghanistan, Libya, Iraq, and Sudan. But the main reason they hate us and want to kill us is that we support Israel.'

The Jewish defense organizations have worked hard to counteract this perception. For example, the ADL conducted surveys to determine whether the American public blamed the attack on the United States' close relationship with Israel. According to the study, 63 per cent of those surveyed rejected the notion (ADL 2001b). The American Jewish Committee issued briefings that argued that Islamic extremism predates the state of Israel and is thus a side issue to the current terrorist campaign (AJC 2001). Finally, the Simon Wiesenthal Center announced a two-prong strategy consisting of an expansion of its worldwide monitoring coupled with increased sharing of this information with government officials, the media, and other important international figures (SWC 2001).

It is axiomatic to say that Anti-Semitism looms large in the racialist segment of the far-right milieu. Likewise, many Islamic extremists hold a similar worldview, known as anti-Zionism. Thus, there is clearly a meeting of the minds between the two political movements. Furthermore, both movements direct their animus at identical or similar targets, including globalization, the United States government, Zionism, cultural decadence, and secularism. Collusion between the far right on the one hand and Arab and Islamic extremists on the other has occurred in the past but with little effectiveness.[19]

The watchdog organizations were quick to point out the ideological similarities between far right and Islamic extremists. Some even feared the start of an operational alliance between the two movements. Mark Potok of the SPLC opined that both far rightists and Islamic extremists share common enemies in globalization and multiculturalism. This potential for collaboration has not gone unnoticed by the government. US authorities, including Homeland Security Director Tom Ridge, announced through a spokesman that the FBI has stepped up its efforts to monitor groups for such an eventuality (Solomon 2002).[20] Finally, the spate of anthrax-laden letter attacks heightened suspicion that right-wing terrorists might be coordinating their efforts in a synergistic way with foreign terrorists.[21]

Conclusions

Why have watchdog groups been able to set so much of the agenda in this field of public policy? First, unlike other public policy issues, this area of public policy is basically a no-lose proposition for lawmakers. By supporting policies such as hate crime legislation, anti-paramilitary training statutes, and tougher counter-terrorist measures, lawmakers send symbolic messages that they are taking a tough stand against bigotry and support law and order. By doing so, they please the interest groups that advocate these policies. Furthermore, with the exception of some of the new counter-terrorist initiatives, these policy measures usually do not involve significant fiscal costs and hence do not really raise issues of tax increases or sacrificing funding from other programs to implement them.[22]

Second, there really is not much competition or countervailing power on the other side of this issue. The far right, although it episodically experiences spurts of growth, is still small, organizationally fragmented, and has little popular support. By contrast, the watchdog groups have formidable resources at their disposal, including money, membership size, leadership, political expertise, motivational resources and political reputation.[23]

Table 8.1 lists the most recent available financial data on assets and annual income of the eight most important NGOs in this area of policy. As these data indicate, they collectively command assets of over $309 million and collectively receive an annual income of over $154 million. By comparison, virtually all far-right organizations are poorly financed. Furthermore, the success of interest groups depends largely on their position in the social structure and access to powerful political institutions (Malecki and Mahood 1972, p. 152). Several of the watchdog groups – most notably the ADL, the Simon Wiesenthal Center, and the SPLC – have received access to, and support from, high level public figures including politicians, celebrities, and other influential opinion makers. Because of this imbalance, watchdog groups dominate this area of public policy unimpeded by strong opponents.

Third, another way in which interest groups can enhance their success is by framing their concerns as part of the larger national interest (Malecki and Mahood 1972, p. 303). Watchdog groups have effectively persuaded much of the American public and policy makers that their agenda is consistent with the national interest. Representatives from the ADL and SPLC are often called upon to give expert testimony and advice on such issues as terrorism and hate crime legislation. By doing so, they have raised the

Table 8.1 Financial assets and annual income of leading watchdog groups (fiscal year 2000)

	Assets ($)	Annual income ($)
Jewish Defense Organizations		
Anti-Defamation League	17,737,259	48,693,379
American Jewish Committee	70,055,959	39,793,811
Simon Wiesenthal Center	72,576,026	31,619,393
Civil Litigation Watchdog Group		
Southern Poverty Law Center	147,441,903	32,520,416
Progressive-Oriented Watchdog Groups		
Center for Democratic Renewal	102,290	543,282
Political Research Associates	737,022	708,556
Regional Watchdog Groups		
Northwest Coalition Against Malicious Harassment	142,124	442,710
Center for New Community	507,450	256,886
Total	309,300,033	154,578,433

Source: guidestar.org.

salience on these issues about which they feel strongly and influenced public opinion. Watchdogs have done much to brand the far right as beyond the bounds of acceptability in American society and depict it as a threat to be contained. The anti-terrorist measures advocated by these NGOs are seen as dovetailing with domestic security. Slighting the civil liberties of unpopular groups is seen as an acceptable price for increased national security.

The cumulative effect of the various efforts discussed above has done much to neutralize the far right in America. Admittedly it is very speculative to say just how influential and/or dangerous the American far right would be in the absence of their watchdog opponents. At the present time it is virtually inconceivable that a significant right-wing terrorist group could emerge in the United States. Watchdog groups would almost undoubtedly alert authorities to such a development and persuade them to take resolute action. Previously, some right-wing extremist groups (the Order) have demonstrated revolutionary and other violent ambitions. It is not unreasonable to assume that they would have had a much better chance of achieving their goals in the absence of the watchdog organizations. As in other areas of public policy, the government is more likely to act resolutely, when prodded by interest groups.

Just prior to the September 11 attacks, the American far right appeared to have suffered several setbacks. Just one year earlier, the Aryan Nations lost a $6.3 million civil suit filed by the SPLC. In November 2000, the FBI arrested Alex Curtis and, in doing so, silenced the most strident advocate of the leaderless resistance approach. Finally, in the summer of 2001, one of the most important and enduring institutions of the American far right, the Liberty Lobby, was forced to shut down as a result of a civil judgment awarded to its erstwhile subsidiary, the Institute for Historical Review. However, the September 11 attacks appear to have reinvigorated the American far right, and more importantly, increased the salience of the issues about which it feels strongly. It is conceivable that the far right could exploit the current crisis as a way to call attention to its critique of America. If the war on terror should falter, increased public support could redound to the favor of the far right. The government has also been galvanized by the crisis and appears to be more vigilant in combating terrorism. These efforts could conceivably spill over into the area of domestic extremism as well. Finally, the NGOs are keeping a close watch on the current crisis and are responding accordingly. As a result, these various developments presage added potential for confrontation in the future.

Notes

1 Interview with Chip Berlet, August 31, 2000.
2 For more on the political backgrounds of the staffs of the CDR and PRA see Wilcox (1999).
3 Interview with Todd Ferguson, February 2, 2001.
4 COINTELPRO is an oft-used acronym for the FBI's now defunct 'Counter-intelligence Program', which officially ran from 1956 to 1971. In essence it was a secret program that sought to disrupt extremist groups falling into the following five categories: Communist Party, USA; Socialist Workers Party; 'White Hate Groups'; 'Black Nationalist Hate Groups'; and 'New Left'.
5 According to the new guidelines, in order to commence an investigation of a dissident group, evidence of a criminal predicate (i.e. the evidentiary criterion is slightly below the threshold of 'probable cause' which is less than absolute certainty but greater than mere suspicion or 'hunch') was required. An investigation could not be opened solely on activities protected by the First Amendment.
6 Dr James O'Connor, a former deputy assistant director or the FBI and currently a professor of criminology, communicated to me that the idea for the Hostage Rescue Team was conceived by the Training Division of the FBI. Phone Conversation with Dr James O'Connor, June, 2002.
7 According to independent researcher Laird Wilcox, the ADL played a major part in the Fort Smith trial and consulted with prosecutors. Irwin Suall, the ADL's chief investigator, at that time, flew to Arkansas when it looked bad for the prosecution. Letter from Laird Wilcox, April 29, 1999. This was corroborated by defense attorney Kirk Lyons, who pointed out that Suall had a personal interview with Judge Morris Arnold in the latter's chamber. Interview with Kirk Lyons, August 17, 2000.
8 For example, reportedly a coalition of 32 conservative organizations called on House Speaker Dennis Hastert of Illinois to obtain an un-redacted classified version of the report. One of the questions that the coalition posted to Hastert was whether or not the report had been authored by an outside advocacy groups including the ADL and SPLC (see O'Mera 1999).
9 Greg Rampton, the Assistant Special Agent in charge of the Denver FBI field office made this denial in an interview with Don Wiederman on the Freedom Forum radio-call in show (see American NewsNet, 23 November 1999).

10 The alleged offenses include placing racist stickers at some of the victims' offices; placing a snake skin in the mail slot of Congressman Filner's office; spray painting anti-Semitic words and symbols on a synagogue; and perhaps the most serious act, placing an inactive hand grenade at Mayor Madrid's residence. For more on this investigation see the FBI's report 'Operation Lone Wolf,' 2000, http://www.fbi.gov/majcses/ lonewolf1/htm.

11 For example, in the Senate by a vote of 98–0, and in the House of Representatives by a vote of 420–1, Congress passed a joint resolution authorizing President Bush to use 'all necessary and appropriate force' for those responsible for the September 11 terrorist attack.

12 A 2000 SPLC report stated that known common law courts have fallen from 31 in 1998 to just four in 1999.

13 According to two researchers, hate crime perpetrators rely upon far right organizations for 'slogans, mottoes, and guidance,' which can persuade them to commit hate crimes (Levin and McDevitt 1993, p. 104).

14 In 1995 the SPLC reported that 15 per cent of those offenders arrested for hate crimes belonged to organized far right groups (Dees and Bowden, n.d.). This statistic must be taken with some caution in that these links are often very tenuous and consist of little more than subscribing to and reading extremist newsletters and literature, etc. The amorphous nature of the American far right makes such claims of affiliation very difficult.

15 For example, the San Diego Police Department works very closely with the ADL in the area of hate crimes. Police officers are instructed to contact immediately an ADL crisis interventionist when a hate crime occurs. The crisis interventionist works directly with the victims at the scene of the crime to determine any support that they might need (Wessler 2000, p. 7). More recently, the ADL distributed clipboard cards imprinted with guidance on responding to hate crimes to over 2,000 members of the Boston Police Department (Meek 2000).

16 Kenneth Stern (1999) from the American Jewish Committee cites two studies on this issue. *The Ottawa Citizen* estimated approximately 600, while Gina Smith estimated 800. The Simon Wiesenthal Center puts the number at 2,100. For more see the SWC's site at www.wiesenthal.com.

17 Independent researcher Laird Wilcox (1999) has thoroughly examined various FBI and ADL memoranda, which indicate a close working relationship between the two entities. My review of Wilcox's archives on this subject confirms his assertion.

18 For more on the ADL's analysis of these rumors see ADL, 'Conspiracy theories and criticism of Israel in the aftermath of Sept. 11 attacks,' November 1, 2001, and '4,000 Jews Absent During World Trade Center Attack,' downloaded November 15, 2001. Both are available on the ADL's website at http:www.adl.org. For more on David Duke's allegations see Duke (2001).

19 For example, George Lincoln Rockwell made overtures to President Gamal Abdel Nasser of the United Arab Republic and even considered becoming a registered foreign agent for Arabic governments. During the late 1970s and early 1980s, members of a small German neo-Nazi group, *Wehrsportgruppe-Hoffmann*, reportedly received paramilitary training in PLO camps in Jordan (see Hoffman 1984, pp. 6–7). In 1989, Libyan leader Mu'ammar Qadhafi hosted various far right individuals from North America and Europe in an effort to create an anti-Zionist united front (Kinsella 1995).

20 Adding credence to these suspicions was the case of Ahmed Huber, a 75-year old Swiss national, who was reputed to be the liaison between European right-wing extremists and Islamic extremists.

21 According to one account, some top CIA and FBI officials had suspected that domestic extremists were responsible for the anthrax attacks (CNN 2001).

22 Jacobs and Potter (1998, pp. 77–78) made this argument with regard to hate crime legislation and I believe that it is applicable to the other legislative initiatives watchdogs groups have sponsored as well.
23 Ornstein and Elder (1978, pp. 70–79) identified these various resources as crucial for attaining success in lobbying.

Bibliography

ADL (Anti-Defamation League) (1965) *Not the Work of a Day: The Story of the Anti-Defamation League of B'nai B'rith*. New York: Anti-Defamation League.
ADL (1980) 'ADL memorandum to FBI Director William H. Webster', *FBI File Number 100–530–526*, 10 December.
ADL (1985) *Computerized Networks of Hate*. New York: Anti-Defamation League.
ADL (1995) *The ADL Anti-Paramilitary Training Statute: A Response to Domestic Terrorism*. New York: Anti-Defamation League.
ADL (1996) *Web of Hate*. New York: Anti-Defamation League.
ADL (1997a) *Vigilante Justice: Militias and 'Common Law Courts' Wage War Against the Government*. New York: Anti-Defamation League.
ADL (1997b) *High-Tech Hate*. New York: Anti-Defamation League.
ADL (1998a) 'Press Release: ADL commends president for domestic anti-terrorism initiative calls on 26 states to enact anti-paramilitary training statutes, 24 April.
ADL (1998b) *1999 Hate Crime Laws*. New York: Anti-Defamation League.
ADL (1999a) *Poisoning the Web*. New York: Anti-Defamation League.
ADL (1999b) 'Statement of the Anti-Defamation League on hate on the Internet before the Senate Committee on the Judiciary', 14 September.
ADL (2001a) 'ADL applauds President Bush for signing into law landmark anti-terrorism bill', 26 October.
ADL (2001b) 'New ADL poll shows no anti-semitic and blame Israel fallout from Sept. 11 attack', 2 November.
ADL (2002a) 'ADL calls Bush administration military commission guidelines "A significant step forward"', 25 March.
ADL (2002b) 'ADL Press Release: ADL Definitive Guide to Extremism in America now on CD-ROM. Resource will be widely distributed to law enforcement agencies nationwide', 15 April.
AJC (American Jewish Committee) (2001) 'Talking Points: The agenda of Islamic extremism, the war on terrorism and the U.S.-Israel alliance', 8 October.
American NewsNet, 23 November 1999, at: http://www.amerifree.com/front/front05.htm.
Ammerman, N.T. (1995) 'Waco, law enforcement, and scholars of religion', in Wright, S.A. (ed.) *Armageddon in Waco: Critical Perspectives on the Branch Davidian Conflict*. Chicago: University of Chicago Press, pp. 282–296.
Arent, L. (1999) 'Net group stalks L.A. gunman', *Wired News*, 11 August, at: http//www.wired.com/news/news/politics/story/21163.html.
Blitzer, R.M. (1997) 'FBI's role in the Federal response to the use of weapons of mass destruction: statement of Robert M. Blitzer, Chief Domestic Terrorism/Counter-terrorism Planning Section FBI before the U.S. House of Representatives Committee on National Security', 4 November.
Brackman, H. (2001) *9/11 Digital Lies: A Survey of Online Apologists for Global Terrorism*. Los Angeles: Simon Wiesenthal Center.

CNN (2001) 'Report: anthrax could be from domestic extremists', on *CNN*, 26 October.
Coulson, D.O. and Shannon, E. (1999) *No Heroes: Inside the FBI's Secret Counter-Terror Force*. New York: Pocket.
Davis, J.K. (1992) *Spying on America: The FBI's Domestic Counterintelligence Program*. Westport, CT: Praeger.
Dees, M. (1993) *Hate on Trial*. New York: Villard.
Dees, M. and Bowden, E. (n.d.) 'Taking hate groups to court', at: http://www.splcenter.org/legalaction/la-3.html.
Duke, D. (2001) 'How Israeli terrorism and American treason caused the September 11 Attack', in *The David Duke Report* 52, November.
FBI (1964) 'FBI Internal Memorandum', *File Number 438611424445*, 8 September.
FBI (1985) 'FBI Internal Memorandum', *File Number 44-0-1204*, 4 February.
FBI (1998) *Terrorism in the United States 1997*. Washington, DC: FBI.
Ferguson, T. (2000) 'Youth against hate: anti-racist action as a new citizens' movement', unpublished paper.
Finch, P. (1983) *God, Guts and Guns*, New York: Seaview/Putnam.
Forster, A. (1988) *Square One: The Memoirs of a True Freedom Fighter's Lifelong Struggle Against Anti-Semitism, Domestic and Foreign*. New York: Donald I. Fine.
Freeh, L. (1999) 'The Threat to the United States Posed by Terrorists. Testimony before the U.S. Senate Committee on Appropriations', 4 February.
Herman, S. (n.d.) 'The USA PATRIOT Act and the U.S. Department of Justice losing our balances', in *Jurist*, at: http://law.pitt.edu/forum/ formnew40htm.
Hoffman, B. (1984) *Right-Wing Terrorism in Europe since 1980*. Santa Monica, CA: The Rand Corporation.
Jacobs, J.B. and Potter, K. (1998) *Hate Crimes: Criminal Law and Identity Politics*. New York: Oxford University Press.
Jones, S. with Israel, P. (1998) *Others Unknown: The Oklahoma City Bombing Case and Conspiracy*. New York: Public Affairs.
Kaplan, D.E. and Tharp, M. (1997-8) 'Terrorism threats at home', in *U.S. News & World Report*, 123 (25), 29 December-5 January, pp. 22-27.
Kinsella, W. (1995) *Web of Hate: Inside Canada's Far Right Network*. Toronto: Harper Perennial.
Klaidman, D. and Isikkoff, M. (1996) 'The Feds' quiet war: inside the secret strategy to combat the militia threat', in *Newsweek*, 128, 22 April, p. 47.
Kopel, D.B. and Blackman, P.H. (1997) *No More Wacos: What's Wrong with Federal Law Enforcement and How to Fix It*. Amherst, NY: Prometheus.
Levin, J. and McDevitt, J. (1993) *Hate Crimes: The Rising Tide of Bigotry and Bloodshed*. New York: Plenum.
Malecki, E.S. and Mahood, H.R. (1972) *Group Politics: A New Emphasis*. New York: Charles Scribner's Sons.
Meek, J.G. (2000) 'Cops get guides to hate crimes', *APB News*, 14 December.
O'Mera, K.P. (1999) 'FBI targets "right wing"', in *The Washington Times*, 27 December.
Ornstein, N.J. and Elder, S. (1978) *Interest Groups, Lobbying and Policymaking*. Washington, DC: Congressional Quarterly Press.
Padilla, M.T. (1999) 'Race violence leads to rise in anti-racism groups', in *Salt*

Lake Tribune, 22 August, at http://www.sltrib.com/1999/aug/08221999/nation_w/17231.htm.

Redden, J. (2000) *Snitch Culture*. Venice, CA: Feral House.

Revell, O. (1998) *A G-Man's Journal*. New York: Pocket Star Books.

Rosenlum, R. (1999) 'FBI surveillance of hate groups critical, Jewish leaders assert', in *Jewish Bulletin of Northern California*, 3 September.

Schachner, N. (1948) *The Price of Liberty: A History of the American Jewish Committee*. New York: The American Jewish Committee.

Schonbach, M. (1958) *Native Fascism during the 1930s and 1940s: A Study of Its Roots, its Growth, and its Decline*. Los Angeles: UCLA, unpublished PhD.

Seymour, C. (1991) *Committee of the States: Inside the Radical Right*. Mariposa, CA: Camden Place Communications.

Shapiro, J.P. (1999) 'Hitting before hate strikes', in *U.S. News & World Report*, 6 September, pp. 56–57.

Silverstein, K. (2000) 'The church of Morris Dees: how the Southern Poverty Law Center profits from intolerance', in *Harper's Magazine*, November, pp. 54–57.

Solomon, J. (2002) 'U.S. extremists' links with terror groups watched', 28 February, at: http://www.Salon.com.

SPLC (2000) 'Red hot patriot movement cools down', in *Intelligence Report*, Issue 98. http://www.splcenter.org/cgi-bin/goframe.pl?dirname=/.&pagename=sitemap.html.

Stern, K. (1999) *Hate on the Internet*. New York: American Jewish Committee, at: http://www.ajc.org/pre/interneti.htm.

SWC (Simon Wiesenthal Center) (2001) 'Trans-national hate: technology unites anti-semites and haters around the globe', 27 February.

Taylor, J. (2001a) 'Will America learn its lessons? Paying the price for foolish policies', *American Renaissance*, 12, 11: 1–8.

Taylor, J. (2001b) 'Teaching more millions to hate us', *Battleflag*, October, p. 4.

Wessler, S. (2000) *Promising Practices Against Hate Crimes: Five State and Local Demonstration Projects*. Washington, DC: Bureau of Justice Assistance. http://www.ncjrs.org/pdffiles1/bja/181425.pdf.

Wilcox, L. (1999) *The Watchdogs: A Close Look at Anti-Racist 'Watchdog' Groups*. Olathe, KS: Laird Wilcox Editorial Research Center.

Wright, S.A. (1995) 'Construction and escalation of a cult threat', in Wright, S.A. (ed.) *Armageddon in Waco: Critical Perspectives on the Branch Davidian Conflict*. Chicago: University of Chicago Press, pp. 75–94.

Conclusion
Defending democracy and the extreme right

Cas Mudde

Introduction

Western democracies have been challenged by a broad variety of political actors over the past decades: Communist political parties, skinhead gangs, separatist terrorists, religious sects, etc. In this volume we have focused on the challenge from the 'extreme right', which increasingly during the last two decades has come to be perceived as the main threat within Western democracies (at least before September 11). The preceding chapters have addressed various issues relating to the ways Western democracies deal with the extreme right, on the one hand, and how the extreme right deals with the inherent tensions of functioning in a (hostile) liberal democracy, on the other.

The aim of this concluding chapter is twofold: first, to provide an overview of the main points made by the different authors in this volume; second, to combine and follow-up some of these insights, raising issues and topics for future research. Although much work surely remains to be done, some important preliminary conclusions clearly emerge.

Right-wing extremism in contemporary democracies

Whether contemporary extreme right groups are indeed anti-democratic or not, there is no doubt that (serious) tensions exist between the extreme right and Western democracies. Most extreme right groups are highly critical of (key) elements of liberal democracy, while liberal democracies tend to treat the extreme right as threats or, at the very least, unwelcome participants. Consequently, extreme right groups face what Jaap van Donselaar (1995, p. 13) has called an 'adaptation dilemma': to become accepted by the mainstream, and prevent repression by the state, they need to moderate, but to satisfy their hard-core members, and to keep a clear profile, they need to stay extreme.

194 *Cas Mudde*

Extreme right parties and the adaptation dilemma

Either explicitly or implicitly, the adaptation dilemma is the focus of all three chapters of the first part of the book. Alexandre Dézé provides a comparative study of the ways in which four extreme right parties try to deal with the inherent tension. His conclusion is that all of them adapt to democracy, but that this always leads to internal problems. As examples he refers to the recent developments within the French National Front (FN) and the Austrian Freedom Party (FPÖ). However, if all four parties are taken into account, a more complex picture emerges, as both the Belgian Flemish Block (VB) and the Italian National Alliance (AN) adapt to democracy, although to different degrees, yet they are confronted far less with internal dissent. I believe this can be explained, at least in part, by accounting for the level of openness of the 'democratic' parties to their 'extremist' counterparts.

In Italy, the political environment was most conducive to the integration of the extreme right into the democratic mainstream. Since the fall of the 'First Republic', the Italian Social Movement (MSI) and its successor, the AN, have been accepted unconditionally by the new mainstream right-wing party, *Forza Italia* of Silvio Berlusconi. This has so far led twice to the inclusion into the Italian government of the AN, *and* to the transformation of the neo-fascist MSI into the 'post-fascist' AN (see Ignazi 1996). Indeed, today many commentators no longer include the AN into the groups of extreme right parties, taking the party at its word that it has transformed into a conservative right-wing party similar to the French Gaullist Rally for the Republic (RPR).

In Austria, the FPÖ was conditionally accepted by the mainstream right, i.e. the Christian democratic Austrian People's Party (ÖVP). Unlike in Italy, it was never a marriage of love, but rather of convenience (this applies both to the 2001 and, even more, to the 2003 government). From the outset, the FPÖ was put under probation, both by the ÖVP and by the international community (see below). Consequently, the FPÖ clearly moderated itself in government, but also became more divided internally. In the end, this led to a showdown between the real leader of the party, Jörg Haider, who had given up his party chairmanship under international pressure, and his successor, official party leader Susanne Riess-Passer. The end result was the fall of the government, a major setback in the 2002 elections, and an internally divided party.

In France the political environment is generally hostile, though there are some 'friendly zones', most notably in the South of the country and within the RPR party (see Chapter 6). This almost schizophrenic situation of being ostracized at the national and (in most cases) the sub-national levels, yet being courted and accepted into coalitions in some regions and communities, is partly the result of strategies by the FN itself. However, while the conciliatory approach of Bruno Mégret led to an initial victory when the mainstream right split over the issue of cooperation with the FN (see Knapp 1999), it ended in a major defeat. After the right had regrouped, the issue became a major bone of contention within the FN itself, with one faction (around Jean-Marie Le Pen) opposed to cooperation with the right, and one group in favor (around Mégret). The result was a fractionalized extreme right, now divided into two smaller and less relevant parties (see Chapters 1 and 6).

In Belgium, or more specifically the Dutch speaking part of Flanders, the VB operates in an almost completely hostile environment.[1] All the major Flemish 'democratic' parties participate in a *cordon sanitaire* around the VB, which is enforced at all governmental levels (local, regional, federal, supranational). The cordon holds that 'no political agreements will be made with the Vlaams Blok', neither in the various councils, nor in elections (Daemen 1998, p. 78). Consequently, the VB is not forced to compromise and can remain both open and vague about its willingness to adapt, without creating internal divisions. The result is an internally united and ideologically radical party, which goes from strength to strength in various elections.

To be sure, the relationship between the openness of the 'democratic' parties and the moderation of the 'extremist' party is not as straightforward as these four cases seem to indicate. For example, Germany and the Netherlands have witnessed the combination of an informal *cordon sanitaire* and a weak and internally divided extreme right. The situation in Britain is fairly similar, as Roger Eatwell's chapter vividly describes, even though the political and social rejection of the extreme right is perhaps less vehement. Still, what the four cases do show is the importance of the position of the 'democratic' parties in the way extreme right parties deal with the adaptation dilemma.

From support to opposition

With regard to the non-party political extreme right, Chapter 2 by Mark Potok also points to the possible negative side-effects of state repression to (non-violent) extremists. After all, the radicalization of the militias, and in their trail terrorists like Timothy McVeigh, was at least in part a reaction to the dramatic state actions against alleged extremists such as Randy Weaver (Ruby Ridge) and David Koresh (Waco).

While it is certainly true that the American case is typical, and differs significantly from the general European situation, there are also striking similarities. For example, the recent wave of increased state repression against the militant extreme right scene in Germany seems to have led to the intended decrease of militants, but also to the unintended hardening of the remaining activists (Maegerle 2002). In other words, the militant extreme right became leaner but meaner.

Another trend that Potok observes for the US is the changed relationship to the state, from (passive) support to (armed) opposition. This development can also be observed in Europe, where right-wing extremists see the state increasingly as the enemy. This can be noted at the rhetorical level, i.e. in the propaganda of various extreme right groups, which blame the state/political elite rather than the immigrants themselves for the 'immigration drama' (see Mudde 2000). But it is even clearer in the recent shift within the most dangerous part of the extreme right, the (potentially) violent extra-parliamentary extreme right movement, most notably the neo-Nazi and white supremacist groups. In countries such as Germany or Sweden these groups increasingly brand the state and their representatives as their main enemy, as hit lists seized by the security forces testify (e.g. Willems 2002; Bjørgo 1997).

Democratic responses to extremism

The second part of the book addresses the ways in which democracies deal with extremist challenges, a topic so far largely ignored in the political science literature. In the little comparative academic literature available on the topic, one often finds a distinction between two (ideal) types: typically, the American and the German model (see also Chapter 5).

In the American model, obviously based upon the US experience, the state provides for as much freedom as possible. This means that all *ideas* are accepted in the democratic 'marketplace of ideas', whether they are democratic or not. An example is the famous Skokie case, where the racist Ku Klux Klan won a court case to demonstrate through a predominantly Jewish neighborhood (Chapter 5). However, not all *actions* are accepted, and violent political groups are the subject of serious state repression (Chapters 2 and 8).

The German model is officially called *streitbare* or *wehrhafte Demokratie*, which roughly translates as 'militant democracy' (e.g. Jaschke 1991; Backes 1989). It is based on the legal system in post-war Germany, which has largely been influenced by the Weimar legacy and the Allied (and German elite's) distrust of the German population. As in the American model, anti-democratic *actions* are severely punished. But the German state has also explicitly defined 'the fundamental principles of the free democratic order', and prohibits not only actions, but also ideas that are opposed to these principles.

Ideal types

As is the case with ideal types, most countries do not neatly fit into any of them. Many of the Western democracies are, on paper, closer to the American model, yet in practice follow the militant route. This is even the case in the Eastern Europe, where most post-communist democracies initially held on to their newly won freedoms, despite the growing visibility of extreme right actors. At the beginning of the twenty-first century, however, most of these countries are (rapidly) moving into the direction of militant democracies (see ECRI 1998), often explicitly encouraged by international organizations such as the European Union and United Nations (see below). In fact, even the US increasingly fails to live up to the American model (e.g. Michael 2003).

The legal and political frameworks of countries are the result of compromises, ever in flux and under discussion. They are much influenced by national and international developments. Most recently, the terrorist attacks of September 11 have led to an unprecedented wave of legal reform across the globe, not in the least in Western democracies. What these reforms have in common is that they 'extend the illegal areas, increase the punishments, ease the burden of proof, limit the chances of the defense, and obstruct the control on legislation' (Hassemer 2002, p. 11). In terms of our two ideal types, the reforms conform more to the German than to the US model. How they will also impact on the relationship with the extreme right will be a topic for future research.

As Pedahzur has convincingly argued, the ideal types focus too much attention on the strict formal side of anti-extremist measures. This somewhat ignores the informal, and sometimes even illegal, sides. Take, for example, the case of the Netherlands in the 1990s, when the country was faced with two small extreme right parties, the Centre Democrats (CD) and the Centre Party'86 (CP'86). On paper, the Netherlands is not a militant democracy, like its big neighbor to the East (Bolsius 1994). Nevertheless, the Dutch are one of the few countries that banned an extreme right political party in recent years: the CP'86 in 1998 after having been considered a 'criminal organization' by the Amsterdam court (see Mudde 2000).

But there are many 'anti-extremist' measures that are more subtle, although nonetheless effective. For example, during most of the 1980s and 1990s the Dutch extreme right was unable to hold any public demonstration. What happened was always the same: an extreme right party would ask for permission to demonstrate in a city, anti-fascists would announce a counter-demonstration (not always asking for permission), and the mayor of the city would ban both demonstrations for fear of public disturbances – thereby sidestepping the provision in the law that does not allow the administration to ban a demonstration on the basis of the ideology of the organizers and participants (e.g. Mudde 1995). Ironically, in sharp contrast, in the militant democracy of Germany, some 2000 policemen and women have been mobilized to separate a similar number of participants to the annual meeting of the German People's Union (DVU) in the south German city of Passau from some few hundred anti-fascists.[2] This in spite of the fact that the DVU is officially labeled as 'extremist' by the German state, while the Dutch CD was allegedly not even monitored by the Dutch security service.

The role of the 'democratic' parties

Given that Western democracies are all *party* democracies, it is obvious that the behavior of the 'non-extremist' parties, often self-described as the 'democratic' parties, is crucial for the way the state deals with extremist parties. This is not just the case in contemporary democracies. On the basis of a comparative study of democratic responses in the inter-war period, Giovanni Capoccia in Chapter 4 concludes that the behavior of 'democratic' party leaders, most notably of so-called 'border parties' (in this case, the mainstream right), was the key factor distinguishing between democratic breakdown and survival in Europe.

Other authors in this volume have also dealt with the inter-party relations. Dézé approached the subject primarily from the viewpoint of the 'extremists', while Kestel and Godmer took the perspective of the 'democrats'. The latter sketched the two extreme models, the exclusionary German and the inclusionary Austrian models, before analyzing the more ambiguous and complex French situation. Some countries fit one of the two extremes, most notably the German model (e.g. Czech Republic, the Netherlands), but most are somewhere between the two. Think of the way the Swedish parties dealt with New Democracy (see Chapter 7), or the ambiguous manner in which the former Hungarian premier 'distanced' himself from the extreme right Hungarian Justice and Life Party.

While we know something (although still far too little) about the relationships between 'democratic' parties and 'extremist' parties in different countries, we know precious little about the reasons behind these relationships (and their changes). Kestel and Godmer argue that ideology plays an important role in the exclusion of extremist parties, but not in their inclusion. This is a popular view, particularly within the anti-extremist camp, but not necessarily always the case.

If one is to judge purely on the level of *rhetoric*, then ample evidence can be provided. For example, in the early 1980s, conservative parties in various countries treated the Green party as 'left-wing extremists' and called for its exclusion from the mainstream; within the German Christian Democratic camp there were even powerful voices that called for a ban. With regard to the extreme right, calls for exclusion have most quickly and consistently come from the left (both the extreme and the mainstream). Still, there are many significant exceptions. Jacques Chirac, leader of the right-wing RPR, has been one of the most outspoken proponents of exclusion of the FN. The Czech Social Democratic Party has been as opposed to cooperation with the Communist Party of Bohemia and Moravia as to an understanding with the right-wing parties, even adopting the so-called 'Bohunin Act' which bars the party from officially cooperating with the Communists.

In terms of *policies*, the relationship is not straightforward either. Some people have argued that there is a link between the ideology of the party that is in power and the way the extreme right (or left for that matter) is treated. Intuitively, it would make sense that mainstream right-wing parties will be more accommodating to the extreme right, yet more vigilant to the extreme left, while the mainstream left will be more accommodating to the extreme left and more vigilant to the extreme right. Unfortunately, there is not much empirical research available on this issue. Moreover, in most European countries straightforward analysis is hindered by the practice of coalition governments, which means that pure right-wing and left-wing governments are rare. Instead, most governments are centre-right and centre-left, having more in common than sets them apart.

In the US, one of the few countries with a single party government, Donald P. Haider-Markel and Sean P. O'Brien (1997, p. 562) found that 'the presence of more conservative Republicans appears to make the adoption of anti-paramilitary laws more difficult.' In Germany, on the other hand, no clear relationship was found between the political color of the (state) government and the ways the (left-wing or right-wing) extremists are dealt with (Backes 2000). Moreover, both the decisive call to have the 'Republicans' (REP) labeled as extremist, and therefore monitored by the Federal Bureau for the Protection of the Constitution (BfVS), and the initiative to apply for a ban of the NPD came from the conservative Bavarian Christian Social Union (Henckel and Lembcke 2001).

In conclusion, there can be convincing ideological arguments for the inclusion of 'extremists' ('democracy is for all'), and there can be strategical (indeed, cynical) reasons for their exclusion – party competition, for example. At this stage, the importance of the various possible factors is largely unknown, and further comparative research will have to discover what explains the (change in) relationships between 'democratic' and 'extremist' parties.

The role of civil society

Some of the chapters have touched upon the role of civil society in dealing with the extreme right. Ami Pedahzur has stressed the importance of an active civil society that counters both the extremists and the state, in cases of overzealous reactions to (alleged) extremists. His type of the 'immunized democracy' entails such a balanced and strong civil society. It would be interesting to see more (comparative) studies of the role of civil society in this respect, and in particular of watchdog organizations that monitor the state responses. For example, I doubt one can find many organizations similar to the powerful American Civil Liberties Union outside of the US.

George Michael provides a very welcome first study of the role of nongovernmental organizations (NGOs) in the 'struggle' against the extreme right in the US (see also Michael 2003). His analysis shows the financial and organizational strength of these watchdog organizations, which can clearly outspend the extremist organizations. He also shows the profound influence of particular groups, most notably the Anti-Defamation League and the Southern Poverty Law Center, in not only co-setting the agenda, but also in providing many of the answers to the political questions. This raises not only serious democratic concerns, but also interesting academic questions. Is the situation in the US indeed 'unique', as Michael argues, or can similarly strong NGOs be found outside of the US?

While quite some work has been done on (individual and comparative) anti-racist and anti-fascist groups – though quite often by strongly pro-biased authors – there is little consensus over their effects on both democracy and the extremists. While anti-fascists themselves claim victory after victory in their 'battle with the fascists', impartial observers are far less positive. Some straightforwardly deny the alleged success the movements claim (e.g. Eatwell in Chapter 3; Husbands 1998; Kowalsky 1992), while others point to a far more worrying aspect. According to them, the often violent approach of anti-fascists only strengthens the extreme right, by making them into victims or underdogs, and leads to a dangerous spiral of violence (e.g. Mletzko 2001).[3]

Comparatively, there is little known about the role of the more traditional NGOs in policies against right-wing extremists. Still, it is known that organizations like the Anne Frank Foundation (AFS) and Forum in the Netherlands are consulted by (governmental, party, parliamentary) commissions on issues related to right-wing extremism. In addition, NGOs like the AFS and the Centre for Information and Documentation about Israel have at times initiated litigation against extreme right organizations, such as the Centre Party and the (Flemish) revisionist Free Historical Research (see Van Donselaar 1995). Even in some of the new democracies of Eastern Europe, civil society plays its role in pushing states to change their initial post-communist *laissez-faire* approach to the extreme right in favor of a more militant democracy (on Hungary, see Szôcs 1998).

There is no doubt that (civil) society does play a role in the way Western governments deal with (right-wing) extremists, and so it should be in a democracy. Indeed, Van Donselaar (1995) has claimed that *social* pressure is one of the most important variables in the adaptation dilemma of the extreme right, and has pointed specifically to the situation in Germany and the Netherlands. In these countries social pressure is among the highest in Europe, while the extreme right has always been weak and divided (e.g. Backes and Mudde 2000; Schikhof 1998). Still, this aspect of the adaptation dilemma is also difficult to prove scientifically, as most countries have had fairly constant levels of social pressure on right-wing extremists; and without fluctuation the thesis might actually hide more than it shows. In one of the few countries where the political and social situation did change drastically, Belgium, the extreme right VB has so far not suffered from the strongly increased pressure (neither electorally, nor organizationally). This could point to a certain threshold value, i.e. the political and social pressure only works in the developing stage of a political party.

But even if we accept that the adaptation dilemma does exist for all extremist groups, it seems questionable that it can really work in countries where the exclusion of extremists is complete (such as in Germany and the Netherlands)[4] given that the dilemma only exists as long as there is *choice*. And once you exclude extremists permanently – either by banning the party or by essentially arguing 'once an extremist, always an extremist' – there is no choice. Consequently, 'extremists' and 'moderates' can easily sit together in extreme right organizations, growing from strength to strength in their isolation (see the VB in Flanders).

Defending democracy against different types of extremist threat

Another shortcoming in most literature is that it describes general models of 'defending democracy' without considering the different forms of extremism. In this respect, Anders Widfeldt in Chapter 7 makes two very important contributions. First, he presents a typology of responses to political extremism that is also applicable to sub-groups within the state. So, whereas the American and German models describe the responses of the state as a whole, as do the similar models presented by Pedahzur, Widfeldt's typology can be applied to (individual) political parties or civil society groups *within* the state. In this way, the various individual responses to extremist challenges that make up the often hugely simplified picture of the one coherent state response, that typifies the 'national' models, can be studied and understood.

Second, he points to the difference between parliamentary and extra-parliamentary challengers. In the 'diversified approach' in Sweden the state dealt relatively mildly with the parliamentary extreme right, yet rather strictly with the extra-parliamentary 'parties'. A similar situation could be found in Austria, where the parliamentary FPÖ has always been treated with caution, whereas the extra-parliamentary National Democratic Party (NDP) was eventually banned. Likewise, in the Netherlands, the parliamentary CD were ostracized, but never seriously faced the risk of being banned, unlike the extra-parliamentary CP'86.

The question is whether it is actually the parliamentary status of an organization that decides the state response. Perhaps it is rather the group's ideological extremity. The FPÖ and the CD were clearly more moderate in terms of ideology than the NDP and CP'86 respectively. Still, in the public debate one often hears the argument that parliamentary parties should not be banned because they represent a (significant) section of the population.

The German militant democracy makes an important legal distinction between political parties and other political organizations. Non-party organizations can be banned by the (federal or state) Minister of Interior. At the federal level alone, this procedure has been applied 18 times in the 1990s (BfVS 1999, p. 13). Political parties, on the other hand, can only be banned by the Federal Constitutional Court, a very demanding procedure that depends on the verdict of an independent organization. So far, 'only' two parties have been banned in post-war Germany, the extreme right Socialist Reich Party and the Communist Party of Germany (Lovens 2001).

Dézé raises the interesting idea of comparing the way democracies deal with challenges from the extreme left and the extreme right. Indeed, in many countries this is a hot issue in the public and political debate, and nowhere more so than in Germany. Many on the left of the political spectrum have accused the German state of being 'blind in the right eye', meaning that they do not adequately deal with right-wing extremists. They substantiate this argument by pointing to the considerable state repression that was used in the 1960s and 1970s against the extreme left, most notably terrorist groups like the Red Army Faction and the Baader-Meinhof Group, and compare this to the alleged soft manner in which right-wing extremists have been dealt with in recent times. Some preliminary research rejects this thesis (e.g. Backes 2000; Prützel-Thomas 2000), but more (comparative) research is surely needed.

This applies not only to the comparison of right and left terrorism, but also to non-violent extremist groups. In various countries, commentators – generally though not exclusively on the right – have complained about the double standards that are being applied to the treatment of left-wing and right-wing extremists. At first glance, it looks indeed to be the case that extreme left parties (and groups more general) have been treated more sympathetically than their extreme right counterparts. For example, in the Netherlands the extreme right has been the object of considerable legal, political and social repression, while the extreme left has been shunned by the mainstream right, but accepted by the majority of the mainstream left. A similar situation can be found in France, where the Communist Party of France has long been an accepted coalition partner of the Socialists, while the FN is, for the most part, rejected by 'democratic' parties of both the right and left (see Chapter 6). Similarly, in Germany, the 'post-communist' Party of Democratic Socialism is, in most Eastern states, accepted as *koalitionsfähig*, despite occasional anti-extremist rhetoric from the mainstream right, while extreme right parties like the DVU and REP are still excluded by all (e.g. Backes 2000).

Another interesting comparison would be between political extremism and religious extremism, or fundamentalism. This will be problematic at the parliamentary level, as religious fundamentalist political parties are rare in Western democracies. The example of the orthodox Protestant Political Reformed Party (SGP) in the Netherlands indicates a far larger acceptance of Christian fundamentalists than of (right-wing) extremists (Voerman and Lucardie 1992). Despite being openly anti-democratic, and excluding women from its membership, the SGP is treated as part of the 'democratic' block and included in several local coalitions. In other countries, Christian fundamentalists constitute influential factions within large mainstream parties, such as *Opus Dei* in the Spanish Popular Party or the Christian right in the US Republican Party.

At the extra-parliamentary level, more fruitful comparisons could be made, particularly given the growing relevance of Islamic fundamentalist groups in the West (e.g. Israeli 2001). It seems that, in recent years, and most notably since the terrorist attacks of September 11, Islamic fundamentalists have overtaken even the extreme right as 'public enemy number one' in Western democracies. Consequently, it is these groups that are feeling the full might of 'defending democracy', at a level that the extreme right (or left) probably never did.

At a local level, this can be observed recently in the city of Antwerp, where small groups of Belgian youths of Moroccan descent were involved in 'riots' in November 2002. After the media had documented the presence of Dyab Abou Jahjah, the charismatic leader of the Arab European League (AEL), a tiny organization that blends Arab nationalism and relatively orthodox Islam, Belgian politicians competed almost *ad absurdum* in their anti-AEL statements. Within a year of its existence, the AEL was already faced with the possibility of serious legal restrictions. The main protagonist of harsh measures against the 'anti-democratic AEL' was, how ironic, the VB, the only party that shares some of the main points of the AEL (e.g. rejection of integration of minorities) and much of the same hostility by the mainstream politicians. Still, it took the 'democratic' parties more than ten years to establish a *cordon sanitaire* around the VB, yet less than a year to ostracize the AEL.

Finally, the way 'defending democracies' deal with the extreme right can be compared with the treatment of separatist-irredentist groups. In this respect, it seems again that the extreme right is treated fairly moderately. Great Britain and Spain, two of the countries faced with the strongest separatist challenges, have adopted far-reaching legislation to repress these groups. Most recently, Spain temporarily banned the Basque separatist party, *Batasuna*, the political wing of ETA[5] – a fate which has befallen no parliamentary extreme right party. In addition, many other countries (e.g. Bulgaria, Slovakia, Turkey) have laws that prohibit political parties that 'threaten the territorial integrity of the state' (see Venice Commission 2000).

A multilevel relationship

While most chapters are mainly, if not exclusively, concerned with relationships between extremism and democracy at the national level, two chapters stress the importance of the sub-national level. While Eatwell provides an insightful study of the importance of 'community politics' for the British National Party (BNP), Laurent Kestel and Laurent Godmer show, on the basis of a comparative study of three European countries (Austria,

Germany and France), that the political inclusion of extreme right parties often starts at the sub-national (i.e. regional or local) level. The Belgian case teaches us that the opposite can be the case as well. It was the electoral breakthrough of the VB in Antwerp in 1988 that triggered the self-proclaimed 'democratic parties' in Flanders to establish the *cordon sanitaire* to exclude the VB (Daemen 1998).

Also, in terms of the development of anti-extremist policies, the sub-national levels play an important role. Given that most militant extreme right groups tend to be only small and very locally organized, it is often the local communities that are confronted with them first. For example, in a study of racist violence in Finland, Timo Virtanen (n.d.) argues that 'in the absence of consistent state policies on issues connected with racism and intolerance, a great deal of anti-racist responses has depended on the awareness and consciousness of local authorities in Finland.' The same situation existed in Sweden, where the experiences of cities such as Trollhättan and Karlkrona had a profound effect on the way other local communities and even the national government would deal with extreme right challenges (see Chapter 7).[6]

The sub-national level is not the only important non-national level that influences the relationships between extremism and democracy. At times even more important is the supranational level. Think of the international treaties that most Western democracies have signed, such as the European Convention on Human Right and Fundamental Freedoms (1963) or the UN International Convention on the Elimination of All Forms of Racial Discrimination (1966). Some of these treaties contain very concrete stipulations on how the state should deal with extreme right organizations. For example, Article 4b of the International Convention on the Elimination of All Forms of Racial Discrimination states that all signatories '(s)hall declare illegal and prohibit organizations, and also organized and all other propaganda activities, which promote and incite racial discrimination, and shall recognize participation in such organizations or activities as an offence punishable by law'.

Since the introduction of the International Convention, the UN's Committee on the Elimination of Racial Discrimination (CERD) has been monitoring and reviewing actions by signatory states to fulfill their obligations under the International Convention. During that period, it has criticized countries as diverse as Australia and Norway for not living up to their commitments. In its 2002 report, for example, it called upon Denmark 'to take decisive steps to prohibit [neo-Nazi] organizations in accordance with article 4 (b) of the Convention' (CERD 2002). The Committee's critique has led to heated debates in the countries concerned, but also to the introduction of many new anti-discrimination policies (Van Donselaar 1995; Bolsius 1994). In Belgium, for example, CERD pressure was an important factor in the introduction of financial sanctions for racist political parties and organizations.

In more recent times, the European Union has become a major actor in the domestic politics of its member states (and those who want to join). Particularly with the adoption of the Copenhagen criteria, or the *acquis communautaire*, extremist behavior has become a specific concern of the EU. The most remarkable example of this, even though it was not an official EU action, were the sanctions imposed by the 'EU 14' against Austria (Merlingen *et al.* 2001). Although they were not able to prevent the inclusion of the FPÖ into the Austrian government, their pressure did have a moderating effect on the party's ministers and even a dividing effect on the party itself. Haider resigned as party leader under the pressure of the EU 14, was succeeded by what he thought was his trustee, Riess-Passer, who then increasingly turned away from Haider and closer to the EU 14.

Finally, there can be an international *economic* dimension. This has been argued most forcefully with regard to some of the repressive measures against the extreme right that the German government issued after the racist attacks in 1991–3 – and later, although less comprehensive, after the CDU's infamous 'Kinder statt Inder' (children instead of Indians) debate in reaction to the government plan to provide green cards to IT specialists (who would come mainly from India). According to Hans-Gerd Jaschke (2000, p. 29), the German state has at times used its possibilities to fight right-wing extremism 'to reestablish the reputation of the investment location of Germany, which had been ruined by political wrong decisions.'

Extreme right parties and violence

Finally, one of the most relevant and hotly debated topics with regard to the issue of 'democratic defence' is the relationship between extreme right parties[7] and extreme right or racist violence (Van Donselaar and Wolff 1996). Whereas state repression on the basis of an extreme right or racist *ideology* is often a controversial issue (e.g. Fennema 2000), there is a broad consensus in democratic societies that violence should be dealt with severely. Therefore, the question whether extreme right parties are involved in violence has both academic and practical significance.

According to many of the opponents of the extreme right the relationship is clear-cut: extreme right parties are both directly and indirectly responsible for racist violence. In Germany, anti-fascist magazines like *Blick nach Rechts* and *Der Rechte Rand* publish article after article about members of extreme right parties who are allegedly involved in racist violence or in violent neo-Nazi groups. In Great Britain, *Searchlight* magazine has published many articles on the alleged overlap between the membership of the BNP and the neo-Nazi paramilitary group Combat 18 (see also Chapter 3).

Not only anti-fascists claim the existence of a strong relationship between extreme right parties and violence: journalists and (at times prominent) politicians do as well. While Tony Blair was careful not to name the BNP when commenting on the 'race riots' in Northern England of 2001, instead blaming 'white extremists' (*Guardian* 31 May 2001), various local politicians and prominents did (Eatwell in Chapter 3; Mudde 2002b). For example, the Labour MP for Clwyd South, Martin Jones, called the riots 'a direct result of agitation by the BNP and other right-wing groups' (BBC 2001).

In the few cases that extreme right parties were banned, e.g. the NPD and CP'86, the direct involvement of party members in violence was always looming in the background, although it was hardly used as an argument in the actual court cases. Similarly, the recent application of the German parliament to the Federal Constitutional Court to ban the NPD does not explicitly mention the party's alleged violent track record. Still, the main reason for the federal government to ask for a ban of the NPD was its 'active, aggressive basic attitude' to the free democratic basic order in Germany (Lovens 2001, p. 565).[8]

Despite all these strong statements, and the clear practical implications, very little academic research exists on this fundamental relationship between extreme right parties and extreme right or racist violence. It is a known fact that *members* of extreme right parties have at times been involved in racist violence. One of the (four) culprits of the firebombing of a house in the German town of Solingen in 1993, in which five Turkish women and girls were killed, was a member of the DVU. Baruch Goldstein, who massacred 29 Palestinians in 1994, was a member of the Kach party (Pedahzur in Chapter 5, Sprinzak 2001). And Maxime Brunerie, the young man who attempted to assassinate French president Chirac in 2002, had been a candidate in local elections for the National Republican Movement of Bruno Mégret.

However, this all does not necessarily prove that the parties as such were involved in the violence. First of all, in none of these cases is there proof that the party leadership knew about the planned activities, let alone that they would have instructed their members to carry out these violent acts. Second, none of the perpetrators was a prominent party member, who could be seen as representative of the party as a whole. Third, in almost all cases the party in question distanced itself from the violence and the perpetrators, who were generally expelled from the party.

However, in addition to the direct relationship between extreme right parties and violence, there might also be an *indirect* relationship. In different countries a wide variety of actors have claimed that a strong extreme right party creates a 'racist atmosphere' that stimulates racist violence.[9] This was argued, for example, in the case of Franz Fuchs, who, under the name of the fictitious Bavarian Liberation Army, carried out a murderous racist bombing campaign in Austria between 1993 and 1996 (e.g. Scharsach and Kuch 2000). Some initial research seems to indicate that a relationship does exist between the discourse of the public debate and the level of extreme right violence, but that it is far more complex than is generally suggested (Koopmans and Olzog 2002).

In one of the few comparative studies of racist violence, Ruud Koopmans has found an inverse relationship between the level of electoral success of extreme right parties and the level of racist violence in a country. From this correlation, he concluded: 'In general, strong extreme right parties serve to limit the potential for extreme right and racist violence' (Koopmans 1996, p. 211). Although definitely a plausible conclusion, there are too many weaknesses in his study to take this conclusion at face value. Most notably, as Koopmans himself acknowledges, the data on racist violence are very country-specific and are therefore badly suited for strict cross-national comparisons. There might also be some intervening variables, such as the political culture of a country, or the fact that people might be less willing to declare a crime to be racist or extreme right in countries were extreme right parties are very successful. That said, so far Koopmans' study is the best available, and until we have been able to replicate it on the basis of a better data set, we should take his conclusion at least as a good starting point for further research.

In the debate about party bans, another relationship between extreme right parties and violence is also claimed. The argument goes that extreme right parties should not be banned because then some of its members will go 'underground' and get involved in extreme right violence (or even terrorism). This argument is very hard to substantiate, if only because 'the underground' is by definition difficult to study. However, as far as we can see, the bans of the NPD and CP'86 have not led to the development of a terrorist 'underground'.[10] Indeed, in the case of the NPD a terrorist underground existed *at the same time* as the political party.

Extreme right party leaders like to claim that if they are allowed to function normally, they will be able to re-integrate these potentially violent members into 'democratic politics'. A fairly suspicious statement, but nevertheless worth serious consideration, as it could be of great importance to the ways democracies should respond to some extremist challenges. There are indeed examples of former terrorists who have transformed themselves into more or less democratic politicians – although often only after having served an extensive prison sentence, and mostly from the extreme left rather than the right.

What should be clear is that the relationship between extreme right parties and violence, either direct or indirect, is too important to be ignored by academia. So far, there are only a few studies available, and then mostly on perpetrators of extreme right and racist violence – of whom only a minority is in any way linked to an extreme right party (see Wahl 2001; Willems 2002). Other studies have simply claimed that extreme right parties create a 'climate of hate' without ever proving how this has influenced people to commit extreme right and racist attacks. Obviously, this is also a potential academic minefield, as it deals with the complex issue of (indirect) influence. However, this should not keep us from trying to study it, as good or bad as it goes. After all, everything is better than simple prejudice.

Conclusions

Despite the huge academic interest in extreme right politics, still very little is known about the various ways in which democracies and the extreme right interact with each other. Recently, some young researchers, most of them included in this volume, have ventured into this *terra incognita*, producing important and interesting first conclusions (e.g. Michael 2003; Pedahzur 2002; Capoccia 2001). We believe that they and the other contributors to this volume have raised some pertinent questions, and even answered some in this volume. Moreover, we hope that this book will stimulate more widespread academic interest in this important and rich field of study.

The developments since September 11 have made the 'democratic dilemma', or the 'liberty–security balance' (Taylor 2003, p. 26), even more relevant. Even though, for the moment at least, 'Islamic fundamentalism' has taken over the position of 'public enemy number one' from the extreme right, the ongoing debate on how democracies should defend themselves has, and will have, profound effects on the relationships between democracies and the extreme right. Therefore, scholars of extremism and democracy should become more involved in studying, and perhaps even solving, the dilemma that has been summarized in a succinct and simple way by Hans-Gerd Jaschke (2000, p. 22): 'Too much state is dangerous, too little as well.'

Notes

1 Although in recent months there has been some opposition against the *cordon sanitaire*, most notably from two new political parties: the small moderate nationalist New Flemish Alliance and the new liberal break-away Liberal Appeal of Ward Beysen.
2 Although in recent years the German state (and *Länder*) has become far less willing to protect meetings and demonstrations of extreme right organizations, including parties like the DVU and REP (Jaschke 2000).
3 Similar concerns have been raised about a spiral of violence that has developed as a consequence of conflicts between often local gangs of 'white' and 'foreign' youths (e.g. Virtanen n.d.; Bjørgo 1997).
4 Obviously, this does not refer to the List Pim Fortuyn, which is not an extreme right party, as is so often wrongly asserted, but rather an odd mix of neo-liberal populism (see Mudde 2002a).
5 Earlier, in 1997, the Spanish state had already imprisoned the leaders of the predecessor of Batasuna, *Herri Batasuna* (People's Party), for 'condoning terrorism' (Holmes 2001, p. 210).
6 This could also be seen from the great emphasis that was put on local experiences and studies at the Stockholm International Forum Combating Intolerance, Stockholm, 29–30 January 2001.

7 I refer here only to *serious* extreme right parties, i.e. organizations that strive for parliamentary influence through contesting elections, and not the many groups that are called 'party' but that hardly act as such (e.g. the Free German Workers' Party).
8 The Federal government (*Bundesregierung*), the Federal Council (*Bundesrat*), and the Federal Parliament (*Bundestag*) all submitted their own application to ban the NPD to the Federal Constitutional Court in Karlsruhe (see Lovens 2001).
9 Incidentally, the accusation of creating a 'racist climate' has not only been made against extreme right politicians. For example, in Britain, both Liberal Democrats and Labour backbenchers have accused then Tory leader, William Hague, of playing 'the race card' and directly linked this to the alleged rise in racist crime in the country (e.g. *The Independent* 12 January 2001; *Guardian* 31 May 2001).
10 In the case of bans of militant although still non-violent non-party political organizations, the danger might be more realistic, however. According to Armin Pfahl-Traughber (1997, p. 169), there is no concrete evidence for the thesis that the various bans by the Minister of Interior in the 1990s have led to the development of right-wing terrorist structures, but there are some 'indications'.

Bibliography

Backes, U. (2000) 'Probleme der Beobachtungs – und Praxis der Verfassungsschutzämter – am Beispiel von REP und PDS', in Bundesamt für Verfassungsschutz (red.), *Bundesamt für Verfassungsschutz. 50 Jahre im Dienst der inneren Sicherheit*, Cologne, etc: Carl Heymanns, pp. 213–231.

Backes, U. (1989) *Politischer Extremismus in demokratischen Verfassungsstaaten. Elemente einer normativen Rahmentheorie*, Opladen: Westdeutscher.

Backes, U. and Mudde, C. (2000) 'Germany: extremism without successful parties', *Parliamentary Affairs* 53, 3: 457–468.

BBC (2001) 'Welsh BNP festival "unwelcome"', available at: http://news.bbc.co.uk/1/hi/wales/1434278.stm (Last accessed on 13 April 2003).

BfVS (1999) *Verfassungsschutz gegen Rechtsextremismus*, Berlin: Bundesministerium des Innern.

Bjørgo, T. (1997) *Racist and Right-Wing Violence in Scandinavia: Patterns, Perpetrators, and Responses*, Oslo: Tore Aschehoug.

Bolsius, E. (1994) *Racistische partijen met recht verbieden. Een onderzoek naar de juridische mogelijkheden om extreem-rechtse en racistische partijen te verbieden of te ontbinden, naar Belgisch, Duits en Nederlands Recht*, Utrecht: Wetenschapswinkel Rechten.

Capoccia, G. (2001) 'Defending democracy: strategies of reaction to political extremism in inter-war Europe', *European Journal of Political Research* 39, 4: 431–460.

CERD (2002) 'Note on the 60th session – (4–22 March 2002)', available at: http://193.194.138.190/html/menu2/6/cerd.htm (Last accessed on 16 April 2003).

Daemen, S. (1998) 'Strategieën tegen extreem-rechts: het cordon sanitaire rond het Vlaams Blok', Antwerp: unpublished MA thesis.

ECRI (1998) *Legal Measures to Combat Racism and Intolerance in the Member States of the Council of Europe*, Strasbourg: Council of Europe.

Fennema, M. (2000) 'Legal repression of extreme right parties and racial discrimination', in Koopmand, R. and Statham, P. (eds) *Challenging Immigration and Ethnic Relations Politics – Comparative European Perspectives*, Oxford: Oxford University Press, pp. 119–144.

Haider-Markel, D.P. and O'Brien, S.P. (1997) 'Creating a "well regulated militia": policy responses to paramilitary groups in the American states', *Political Research Quarterly* 50, 3: 551–565.

Hassemer, W. (2002) 'Zum Spannungsverhältnis von Freiheit und Sicherheit. Drei Thesen', *vorgänge*, 41, 3, 10–15.

Henckel, M. and Lembcke, O. (2001) 'Die Dilemmata des Parteiverbotes. Probleme der wehrhaften Demokratie im Umgang mit dem Rechtsextremismus', *Zeitschrift für Parlamentsfragen* 32, 3: 572–587.

Holmes, J. (2001) *Terrorism and Democratic Stability*, Manchester: Manchester University Press.

Husbands, C.T. (1998) 'De Centrumstroming in perspectief: hoe verschillend is Nederland?', in Van Holsteyn, J. and Mudde, C. (eds) *Extreem-rechts in Nederland*, The Hague: Sdu, pp. 175–191.

Ignazi, P. (1996) 'From neo-Fascists to post-Fascists? The transformation of the MSI into the AN', *West European Politics* 19, 4: 693–714.

Israeli, R. (2001) 'Western democracies and Islamic fundamentalist violence', in Rapoport, D. and Weinberg, L. (eds) *The Democratic Experience and Political Violence*, London: Frank Cass, pp. 160–173.

Jaschke, H.-G. (2000) 'Sehnsucht nach dem starken Staat. Was bewirkt Repression gegen Rechts', *Aus Politik und Zeitgeschichte*, B 39, 22–29.

Jaschke, H.-G. (1991) *Streitbare Demokratie und Innere Sicherheit. Grundlagen, Praxis und Kritik*, Opladen: Westdeutscher.

Knapp, A. (1999) 'What's left of the French right? The RPR and the UDF from conquest to humiliation, 1993–1998', *West European Politics*, 22, 3: 109–138.

Koopmans, R. (1996) 'Explaining the rise of racist and extreme right violence in Western Europe: grievances or opportunities?', *European Journal of Political Research*, 30, 2, 185–216.

Koopmans, R. and Olzog, S. (2002) 'Right-wing violence and the public sphere in Germany: the dynamics of discursive opportunities', available at: http://www.stanford.edu/dept/soc/PDF/GermanViolence.pdf (Last accessed on 14 April 2003).

Kowalsky, W. (1992) *Rechtsaußen ... und die verfahlten Strategien der deutschen Linken*, Frankfurt a.M.: Ullstein.

Lovens, S. (2001) 'Parteiverbote in der Bundesrepublik Deutschland. Zur verfassungsrechtlichen Ausgangslage der Anträge gegen die NPD', *Zeitschrift für Parlamentsfragen* 32, 3: 550–572.

Maegerle, A. (2002) 'Rechtsextremistische Gewalt und Terror', in Grumke, T. and Wagner, B. (eds) *Handbuch Rechtsradikalismus. Personen – Organisationen – Netzwerke vom Neonazismus bis in die Mitte der Gesellschaft*, Opladen: Leske + Budrich, pp. 159–172.

Merlingen, M., Mudde, C. and Sedelmeier, U. (2001) 'European norms, domestic politics and the sanctions against Europe', *Journal of Common Market Studies* 39, 1: 59–77.

Michael, G. (2003) *Right-Wing Terrorism and Extremism in the USA*, London: Routledge.

Mletzko, M. (2001) 'Gewaltdiskurse und Gewalthandeln militanter Szenen Teil 1', *Kriminalistik*, 8–9: 543–548.
Moore (1994) 'Undercover surveillance of the Republikaner Party: protecting a militant democracy or discrediting a political rival', *German Politics* 3, 2: 284–292.
Mudde, C. (1995) 'De paria van de rechtsstaat. Extreem-rechts in Nederland', *Socialisme & Democratie* 52, 5: 246–248.
Mudde, C. (2000) *The Ideology of the Extreme Right*, Manchester: Manchester University Press.
Mudde, C. (2002a) 'The Pink Populist: Pim Fortuyn for beginners', *e-Extreme*, 3, 2, available at: http://www.bath.ac.uk/esml/ecpr/newsletter/News3_2.htm (Last accessed at 22 April 2003).
Mudde, C. (2002b) '"England belongs to me": the extreme right in the UK parliamentary election of 2001', *Representation* 39, 1: 37–43.
Pedahzur, A. (2002) *The Israeli Response to Jewish Extremism and Violence*, Manchester: Manchester University Press.
Pfahl-Traughber, A. (1997) 'Die Neonationalsozialistischen-Szene nach den Verbotsmaßnahmen', in Backes, U. and Jesse, E. (eds) *Jahrbuch Extremismus & Demokratie*, 9, Baden-Baden: Nomos, pp. 156–173.
Prützel-Thomas, M. (2000) 'German criminal justice and right-wing extremists: is justice in Germany "Blind in the right eye"?', *Debatte* 8, 2: 209–225.
Scharsach, H.-H. and Kuch, K. (2000) *Haider. Schatten über Europa*, Cologne: Kiepenheuer & Witsch.
Schikhof, M. (1998) 'Strategieën tegen extreem-rechts en hun gevolgen', in Van Holsteyn, J. and Mudde, C. (eds) *Extreem-rechts in Nederland*, The Hague: Sdu, pp. 143–156.
Sprinzak, E. (2001) 'Extremism and violence in Israeli democracy', in Rapoport, D. and Weinberg, L. (eds) *The Democratic Experience and Political Violence*, London: Frank Cass, pp. 209–236.
Szôcs, L. (1998) 'A tale of the unexpected: the extreme right vis-à-vis democracy in post-communist Hungary', *Ethnic and Racial Studies* 21, 6: 1096–1115.
Taylor, Jr., S. (2003) 'Rights, liberties, and security. Recalibrating the balance after September 11', *Brookings Review*, Winter, pp. 25–31.
Van Donselaar, J. (1995) *De staat paraat? De bestrijding van extreem-rechts in West-Europa*, Amsterdam: Babylon-De Geus.
Van Donselaar, J. and Wolff, R. (1996) *Reacties op racistisch geweld: het perspectief van allochtonen*, Amsterdam: Het Spinhuis (TWCM voorstudie 6).
Venice Commision (2000) 'Guidelines on prohibition and dissolution of political parties and analogous measures', adopted by the Venice Commission at its 41st plenary session, Venice, 10–11 December 1999.
Virtanen, T. (no date) 'The dynamics of racist violence and harassment among youth in Finland: victims, perpetrators, and anti-racist actions', in Virtanen, T. (ed.) *Youth, Racist Violence and Anti-Racist Responses in the Nordic Countries*, unpublished manuscript.
Voerman, G. and Lucardie, P. (1992) 'The extreme right in the Netherlands. The centrists and their radical rivals', *European Journal of Political Research*, 22: 35–54.
Wahl, K. (ed.) (2001) *Fremdenfeindlichkeit, Antisemitismus, Rechtsextremismus. Drei Studien zu Tatverdächtigen und Tätern*, Berlin: Bundesministerium des Innern.

Willems, H. (2002) 'Rechtsextremistische, antisemitische und fremdenfeindliche Straftaten in Deutschland: Entwicklung, Strukturen, Hintegründe', in Grumke, T. and Wagner, B. (eds) *Handbuch Rechtsradikalismus. Personen – Organisationen – Netzwerke vom Neonazismus bis in die Mitte der Gesellschaft*, Opladen: Leske + Budrich, pp. 141–157.

Index

adaptation dilemma xii, 20–1, 193–5, 201; of BNP 77; of National Front (France) 26
Alleanza Nazionale *see* National Alliance.
Almirante, Giorgio 22, 23
anti-Americanism 11, 71–2
Anti-Defamation League (ADL) xiii, 126, 173, 176ff passim, 200
Anti-Fascist Action (AFA) 67, 167
Anti-Nazi League (ANL) 64
Anti-Racist Action 174–5
anti-semitism (anti-Zionism) xii, 2, 10, 11, 48, 51, 52, 57–8, 68, 69, 185; *see also* Holocaust Denial
Armed Revolutionary Nuclei (NAR) 6, 8, 14
Aryan Nations 174, 183, 187
Austrian Freedom Party (FPÖ) 1, 6, 10, 11, 19, 29ff, 133, 153, 194, 201, 205; adaptation, differentiation and distinction of 29–32; conservative collaboration and entry into Government 134–5; maximum institutional inclusion in Austria 136–7; radicalization 30–1, 136; relations with Christian church 32

Bossi, Umberto 12
British National Party (BNP) 1, 2, 9, 10, 62ff, 203, 205–6

Bundesverfassungsgericht *see* Federal Constitutional Court
Bundesverfassungsschutz *see* Federal Bureau for the Protection of the Constitution
Center for Democratic Renewal 174
Center for New Community 174
Centre Democrats (CD) 197, 201
Centre Party'86 (CP'86) 197, 201, 206, 207
charisma 1, 12, 63, 68
Christian Identity 2, 52, 57, 58, 174
civil society xiv, 125–7, 199–201; and uncivil society 114
Combat 18 (C18) 5, 14, 67, 74, 205
conspiracy theory 9, 10, 45, 47ff
Council of Europe's Venice Commission for Democracy through the Law 4
Covenant, Sword, and the Arm of the Lord, CSA 177

Danish People's Party 150, 153
De Benoist, Alain 2, 9, 65
'defensive democracy' ('*streitbare/wehrhafte Demokratie*') xii, 84, 195; inclusive mechanisms ('appeals to the public') 99–102; militant democracy 109, legacy of 103; repressive strategies 98–9

214 Index

democratic dilemma (liberty-security balance) 84–5, 108–9, 209; general and specific accommodation and marginalization 152–5
Dewinter, Felip 4–5, 33–5
Dillen, Karel 32, 35
Duprat, François 26, 27

Evola, Julius 22, 65, 68
extreme right: definition of 4, 5ff; and fascism 6–7; and radical right 7–8; and populism 11–13

Federal Bureau of Investigation, FBI: COINTELPRO Counter-intelligence Programme 176; cooperation with NGOs 184; creation of Hostage Rescue Team (HRT) 177; federal investigation of political extremism and domestic terrorism 175–81; post-Oklahoma City bombing 121; Presidential Decision Directive (PDD) 180
Federal Bureau for the Protection of the Constitution (BfVS) 113, 121, 122
Federal Constitutional Court, BVG: and Clause 21 of the Basic Law 119; and NPD ban 4, 120, 199; and Radikalenerlaß (Radicals Decree) 121–2
Fini, Gianfranco 4, 5, 23–4, 25
Flemish Block (VB) 5, 9, 19, 33ff, 194, 200, 201, 203, 204; cordon sanitaire surrounding 3, 34, 147, 154, 195, 203, 204; emergence and ideology 33; impossible integration of 35
Fortuyn, Pim xiv, 1, 2, 4, 12
Forza Italia, FI 147, 194
Freiheitliche Partei Österreich see Austrian Freedom Party

Front National see National Front (France)

General Security Service, GSS 122–3
German People's Union (DVU) 10, 126, 197, 202, 206
globalization xi, 52, 55–6, 65, 71
Griffin, Nick 63, 68ff passim

Haider, Jörg 1, 5, 12, 30–2, 136–7, 194
Hale, Matt 174, 181
Holocaust Denial 3, 27, 35, 41, 64, 65, 66, 72, 142, 155, 174, 188

Immigration (hostility to) 2, 7, 8, 13, 10, 27, 31, 40, 64, 68, 70–1, 150ff passim, 196
international anti-extremist watchdogs/agreements: Committee on the Elimination of Racial Discrimination (CERD) 204; European Monitoring Centre on Racism and Xenophobia (EUMC) 162–3; European Union's Copenhagen criteria 205; International Forum on Combating Intolerance 169; UN Convention on the Elimination of All Forms of Racial Discrimination 204
Internet 174, 180, 183–4; use by BNP 68, 70; use by white hate groups in USA 53, 183ff
Irving, David 64–5, 69, 77
Islam (and the extreme right) x, xiv, 2, 42, 63, 71, 184–5, 203
Italian Social Movement (MSI) 19, 21ff, 194; and Destra Nazionale (National Right, DN) 23; exclusion 21–4; integration 24–5; relations with Forza Italia and Northern League 24–5

John Birch Society 7, 43

Kach Party 119–20, 123, 129
Kahane, Meir (Rabbi) 120, 123
Karlsson, Bert 156, 168
Ku Klux Klan 7, 41–2, 44, 57, 176, 183, 196

leaderless resistance 2, 188
Le Pen, Jean-Marie ix, 1, 4, 5, 10, 12, 25ff passim, 137ff; Le Penization (of politics) 13, 27

media xii, 43, 52, 65, 66, 68, 69, 70–1, 72ff passim, 139, 167, 181, 185
Mégret, Bruno 26, 27, 28, 143, 194–5
militia movement 10, 41–52, 174, 179, 195
Mouvement National Républicain *see* National Republican Movement
multiculturalism xiii, 41, 53, 58

National Alliance, AN (Italy), 4, 10, 11, 13, 19, 24–5, 147, 194; *see also* Italian Social Movement (MSI)
National Alliance (USA) 2, 6–7, 42, 54, 181
National Democratic Party (NPD) 2, 5, 72, 83, 104, 120, 199, 201, 206, 207
National Front (FN) (France) ix, 1, 2, 6, 7, 8, 9, 10, 11, 19, 25ff, 133, 137ff, 194, 195, 198, 202; association with French mainstream right wing 27, 139–44; containment of by parliamentary right 139–42; distinction of by political system 137–8; emergence 25–6, 138–9; model for other parties 24, 34, 68, 74; relation to regional politics 144–6; split and consequences 27–9, 146
National Front (NF) (UK) 62, 69; John Tyndall and creation of BNP 63–8; David Irving's views on 63–5
nationalism 8, 9, 31–2, 33, 52, 56, 72, 103, 125
National Republican Movement/ Republican National Movement (MNR) 28, 29, 143, 206; the Megretist election strategy 26ff, 194–5
National Socialist Front (NSF) 165–6, 169
National Socialist Party of America (NSPA) 118
Neo-Confederate movement 41, 52, 56–7
New Democracy (ND) 150ff passim, 198; cross-bloc agreements 159–60; parliamentary challenge and response of government 155–62, 167–8
New Order (France) 25, 138
New Order (Italy) 22
'New World Order' 13, 42ff passim, 66, 71–2
Northern League (LN) 9, 12, 13, 24, 147
Northwestern Coalition against Malicious Harassment (NWC) 174

Oklahoma City bombing x, 7, 41, 46–7, 48, 49, 121, 172, 178ff

Pierce, William 7, 54, 55
Political Research Associates 174
populism xiii, 1, 3, 11–13, 29, 31, 35, 77, 152
Posse Comitatus 43, 51
Progress Party (FrP) (Norway) 1, 5, 11, 12, 150, 156

racism 1–2, 8, 27, 34, 41, 52ff, 63, 69, 126, 138, 150–1, 157, 164–5, 182; 'differentialist' 10, 26, 65, 69, 77
Radical Unity 4, 5
Rauti, Pino 4, 22, 24
religious fundamentalism x, 3, 13, 48, 52, 54–5, 57–8, 202–3, 209
Republikaner Party 7–8, 135, 199, 202
Riess-Passer, Susanne 32, 194, 205
Ruby Ridge 43–4, 45, 47, 178, 195

Simon Wiesenthal Center 173, 183ff passim
Socialist Reich Party, SRP 119, 135, 202
SOS-Racisme 139
Southern Poverty Law Center (SPLC) 47, 50, 52, 126, 173, 177ff passim, 200

Stirbois, Jean-Pierre 26, 138–9
Sweden Democrats 150, 169–70

Tyndall, John 63ff passim, 73

USA Patriot Act 124, 180–1

Violence (right extremist) 1–2, 8, 43–4, 46–7, 49ff, 64ff passim, 73–4, 150ff passim, 172ff passim, 204–8
Vlaams Blok *see* Flemish Block

Wachtmeister, Ian 156, 157, 159–60, 161, 168
Waco siege 44–5, 47, 177f, 195
White Aryan Resistance, 53, 165, 183
White Power Music 3; in Scandinavia 150, 165; origins in UK 54, 66; in USA 54

Printed in Great Britain
by Amazon